W9-DHT-429

THE POLL TAX
IN THE SOUTH

THE POLL TAX
IN THE SOUTH

By Frederic D. Ogden

1958

UNIVERSITY OF ALABAMA
PRESS

COPYRIGHT 1958
BY UNIVERSITY OF ALABAMA PRESS
DRAWER 2877
UNIVERSITY, ALABAMA

LIBRARY OF CONGRESS CATALOG
CARD NUMBER 58-8773

PRINTED AND BOUND
BY BIRMINGHAM PRINTING COMPANY

HJ
4931
A13
04
1958

To my mother and to my wife
for encouragement, patience and sacrifice

PREFACE

DURING THE 1940's when repeal of the poll tax as a suffrage prerequisite was a live issue before Congress, many sweeping statements were made about the tax. Opponents of the tax blamed it for preventing millions of citizens from voting in the southern states. They charged that it was adopted to disfranchise Negroes, and that it was administered more to their disadvantage than to the disadvantage of the whites. They held it responsible for an excessive amount of political corruption and implied frequently that it was responsible for most of the ills of the South. Supporters argued that the tax requirement prevented ignorant, corrupt, and disinterested citizens from voting but did not stop any citizen who really wanted to vote. They contended that the tax helped to preserve the purity of the ballot box, instead of causing political corruption.

Little proof was given for such statements. This study was undertaken to find out what the poll tax is and how it operates, and to present an objective, factual analysis of the tax as a voting prerequisite. The purpose was to give a complete picture of the tax in the eleven former Confederate States, the states where poll tax payment has been a voting requirement in this century. To this end, the origins of the tax, its form, the way in which it is administered, the relation between the tax and corrupt election practices, its effects upon voting participation, and the movements to repeal it by state and national action were examined. The study was originally submitted as a doctoral dissertation at The Johns Hopkins University.

V. O. Key and Carl B. Swisher were the author's advisors when he prepared the study as a doctoral dissertation. He is indebted to them for their advice and for their care in saving him from numerous errors.

The author was associated with V. O. Key's study, *Southern Politics in State and Nation,* and had access to the files of this study. Material which was collected by interviews is not footnoted because many of the informants did not wish to be identified. The author is indebted to Roscoe C. Martin, formerly Director of the Bureau of Public Administration, University of Alabama, and to V. O. Key for the opportunity to serve on the staff of the *Southern Politics* investigation. Thanks are also due Alexander Heard and Donald S. Strong who collected, by interview, much of the poll tax material for the study of *Southern Politics.* York Willbern, formerly head of the Department of Political Science, University of Alabama, gave encouragement and assistance in preparing *The Poll Tax in the South* for publication.

Final preparation for publication was made possible by a grant from the Research Committee of the University of Alabama. Walter Koch assisted with statistical calculations; Doris Albright and Mary Lou Benson provided secretarial assistance; and Carolyn Bolt prepared the figures for publication.

Special acknowledgment is due my wife, Jessie Cupitt Ogden, who typed preliminary drafts, made the first drawings of the figures, and provided suggestions and assistance at all stages.

No one but myself is responsible for what is contained in the book and for any errors of fact or interpretation.

FREDERIC D. OGDEN

New Delhi, India, May, 1958

CONTENTS

TABLES

FIGURES

1. ROOTS IN THE PAST

THIS STUDY IS CONCERNED with the use of the poll tax in the South as a suffrage prerequisite. Although emphasis is placed on present day poll tax controversies and practices, the current scene can be illuminated by an understanding of historical background. The account of the background in this chapter assumes a knowledge of the complicated problems of race relationships flowing from the presence in the South after the Civil War of a huge population of Negroes recently freed from slavery, people initially largely illiterate and unaccustomed to responsibility for themselves and to participation in democratic government. It assumes knowledge of a sensitive white population writhing from the military defeat of the Civil War, from their consequent impoverishment, and from enforcement upon them of the abandonment of slavery. White southern leaders were convinced that the survival of white civilization in the South required wresting from Negroes the political rights and authority virtually foisted upon them by northern whites during the reconstruction period. With the passage of time, these conditions and attitudes have changed in varying degrees in parts of the South, thereby complicating the later stages of the poll tax story. In its early period, that story must take into account the relation of the poll tax to other suffrage restrictions, and also its use against poorer segments of the white population. Agrarian problems and the Populist movement of the 1890's are involved, as is the threat of national supervision of national elections to protect the voting rights of Negroes.

The poll tax as a revenue measure is an ancient and obsolete device. From the point of view of tax theory it has its drawbacks. In particular, it is a difficult tax to collect. One way of providing an incentive to payment is to link payment to some important privilege, and one such privilege is that of voting. Requirement that poll taxes be paid, and paid within certain periods, and that receipts be preserved and presented at a much later date when offering to vote, inevitably has the effect of excluding some people from the polls.

There are two eras of poll tax requirements for voting in United States history. Following the Revolutionary War, the tax was used in some states to substitute for property qualifications for the suffrage. In this period, the adoption of a tax requirement represented an advance towards a wider manhood suffrage. Gradually tax-paying qualifications were eliminated until by the time of the Civil War few states still possessed them. The second era began after the Civil War, when the poll tax was adopted by southern states as one of a number of devices to restrict the suffrage.[1] Use of the poll tax in the South for suffrage restriction dates back primarily to the period from 1890 to 1908. Adoptions in the former Confederate States came in the following sequence: Florida, Mississippi, Tennessee, Arkansas, South Carolina, Louisiana, North Carolina, Alabama, Virginia, Texas and Georgia. Five of these states retain the tax requirement today, but—and this is indicative of a continuing trend—North Carolina, Louisiana, Florida, Georgia, South Carolina, and Tennessee have abandoned it.

Florida imposed the poll tax as a suffrage qualification by legislative act of 1889 after authorization had been given by the Constitution of 1885.[2] In 1890, payment of a poll tax became a qualification for voting in Mississippi and Tennessee. The Mississippi constitution was re-written with a poll tax provision included in the suffrage plan. In Tennessee, the tax was put into effect by legislative action.[3] In 1892, the voters of Arkan-

---

[1] See Kirk H. Porter, *A History of Suffrage in the United States* (Chicago, 1918), Chapters II, IV and VIII.

[2] *Laws of Florida, 1889*, Chapter 3859, p. 13.

[3] *Acts of Tennessee, 1890*, Chapter 26, p. 67. Poll tax payment as a suffrage prerequisite was authorized by the Constitution of 1870 but legislative action

sas approved a constitutional amendment which added the poll
tax to the election requirements.[4] South Carolina followed the
example of Mississippi and rewrote her constitution in 1895,
including a poll tax payment provision in the suffrage clause.
Louisiana did the same in 1898.

North Carolina in 1900 ratified a suffrage amendment containing a poll tax proviso. In 1901, Alabama adopted a new
constitution and made poll tax payment one of the voting
prerequisites. Virginia followed suit in 1902[5] and Texans
approved a poll tax amendment to their constitution in the
same year.

Georgia, the last Confederate State to alter her suffrage
requirements during this period, did so by means of a constitutional amendment in 1908. This amendment established a

---

was necessary to effectuate it. This provision was not put into effect until the
extra session of 1890. In 1870, a measure requiring poll tax payment was passed
but it was never executed. The following year an act was approved which
lifted the requirement for 1872, and in 1873, the poll tax law was repealed
entirely but no change was made in the constitutional provision. See Verton M.
Queener, "The East Tennessee Republicans as a Minority Party, 1870-1896,"
The East Tennessee Historical Society's Publications, No. 15 (1943), pp. 60-61,
and Stephen B. Weeks, "The History of Negro Suffrage in the South," *Political
Science Quarterly,* IX (December, 1894), 693.

4 The amendment was declared adopted by the Speaker of the House of Representatives in January, 1893. The legality of its adoption was questioned
because it had not received a majority of the total number of votes cast in
the election of 1892 although it had received a majority of the votes cast for
it alone. A federal court decision raised further doubts about the legality of its
adoption. As a result, another poll tax amendment was placed before the
voters in 1908. This amendment, worded in the same way as the 1892 one,
received the necessary majority. Sidney R. Crawford, "The Poll Tax" (Mss.,
M.A. Thesis, University of Arkansas, 1944), pp. 36 and 41-47.

5 Virginia had a poll tax suffrage prerequisite from 1876 to 1882. The tax
encouraged the practice of vote buying through poll tax payment because no
provision was made for a set time of payment before elections. The rise of a
new party, the Readjuster party, led to increased competition for votes and
considerable vote buying by poll tax payment. Political parties discovered that
a large sum of money was needed for paying poll taxes. Experience also disclosed that the tax disfranchised poor whites as well as Negroes. Since the
Readjuster party was essentially the poor man's party in Virginia, it led in
repealing the constitutional amendment which had authorized the tax. See
Charles C. Pearson, *The Readjuster Movement in Virginia* (New Haven,, 1917),
pp. 146 and 156.

literacy test and altered the tax-paying requirement. Since
1789, Georgia had required that voters must have paid all taxes
levied in the year preceding the election. The 1908 amendment altered the tax provision to require that voters must pay
all taxes for which they had been liable since the adoption of
the Constitution of 1877. A poll tax was one of these taxes.[6]

In Alabama, Georgia, Louisiana, Mississippi, North Carolina,
South Carolina, and Virginia, the poll tax was only one of
several measures comprising a general scheme of disfranchisement. Additional restrictive provisions were lengthy residence,
registration, and literacy, the last considerably mitigated by
"understanding clauses" and by property ownership in lieu of
ability to read and write. The "understanding clauses" provided that, although a person could not read, he could be
registered to vote if he could "understand and explain" any
section of the state, and sometimes the United States, constitution, when read to him by the registration officer. Conviction
for any of a long list of crimes was also made a cause for
disqualification from voting. Both temporary and permanent
plans for dealing with the suffrage were formulated in many
of these states. Temporary provisions were adopted to enable
whites unable to meet the new literacy qualifications to become
permanently registered as voters. In no state was poll tax
payment a part of the temporary suffrage requirements.

By contrast with these states, Arkansas, Florida, Tennessee,
and Texas had no formally legalized program of disfranchisement in which the poll tax requirement was but a component
part. These states used the poll tax device as their major
instrument of legalized action. Non-legal action to the same
end, whether in the form of intimidation or otherwise, is a
matter with which we are not here directly concerned.

THE MOVEMENT FOR NEGRO DISFRANCHISEMENT

It is obvious that one reason why southern states adopted the
poll tax and other suffrage restrictions[7] in the period from 1890

6 *Acts of Georgia, 1908*, p. 27, and *Georgia Code of 1926*, sec. 34, pp. 19-20. In
1932, the "all taxes" requirement was replaced by a provision that only all
poll taxes due since 1877 need be paid to be eligible to vote.

7 The entire movement for disfranchisement is considered because the poll tax

to 1908 was to disfranchise the Negro. Federal troops had by this time been withdrawn from the South and congressional reconstruction had come to an end. The former southern leaders or their descendants had regained control from the carpetbaggers, scalawags, and Negroes who had filled offices and wielded political power during the reconstruction period. As these old-time leaders entrenched themselves in power, they turned gradually from illegal to legal, or at least superficially legal, methods of depriving Negroes of political power.

The records of the constitutional conventions held in Mississippi, South Carolina, Louisiana, Alabama, and Virginia during this period show that disfranchisement of the Negro was a major purpose in calling the conventions and a major preoccupation of the members. At the beginning of the Mississippi constitutional convention in 1890, Judge S. S. Calhoon, the president of the convention, discussing the conflict between the races, said:

That is the great problem for which we are called together; that is the great question for you to solve, and the outside world is looking anxiously and our sister States of the South are looking at the solution we arrive at in reference to that question.[8]

The question of the suffrage was the sole cause for having a constitutional convention in South Carolina, according to Benjamin R. Tillman. Tillman declared that the Negroes had furnished the ballots for the reconstruction government. He said:

. . . this must be our justification, our vindication, and our excuse to the world that we are met in convention openly, boldly, without any pretence of secrecy, to announce that it is our purpose, as far as we may, without coming in conflict with the United States Constitution, to put such safeguards around this ballot in future, to so

cannot be divorced from other suffrage measures adopted at the same time. Although in recent times much attention has been devoted to the poll tax, at the time of adoption popular interest was focused upon the literacy qualifications and other registration requirements. The poll tax was largely overshadowed by them.

[8] *Journal of the Proceedings of the Constitutional Convention of the State of Mississippi, 1890* (Jackson, 1890), p. 11.

restrict the suffrage and circumscribe it, that this infamy can never come about again.[9]

In his closing remarks to the Louisiana constitutional convention, Ernest B. Kruttschnitt, president of the convention, frankly said:

We have not drafted the exact Constitution that we should like to have drafted; otherwise we should have inscribed in it, if I know the popular sentiment of this State, universal white manhood suffrage, and the exclusion from the suffrage of every man with a trace of African blood in his veins. . . . What care I whether the test we have put be a new one or an old one? What care I whether it be more or less ridiculous or not? Doesn't it meet the case? Doesn't it let the white man vote, and doesn't it stop the negro from voting, and isn't that what we came here for?   (Applause)[10]

Many similar remarks about Negro disfranchisement could be quoted. Many such statements were made about the poll tax specifically. Those who argued for the tax held that Negroes would be more neglectful in paying it and in preserving their receipts than whites. One of the delegates in the Alabama convention stated that he believed that the poll tax would disfranchise ten Negroes to one white man.[11] Another delegate, who approved using the revenue for educational purposes, thought that the tax would both disfranchise Negroes and educate white children.[12] Other members of this convention regarded the poll tax as the primary solution for their suffrage problem, frequently stated to be that of disfranchising the Negro without at the same time disfranchising any whites.[13]

When the Committee on the Elective Franchise reported to the Virginia constitutional convention, J. C. Wysor, a delegate from Pulaski and Giles counties, submitted a minority report

[9] *Journal of the Constitutional Convention of the State of South Carolina, 1895* (Columbia, 1895), p. 463.

[10] *Official Journal of the Proceedings of the Constitutional Convention of the State of Louisiana, 1898* (New Orleans, 1898), p. 380.

[11] *Official Proceedings of the Constitutional Convention of the State of Alabama, 1901* (Wetumpka, 1940), p. 3368, Mr. Reese of Dallas County. Hereafter cited as *Official Proceedings.*

[12] *Ibid.,* p. 3376, Mr. Bulger of Tallapoosa County.

[13] *Ibid.,* p. 3018, Mr. Porter of Coosa County; p. 3333, Mr. Cunningham of Jefferson County; p. 3394, Mr. Taylor of Perry County; p. 3333, Mr. Reese of Dallas County.

because he opposed the "understanding clause." However, he said of the poll tax:

It will not do away with the negro as a voter altogether, but it will have the effect of keeping numbers of the most unworthy and trifling of that race from the polls. I do not know of anything better in view of the fifteenth amendment.[14]

He recommended increasing the severity of the tax provision by requiring that the tax be cumulative for the entire period of liability.

In the Louisiana convention, opposition arose because the Suffrage Committee did not include a poll tax provision in its plan. Several speakers stated that the problem was to find a lawful method to prevent Negroes from voting and many spoke in favor of a poll tax for this purpose. The plan was recommitted to the committee and, as finally adopted, included a poll tax provision.[15] In Mississippi, payment of the tax was made a voting prerequisite largely because of the belief that whites would be more apt to pay it than Negroes.[16] The situation was similar in Texas.[17]

PURIFICATION OF ELECTIONS

While critics of legalized restrictions on Negro voting may find it hard to discover any high moral tone in such activities, these restrictions reflected a movement for purifying the electoral process in the southern states. In their initial attempts at recovery of control over politics, southern white leaders had resorted to various methods of fraud and violence, to such things as the South Carolina "eight box" law, to the tissue ballot and to the methods of organizations like the Ku Klux Klan. Although legally Negroes and whites had equal access to the polls, actually by 1890 Negro votes were so controlled by

[14] *Report of the Proceedings and Debates of the Constitutional Convention of Virginia, 1901-2* (Richmond, 1906), p. 604. Hereafter cited as *Debates.*

[15] Amasa M. Eaton, "The Suffrage Clause in the New Constitution of Louisiana," *Harvard Law Review,* XIII (December, 1899), 288-91.

[16] William A. Mabry, "Disfranchisement of the Negro in Mississippi," *Journal of Southern History,* IV (August, 1938), 333.

[17] Laura Snow, "The Poll Tax in Texas: Its Historical, Legal and Fiscal Aspects" (Mss., M.A. Thesis, University of Texas, 1936), p. 32.

southern white leaders that the whites ruled and few Negroes held office.

If the Negro's vote was effectively controlled and if the whites had been back in power since about 1876, why did the whites wait until the 1890's to disfranchise the Negro legally? Individuals who participated in the movement insisted that it was necessary to disfranchise the Negro to purify the electoral process. They maintained that intimidation, ballot-box manipulation and other dishonest election methods reached out beyond the bounds of politics and tainted the whole society.

Again and again members of the various constitutional conventions brought this point into their speeches. Judge J. J. Chrisman, a member of the Mississippi constitutional convention, stated that there had not been a full vote and a fair count in Mississippi since 1875 and that as a result of the revolutionary methods which were being used by the white people to preserve their ascendancy, the public conscience had revolted.[18] The president of the Alabama convention, referring to the fact that the younger generation was being taught that it was right to buy and steal votes, said:

The results of such an influence will enter every branch of society; it will reach your bank cashiers, and affect positions of trust in every department; it will ultimately enter your courts and affect the administration of justice.[19]

Carter Glass informed the Virginia convention that the constitutional revision movement had originated because

. . . negro enfranchisement was a crime to begin with and a wretched failure to the end, and that the lawful, but necessary, expedients employed to preserve us from the evil effects of the thing were debauching the morals and warping the intellect of our own race.[20]

Newspapers also emphasized the necessity of purifying elections by finding constitutional means of disfranchising the Negro. The Richmond *Times* declared: "It is more courageous and honorable and better for public morals and good govern-

18 Mabry, p. 319.

19 *Official Proceedings*, p. 9. See also statements of former Governor Oaks, p. 2786, and Mr. Lowe of Jefferson County, pp. 2825-28.

20 *Debates*, p. 293. See Edgar G. Murphy, *Problems of the Present South* (New York, 1904), pp. 191-92, for a viewpoint similar to those stated above.

ment to come out boldly and disfranchise the Negro than to make a pretense of letting him vote and then cheating him at the polls."[21] In Alabama, the Birmingham *News* reported that "the youth of the state were being taught that cheating in elections was excusable, and this was leading on to dishonesty in commercial and social life."[22]

In addition, there was a realization that if fraudulent methods could be used to control the Negro vote, they could be used against fellow whites, and were, in fact, so used. In the Virginia election of 1896, such election tactics were used to discriminate against the "Gold" Democrats.[23] Tom Watson, the Georgia Populist, was defeated time after time following the election of 1892 by means of intimidation and fraudulent practices.[24] The Birmingham *News* declared that "from cheating Republicans and Populists, the Democrats had turned to cheating themselves."[25]

In Arkansas and Texas, the argument was frequently presented that a poll tax payment prerequisite would purify elections by preventing repeaters and floaters from voting.[26] Neither state had a registration requirement and the proponents of the poll tax advocated it as a substitute. The editor of the San Antonio *Express* wrote:

By requiring a poll tax receipt, secured six months previous to an election, fraudulent elections can be prevented almost entirely. No sharp candidate will buy tax receipts for purchasable voters six or eight months in advance. He cannot buy them for floaters who move from county to county to vote, even if he were willing to do

21 As quoted in Ralph C. McDanel, *The Virginia Constitutional Convention of 1901-1902* (Baltimore, 1928), p. 33.

22 July 30, 1902. As quoted in Albert B. Moore, *History of Alabama and Her People* (Chicago, 1927), p. 901.

23 McDanel, p. 32.

24 C. Vann Woodward, "Tom Watson and the Negro in Agrarian Politics," *Journal of Southern History*, IV (February, 1938), 25.

25 July 30, 1902. As quoted in Moore, p. 900.

26 See editorial from Pine Bluff *Commercial*, reprinted in *Arkansas Gazette*, August 26, 1892; editorial, *Arkansas Gazette*, July 14, 1892; letter addressed to editor of Batesville *Guard* and signed by Charles Coffin in *Arkansas Gazette*, August 10, 1892; editorial, Dallas *News*, October 2, 1902, as quoted in Snow, p. 47.

so. The amendment will prevent fraudulent voting. There is no
reasonable doubt as to that.[27]

When interviewed in 1947, Lee Satterwhite, a veteran Texas
politician and member of the legislature in 1901 when the poll
tax amendment was proposed, said that the main reason why
the legislators approved it was to improve the conduct of
elections.[28]

While there is substance to the contention that the southern
disfranchising movement would purify elections, purification
was not the primary motivation.   Much of what was said about
the need for improving the honesty of elections may be classified as pious talk used as a means of winning popular support
for disfranchisement.   The leaders of the movement were too
sophisticated politically to believe all that they said.   Some of
the suffrage provisions encouraged, rather than discouraged,
the use of fraud and discrimination in elections.   The use of
the "understanding clause" and the discriminatory powers given
to election officials indicate that leaders of the disfranchising
movement failed to purify elections significantly.[29]

EFFECT OF POPULIST PARTY

The rise of the Populist party is another important reason
why the southern movement for legalized disfranchisement
occurred at this time.   The entrance of this new party upon the
political scene definitely contributed to the demands for
restrictions upon the suffrage in most of the southern states.
Populism spread rapidly through southern and western states,

[27] October 25, 1902. As quoted in Snow, pp. 47-48.

[28] Erle Pettus, a delegate to the Alabama constitutional convention from Limestone County, also emphasized, when interviewed in 1947, the "purity of elections" factor.

[29] This fact was recognized at the time. A delegate to the Alabama convention
opposed the majority report of the suffrage committee because he believed the
plan contained in it would encourage fraudulent elections. He advised the
convention that "the whole scheme is not in favor of fair elections. I will not
question the motive of those who prepared it, but I declare to you that the
scheme, as presented by the majority of this Committee, permits the most
infamous frauds that were ever planned in Alabama." Mr. Lowe of Jefferson
County, *Official Proceedings*, p. 2828.

obtaining its strength largely from discontented farmers. It reached its zenith in the South by the early 1890's and declined quickly after 1896.[30] Either alone, or in combination with Republicans and Negroes, Populists seriously threatened the supremacy of the Democratic party for the first time since reconstruction. For a brief period, Populists were able to unite dissatisfied elements against the conservative Democratic party controlled by business interests of the New South and remnants of the planter aristocracy. It came close to succeeding where the Republican party had failed. For a short time, it appeared that a two-party system might be restored in the South.

The division of the whites caused by the Populist revolt led to bidding by Democrats and Populists for Negro support. Since the Negro vote was controlled by intimidation and fraudulent methods, nothing prevented overtures from being made for this vote when it was needed to win elections. The Negro was becoming the balance of power between the white groups, and Democrats, their predominance threatened, found it expedient to make vigorous use of the plea for white supremacy. Democratic supremacy and white supremacy were portrayed as synonymous although actually the Democrats were probably more successful than the Populists in obtaining the Negro vote, by fair means or foul.

The close relationship between the rise of the Populist party and the disfranchising movement does not follow a common pattern in all southern states. In Florida and Tennessee, the poll tax was made effective by legislative acts before the Populist party became significant.[31] The Mississippi suffrage plan of 1890 was also adopted before the agrarian revolt had become

---

[30] For a general account of Populism, see John D. Hicks, *The Populist Revolt* (Minneapolis, 1931).

[31] For accounts of Populism in these states, see Kathryn T. Abbey, "Florida Versus the Principles of Populism," *Journal of Southern History*, IV (November, 1938), 462-75, and Daniel M. Robison, *Bob Taylor and the Agrarian Revolt in Tennessee* (Chapel Hill, 1935). There is some indication that one reason for the adoption of the Florida poll tax was a fear of the growing power of the Farmer's Alliance. The Alliance was a precursor of the Populist party and later became a part of it. See Virginia D. Collins, "Florida Election Laws" (Mss., Florida State College for Women, Tallahassee, May, 1946), pp. 26-27.

strong in southern politics.[32]   In Alabama, Virginia, Texas, and
Georgia, the suffrage restrictions were imposed after the threat
of Populism had largely disappeared, but these states, and in
particular Alabama and Georgia, had felt keenly the divisions
caused by the movement.   Populism was not dead in the minds
of the leaders of disfranchisement.   The most direct relationship between the two movements occurred in Louisiana, South
Carolina, North Carolina and, to a lesser degree, Arkansas.

In Louisiana, Populists and Republicans fused in the campaigns from 1892 to 1896, thereby creating formidable
opposition for the Democrats.   Both sides courted the Negro
vote, and the altered political importance of the Negro caused
many to express fears of Negro domination.   Louisiana Democrats were convinced that the election of 1896 was the time for
a settlement, and the legislature, under their control, submitted
a suffrage amendment to the voters.   This amendment called
for educational and property qualifications in addition to poll
tax payment.   The ensuing campaign was marked by disorder
and some bloodshed.   The Democrats gained control of the
legislature but with greatly reduced majorities.   The suffrage
amendment was defeated by methods which were characterized
as "disgraceful."   The excesses of the election and the failure
to adopt the amendment led to passage of a measure which
provided for a referendum on the question of holding a constitutional convention.   This proposal was approved by 36,178 to
7,578 votes on January 11, 1898.

The state election of 1896 marked the end of the Republican-
Populist alliance in Louisiana.   In the presidential campaign
of that year, Populists combined with Democrats to support

---

[32] The leadership in calling the Mississippi constitutional convention came
from the predominantly white counties and the discontented farmers, while
the opposition was concentrated in the predominantly Negro counties and the
conservative Bourbon wing of the Democratic party. In states where there was
a close relationship between the Populist party and the movement for disfranchisement, the counties of small farms and few Negroes tended to oppose
this movement while those of large farms and many Negroes tended to lead it.
See Willie D. Halsell, "The Bourbon Period in Mississippi Politics, 1875-1890,"
Journal of Southern History, XI (November, 1945), 519 and 531-33, and Albert
D. Kirwan, "Apportionment in the Mississippi Constitution of 1890," *Journal
of Southern History*, XIV (May, 1948), 234-35.

William Jennings Bryan. After 1896, the Populist party ceased
to be important in this state. Louisiana Populists did not
participate in any election as a separate party after 1900.[33]

A somewhat different situation developed in South Carolina,
where the agrarians, under the leadership of Benjamin R.
Tillman, captured control of the Democratic party without
organizing an independent Populist party. In an attempt to
regain control, the Conservative Democrats appealed to the
Negroes for their support, and once again a division of the
whites brought the Negro into political prominence. Following
his election as governor in 1890, Tillman undertook to disfranchise the Negro, but it was not until after his re-election in
1892 that he could persuade the legislature to pass a bill
providing for a popular referendum in the election of 1894 on
the question of calling a constitutional convention. In this
election, Tillman campaigned for the constitutional convention
referendum and for a candidate as his successor. A bitter
struggle ensued between the two factions of the Democratic
party, the Tillmanites and the Conservatives. Opposition to
the convention came not only from the Conservatives but also
from some Tillman supporters who feared the consequences to
the illiterate white vote. Tillman had not announced what
he proposed to do regarding the suffrage. The vote on the
convention question was close, 31,402 to 29,523. The Tillman
faction won by less than 2,000 votes.[34]

While a connection between the agrarian revolt of the 1890's
and the disfranchising movement existed in South Carolina, it
was a different relationship from the one in Louisiana. In
Louisiana, Populists combined with Republicans and Negroes
to threaten the supremacy of the Democratic party and the
conservative element led the movement for revised suffrage

---

[33] Based upon the article by Melvin J. White, "Populism in Louisiana during
the Nineties," *Mississippi Valley Historical Review*, V (June, 1918), 3-19.

[34] William A. Mabry, "Ben Tillman Disfranchised the Negro," *South Atlantic
Quarterly*, XXXVII (April, 1938), 171-77; Francis B. Simkins, *Pitchfork Ben
Tillman* (Baton Rouge, 1944) pp. 278-82, and *The Tillman Movement in
South Carolina* (Durham, 1926), pp. 203-07; and David D. Wallace, "The
South Carolina Constitutional Convention of 1895," *Sewanee Review*, IV (May,
1896), 350-51.

requirements. In South Carolina, the disfranchising movement
was headed by the leader of the agrarians who feared that his
conservative opponents would use the Negro vote to defeat him.
The events in this state suggest that a significant factor in the
suffrage reform movement was not so much white supremacy
as such but the supremacy of a particular group of whites.

In North Carolina also, a division among the whites developed and was followed by the adoption of a disfranchising
amendment. In 1894, Republicans and Populists controlled
the legislature. In 1896, they fused on a ticket for state officers
in spite of the fact that Populists were linked with Democrats
in the presidential campaign. Together they gained control of
the legislature, the governorship, and many local offices. Many
Negroes were selected to fill local offices in eastern counties
where the Negro population was heavy. North Carolinians
feared the return of the horrors of reconstruction, and several
riots occurred. Even Populists were affected by the intense
excitement, and many Populist supporters decided that if a
third party was going to mean that Negroes again would be
governing officials, it would be best to abandon the idea.
Consequently, in 1898, a Democratic majority was returned to
the legislature, and this legislature proposed the disfranchising
amendment adopted in 1900.[35]

During the campaign for ratification of the amendment,
Republicans opposed it. At first, the attitude of the Populists
was doubtful. The newspaper of Marion Butler, the Populist
leader, announced that Populists would support it if the
amendment would actually take the Negro issue out of politics.
Serious doubts that it would do so were expressed. Later,
Butler announced that the amendment was unconstitutional
and Populists joined Republicans to oppose Democrats on this
issue.

The amendment was essentially a copy of the suffrage provisions of the Louisiana constitution. Republicans and Populists

[35] Hicks, pp. 391-93, and Simeon A. Delap, *The Populist Party in North Carolina* (Historical Papers of Trinity College Historical Society, Series XIV, Durham, 1922), pp. 61-70. The election of Negroes to office and the resulting
bloodshed which accompanied the rise to power of the Populist party in North
Carolina had an adverse effect upon the party in other sections of the South.

argued that the "grandfather clause"[36] was unconstitutional and that, if it should be so declared, the educational qualification would result in the disfranchisement of many whites. They stressed this point particularly in the western counties which were predominantly white and where there was considerable illiteracy. They also reasoned that the poll tax would bear as heavily on unfortunate whites as on Negroes. The Populist Executive Committee issued the following caveat:

We warn the white people that this amendment will disfranchise approximately as many white men as it will Negroes in this state, and will leave the Negro still a factor in politics, with as much power as he now has. . . . This is a white man's government and always will be; there are two white voters to every colored voter, hence the state is in no danger of Negro supremacy. . . . This amendment if adopted would end popular government in this state. It would turn the offices over to a select few, who would not feel bound to respect the rights of the common man, because the common man would not be able to enforce respect at the ballot box.

The principal argument for the amendment was the familiar one of white supremacy. The Democratic nominee for governor, Charles B. Aycock, led in spreading the idea that ratification was essential for the preservation of white supremacy. The appeal to race was in some cases stronger than party loyalty. Many individual Populists openly supported the amendment despite the fact that the party leadership opposed it. On the other hand, some western Democrats, alarmed over the possibility of white disfranchisement, fought the amendment.

Force, fraud, and intimidation were liberally used in the campaign. Physical terror kept Negroes from voting and social pressure prevented many whites from voting against the amendment. It was called the "Red Shirt Campaign," because red-shirted riflemen were organized, mainly in the eastern section of the state, to intimidate anti-amendment voters and

---

36 This clause permitted a man to register as a voter without complying with the literacy requirement if he or an ancestor was a registered voter on or before January 1, 1867. Since the right to vote had not been extended to Negroes by this date, Negroes could not qualify under the clause but illiterate whites could.

speakers.[37]   The amendment carried with a majority of nearly 54,000 votes.[38]

Thus, in North Carolina as in Louisiana and South Carolina, a division among the whites caused by the rise of the Populist party resulted in the imposition of legal restrictions upon the suffrage.   By combining with Republicans, Populists successfully challenged the supremacy of the Democratic party.   The change in political control was accompanied by a return of Negro officeholders, and this fact enabled Democrats to argue persuasively that the time had come to restrict the suffrage as a means of preserving white supremacy.   The power of this argument led many Populists to support the suffrage amendment.   On the other hand, the leaders of the Republican and Populist parties as well as many Democrats from the western part of the state, opposed it because they feared the effect on the illiterate and low-income white voters.   Since the North Carolina amendment was supported by the Democratic party and opposed by the Republican and Populist parties, the situation here was more nearly comparable to Louisiana than to South Carolina.

The Arkansas poll tax amendment was adopted in 1892, a year when Populism was becoming a threatening force in other states.   Populists were not strong in Arkansas and the Democrats were not seriously worried by them.   In 1892, Democrats, Republicans and Populists each ran a gubernatorial candidate. The Democrats won with apparent ease and without resorting to the tactics employed in Louisiana and South and North Carolina.   The Democratic party supported the poll tax amendment but did not center its campaign on this issue.   The party leaders devoted themselves primarily to the tariff and the

[37] This action was an imitation of the tactics of Wade Hampton and his South Carolina followers in 1876.

[38] Based primarily upon Mabry, *The Negro in North Carolina Politics Since Reconstruction* (Historical Papers of Trinity College Historical Society, Series XXIII, Durham, 1940), pp. 58-71. See also editorial, "The North Carolina Elections," *Outlook*, LXV (August 11, 1900), 841-42; editorial, "North Carolina's Red Shirt Campaign," *Independent*, LII (August 2, 1900), 1874-76; and Marion Butler, "Election in North Carolina," *Independent*, LII (August 16, 1900), 1953-55.

Force Bill, a proposal that the national government should again intervene in congressional elections to protect the Negro's right to vote. Republicans and Populists both opposed the poll tax amendment, and the Populist candidate for governor, J. P. Carnahan, was its most outspoken opponent. The vote revealed considerable opposition with 75,940 for to 56,601 against.[39]

In Alabama the disfranchising movement did not follow so closely on the heels of Populism. Populism had largely run its course there by 1896, while a constitutional convention to revise the suffrage requirements did not assemble until 1901. Nevertheless, a connection did exist between these two movements. When Populism was at its zenith, Negroes were appealed to for their votes just as they had been in other states when whites divided. Fraudulent elections thrived, and the prevalence of dishonesty in elections created demands for reform. In 1893, the Sayre Election Law was passed to improve the elective system by increasing the secrecy of the ballot and by providing for a registration system. Originally, this measure required payment of a poll tax as a condition of registration. The tax provision was struck out while the bill was in committee because many Populists and Jeffersonian Democrats opposed it.[40] In this same legislature, an unsuccessful attempt was made to initiate a constitutional convention.[41] These incidents indicate that the disfranchising movement began when Populists were strong.

With the rise of Populists in Alabama, Conservative Democrats resorted to the magic cry of "white supremacy." The choice was presented to the people as one between white supremacy and a third party. Populism was sacrificed largely on the altar of white supremacy. The way was made ready for calling a constitutional convention whose declared purpose was the disfranchisement of the Negro.[42]

---

[39] William F. Kirby, *A Digest of the Statutes of Arkansas* (Austin, Tex., 1904), p. 109. Other information is based on *Arkansas Gazette*, July, 1892, through September, 1892.

[40] Malcolm C. McMillan, "A History of the Alabama Constitution of 1901" (Mss., M.A. Thesis, University of Alabama, 1940), p. 12.

[41] John B. Clark, *Populism in Alabama* (Auburn, 1927), p. 147.

[42] McMillan, p. 5, and Clark, p. 180.

The Populist party as such did not have the turbulent history in Virginia that it had in most of the southern states.[43] Virginia had a taste of the effects of a division of the white vote during the Readjuster period.[44] Dishonest elections became almost customary when Democrats adopted fraudulent practices to beat the Readjuster leader, Mahone, at his own game. This condition of affairs resulted in the movement for a constitutional convention, and, in this way, the Readjusters set in motion the chain of events which culminated in the Constitution of 1901-02.[45]

The question of calling a convention had been debated for more than ten years. Proposals for calling a convention were defeated by the voters in 1888 and 1896. Finally in 1900, a favorable popular vote was obtained. The knowledge of what was then happening in North Carolina undoubtedly had its effect in this decision. Approval was given by a narrow margin after a light vote, 77,362 to 60,375.[46]

In Texas also, the adoption of the poll tax and Populism were related. Most of the opposition to the 1902 amendment, came from the remnants of the Populist party. The Populist State Headquarters in Dallas issued the following circular on November 2, 1902, two days before the election:

Read this—Lincoln's warning to the American people—"I bid the laboring people beware of surrendering a power which they already have, and which, when surrendered, will close the door of advancement to them and fix new disabilities upon them till all of liberty will be lost."

Lincoln saw the coming evil, and with prophetic eyes he saw what would result. His prophecy is now being fulfilled. On Tuesday next, the laboring people will be called upon to vote for an amendment to our Constitution, which, if carried out, will rob them of their liberties at the ballot box. Every laboring man who loves

---

[43] See William D. Sheldon, *Populism in the Old Dominion: Virginia Farm Politics, 1885-1900* (Princeton, 1935).

[44] See footnote 5 above.

[45] McDanel, p. 8. Cf. Richard L. Morton, *Virginia Since 1861*, Vol. III of *History of Virginia* (Chicago, 1924), p. 218.

[46] McDanel, p. 16. The estimated number of registered voters at this time was 425,000.

liberty, who believes in freedom of suffrage, who prizes his rights of citizenship should vote against the poll tax amendment.

(Signed) Milton Park
State Chairman Allied Peoples Party
J. D. Johnston.[47]

Since Populists were not strong in Texas in 1902 and since only slight opposition came from other groups, the amendment was approved by 200,650 to 107,748 votes.[48] Only 33 of the 226 counties voted against it. They were predominantly white counties in the center of the state and along the Mexican border. Only two had a sizable Negro population.[49] The opposition of unionized labor was evident in Johnson County, where there was a large railroad employee vote. Large majorities for the amendment were recorded in many black belt counties,[50] an indication that Negroes either did not vote or that their vote was controlled. The larger cities of the state strongly favored it.[51]

In Georgia, the situation was somewhat analogous to that in South Carolina. The disfranchising amendment of 1908 had the backing of Tom Watson, the fiery leader of Populism. At first, Watson defended the Negro and tried to unite depressed whites and equally depressed Negroes in the Populist party. The efforts of both Democrats and Populists to gain the Negro vote resulted in fraud, corruption, and bloodshed. Watson's home was in the black belt and Democrats successfully counted

[47] As quoted in Snow, p. 50.

[48] Alexander Heard and Donald S. Strong, *Southern Primaries and Elections, 1920-1949* (University, Ala., 1950), p. 189.

[49] Montgomery and Smith with a Negro population as of 1900 of 38.8 per cent and 42.9 per cent respectively. The other opposition counties were Cameron, Comanche, Delta, Duval, Eastland, Ellis, El Paso, Fisher, Floyd, Hamilton, Henderson, Hidalgo, Hood, Jack, Johnson, Kendall, Kent, Mason, Nolan, Parker, Potter, Rains, Runnels, Scurry, Shackelford, Somervell, Starr, Stephens, Stonewall, Val Verde, Webb.

[50] Those counties with a high proportion of Negroes in the population.

[51] Snow, p. 51. For the county-by-county vote, see Heard and Strong, pp. 189-91. Texas had seven cities with a population over 20,000 in 1900. They were Austin, Dallas, Fort Worth, Galveston, Houston, San Antonio, and Waco. The percentages voting for the amendment in the counties where they were located were Travis, 66.8; Dallas, 65.4; Tarrant, 60.3; Galveston, 68.4; Harris, 57.5; Bexar, 74.1; McLennon, 73.8.

the Negro vote against him.   These defeats caused him to turn
against the Negro and to become a leader in the movement for
disfranchisement.   By the end of the 1890's, Populism had sub-
sided in Georgia, but, in 1906, a serious rift developed within
the Democratic party, a struggle between the conservative and
radical wings.   The chief issue in the campaign that year was
railway regulation.   Hoke Smith, the gubernatorial candidate
of the radical wing, supported regulation of the railroads and
corporations and advocated reforms to bring about more direct
popular government.   His platform was in reality a Populist
one.   Smith also declared for the elimination of the Negro from
politics by legal methods.   Watson supported him, and he won
the election.   In 1908, the disfranchising amendment was added
to the constitution.   Watson justified his desertion of the
Negro on the ground that only by eliminating the Negro vote
could Populism triumph in the South.   As a result of his
experience, he concluded that the whites would not revolt as
long as they could be intimidated by the fear of the Negro
vote.[52]

DISFRANCHISEMENT OF THE POOR WHITE

In recent years, the hypothesis has been advanced that the
Populist party not only caused a demand for Negro disfranchisement but also evoked a desire on the part of conservative
Bourbon Democrats to disfranchise poor and illiterate whites,
thereby cutting into Populist strength.[53]

---

[52] Woodward, pp. 27-28.

[53] In 1940, Ralph J. Bunche wrote: "There seems to be little room for doubt
that the entrenched interests of the South—the southern ruling class of that
period—were fearful of the threat of union between the poor whites—who
were beginning to become articulate in Populism—and the Negroes, and that
this possibility of a united people's movement in the South impressed them as
a revolutionary upsurge that must be crushed at all odds. The poll tax legislation lent itself admirably to this purpose. It made it possible for the South
to maintain and to exploit its white supremacy doctrine and at the same time
keep away from the polls, not only Negroes, but those under-privileged whites
who constituted a new threat to the hegemony of the entrenched interests of
that section." See "The Political Status of the Negro," unpublished research
memorandum for the Carnegie-Myrdal Study, p. 600.

It is relatively simple to find proof for Negro disfranchisement as the major purpose of the poll tax and the other suffrage restrictions.   It is not so easy to establish that disfranchisement of the so-called poor whites was also an intent of the leaders of the movement.   It was popular to talk about Negro disfranchisement.   To discuss limiting the vote of fellow whites was an entirely different matter.   Despite this fact, evidence that there was a desire to disfranchise whites as well as Negroes may be found in the records of the constitutional conventions of this time.

Some members of the conventions frankly believed that some whites should be disfranchised.   In opposing the adoption of a grandfather clause, former Governor Oates of Alabama said: "There are some white men who have no more right and no more business to vote than a negro and not as much as some of them."[54]   A delegate in the Virginia convention declared:

The need is universal, not only in the country, but in the cities and towns; not only among the blacks but among the whites, in order to deliver the State from the burden of illiteracy and poverty and crime, which rests on it as a deadening pall. . . . It is not the negro vote which works the harm, for the negroes are generally Republicans, but it is the depraved and incompetent men of our own race, who have nothing at stake in government, and who are used by designing politicians to accomplish their purpose, irrespective of the welfare of the community.[55]

Frequent remarks were made about depriving the "ignorant and vicious" of the suffrage with little indication whether these descriptive terms were intended to apply only to the Negro.[56]

Many delegates believed that the poll tax would be especially harmful to the whites.   An opponent of the tax in the Virginia convention said: "I have always maintained and believed that

[54] *Official Proceedings*, p. 2789.

[55] *Debates*, p. 2998, Mr. McIlvaine.

[56] The following comment by Mr. Smith from Mobile in the Alabama convention is fairly typical: "It [Suffrage and Elections Committee] has labored diligently, carefully, and honestly not for the purpose, as has been said, by some of the members of the Convention, of depriving all negroes of the right of suffrage, not to avoid depriving any white man of it, but to frame such an Article as will place the ballot, as was said by our President, in the hands of those who are competent to wield it, and take it from the ignorant and the vicious." *Official Proceedings*, pp. 2952-53.

more white people will be stricken from our registration rolls than negroes by such a provision."[57]   A supporter exclaimed:

I am in favor, Mr. Chairman, of the capitation tax, and I do not hesitate to say so, because I believe it will disqualify some white men in Virginia who ought to be disqualified. . . . I want to say to the gentlemen of this body that when they undertake to put an additional capitation tax on the people of Virginia and then provide that it shall be a prerequisite to voting, instead of disfranchising the African, they are disfranchising the Anglo-Saxon.[58]

Another delegate reported that many members of the Suffrage and Elections Committee looked with apprehension upon the poll tax requirement and felt it was impossible to forecast its result. He said:

. . . The report comes to us from large, and from diversified, sections of this State that in many of these communities it will be an exceedingly problematic matter as to whether the poll tax will not strike harder upon the white race six months in advance than it will upon the negro.

He cited the decrease that had occurred in the white vote in Mississippi and stated that this decline may have been brought about at least partly by the poll tax.[59] Another member advised that he had always been against the tax as a suffrage prerequisite because he believed that it would disfranchise, at least in the mountain section and in the cities, as many or more whites as Negroes and that it would be a constant source of dissatisfaction and worry.[60]

A delegate in the Alabama convention who wanted collection of the poll tax enforced stated:

Now, Mr. President, if you make the payment of a poll tax voluntary and put upon it no other condition than he shall vote, I believe a large majority of the best element of the white people in this State will sit by and not take part, and that the politics of this State will fall into the hands of rings and cliques who will operate and run it, pay their poll tax and vote, not for the benefit of the State, but for offices for themselves and their followers.[61]

---

[57] *Debates*, p. 2864, Mr. Flood.
[58] *Ibid.*, pp. 2871-72, Mr. Gordon.
[59] *Ibid.*, pp. 2979-80, Mr. Thom.
[60] *Ibid.*, p. 3010, Mr. Brown.
[61] *Official Proceedings*, p. 3373, Mr. Smith of Mobile.

A member of the Committee on Suffrage and Elections replied that the main purpose of the committee in dispensing with compulsory collection was to allow the poll tax to accumulate "on this very class of voters that we want to get rid of—the vicious voter in Alabama."[62]

A poll tax opponent in this convention advised his colleagues that, although the amount of the tax might seem small to them, "it is an important factor to men of little material substance, but of considerable character in various portions of the hill country of this state."[63] Another opponent declared:

. . . there are a great many people all over the white counties that have not $1.50 at the end of the year, but come out in debt. There are white men in this country who rather than pay $1.50 would surrender their vote. . . .[64]

In those states which held constitutional conventions, promises were made prior to the assembling of the conventions that no whites would be disfranchised. Temporary suffrage plans were formulated to fulfill these promises. The leaders of the disfranchising movement pointed to these temporary provisions and informed illiterate whites that they would still vote. However, they refrained from discussing the long term effects of their schemes upon white suffrage. In each instance, the poll tax was a part of the permanent plan and proof exists that the leaders of disfranchisement incorporated it in their permanent plans to eliminate many whites from the polls.

In 1905, John B. Knox, the president of the Alabama constitutional convention, wrote:

The charge made against us is that we adopted this constitutional provision for the purpose of excluding the negro. The true philosophy of the movement was to establish restricted suffrage, and to place the power of government in the hands of the intelligent and virtuous; and while any provision for restricted suffrage would exclude more negroes than white men, in its practical operation the Alabama provision, so far as the permanent plan is concerned,

---

62 *Ibid.*, p. 3381, Mr. Hood of Etowah.

63 *Ibid.*, p. 3357, Mr. Fitts of Tuscaloosa.

64 *Ibid.*, p. 3397, Mr. Duke of Chambers. For a discussion of the disfranchising effect of the poll tax upon white voters in Texas, see Seth S. McKay, ed., *Debates in the Texas Constitutional Convention of 1875* (Austin, 1930), pp. 168-69, 171-75, 177-79, 183-84, and 189.

and the exaction of a poll tax as a condition to suffrage, so operates as to exclude not only a large mass of negro voters, but quite a number of white voters who do not feel sufficient interest in their own Government to contribute to the school fund the small amount exacted as a poll tax, and who are so indifferent to their own interests as that they fail to meet the provision of the Constitution which requires that any voter under the permanent plan shall be able to read and write any clause of the Constitution in the English language, although the free public schools of the State are open to them.[65]

The same year Francis G. Caffey, a practicing lawyer in Montgomery at the time of the Alabama convention, stated even more directly the long term purpose behind the poll tax. After pointing out that to carry the call for that convention, the leaders in the movement had to promise their fellow whites that they would not be disfranchised and that the constitution would be submitted to the voters for ratification, he continued:

How to get rid of the venal and ignorant among white men as voters was a far more serious and difficult problem than how to get rid of the undesirable among the negroes as voters. While it was generally wished by leaders in Alabama to disfranchise many unworthy white men, as a practical matter it was impossible to go further than was done and secure any relief at all. Hence, as the next best thing, the evils of ignorance and venality among the white electorate were reduced to a minimum by making their further lease of life as short as possible.

The long sway of one party had, naturally, put undue political power into the hands of unworthy white men. To get a new constitution at all, it was necessary to appease this element. This was done by giving those who then had the right to vote the right of registration under the temporary plan. To rid the state eventually, so far as could possibly be done by law, of the corrupt and ignorant among its electorate, white as well as black, the poll tax and vagrancy clauses were put into the constitution.[66]

---

[65] "Reduction of Representation in the South," *Outlook*, LXXIX (January 21, 1905), 171. At the time of the convention, Mr. Knox said that although the delegates were pledged not to deprive any white man of his vote, this pledge did not extend beyond the life of the voters then living unless the convention so chose. See Max B. Thrasher, "The Alabama Constitutional Convention," *Outlook*, LXVIII (June 22, 1901), 437.

[66] "Suffrage Limitations at the South," *Political Science Quarterly*, XX (March, 1905), 56-57.

Further proof that a desire to disfranchise whites as well
as Negroes existed at this time may be found by examining
the movement for calling constitutional conventions where
suffrage reform was secured through constitutional revision.
There was considerable opposition to the conventions due
largely to a fear that whites would be disfranchised along
with Negroes. The whites were definitely not in agreement
on the necessity for these conventions.

Although in Mississippi the leadership for a constitutional
convention came from the white counties,[67] a number of
Democrats from these counties feared that whatever was done
would result in the disfranchisement of many whites. It took
considerable time for the movement to gain enough strength
to be approved. When the convention was authorized, the
call was issued by the legislature without submitting the question to a popular vote. Therefore, there is no record of the
amount and location of the opposition. United States Senator
Edward C. Walthall reflected the opinion of many other
Democrats from predominantly white counties when he objected
to the proposed convention because he did not want "to
restrict the elective franchise by imposing on it any conditions
which would strike down tens of thousands of the best white
Democrats in Mississippi."[68]

That some of Tillman's followers in South Carolina had
a similar fear was noted previously. The popular vote in 1894
on the question of calling a constitutional convention reflected
this opposition. Since it was 31,402 to 29,523, only 51.5 per cent
of those who voted favored a convention.[69]

Many whites in Alabama opposed a constitutional convention to revise the suffrage requirements. The state Democratic
party pledged itself not to deprive any white man of his vote,
but even so experienced great difficulty in obtaining approval
for the convention of 1901.[70] Of the 66 counties, 25 opposed

[67] See footnote 32 above.
[68] As quoted in Mabry, "Disfranchisement of the Negro in Mississippi," p. 321.
[69] Cf. editorial, "South Carolina's Problem," *Nation*, LXI (September 19, 1895),
199, wherein it is stated that the Conservatives claimed the convention was
really voted down.
[70] McMillan, pp. 67-95.

calling a convention. Most of these counties were located in North Alabama and in the extreme southern part of the state. All but one were predominantly white. Butler was the sole black belt county to vote in opposition. The counties which returned the largest majorities for a convention were mainly located in the black belt. The vote was 70,305 to 45,505; 39.3 per cent of those who voted opposed a convention.[71]

There is a significantly close relationship between the vote against calling the convention of 1901 and the vote for Reuben Kolb, the Populist gubernatorial candidate in 1892 and 1894. Kolb's support was concentrated in the northern half of the state and in the extreme southeastern corner. These are the hill counties and the wire grass counties—the less fertile sections, the areas of small farms and a predominantly white population. The chief opposition to Kolb came from the black belt section—that fertile, plantation area with a heavy concentration of Negroes which stretches across the lower central portion of the state. In 1892, although defeated, Kolb carried 37 of the 66 counties. Twenty of them were among the 25 counties which opposed the convention of 1901. In 1894, 34 counties went for the Populist candidate; 21 were among the 25 counties voting against a constitutional convention.[72] Thus, most of the counties which supported the Populist party in 1892 and 1894 opposed the calling of a constitutional convention in 1901. The Populist party was strongest in those areas where the percentage of white illiterates was highest and where agricultural conditions were poorest. Opposition to the convention from this same section indicates the existence of a great fear that its result would be the disfranchisement of many whites, especially those whites who had revolted against the Bourbon Democrats by supporting the Populist party.

In Virginia, also, the opposition to calling a constitutional convention came from the section containing few Negroes and many illiterate and relatively poor whites, i.e., the western

[71] For the county-by-county vote, see *Alabama Official and Statistical Register, 1903* (Montgomery, 1903), pp. 141-42.

[72] For the county-by-county vote in the elections of 1892 and 1894, see Heard and Strong, p. 20.

mountainous region. A student of this convention concluded that "the vote was decidedly sectional, the convention being brought into existence by the cities and the black counties against the rural districts and the white counties."[73] Since the vote was 77,362 to 60,375, only 56.2 per cent of those who voted favored a convention.[74]

The only state where there was not considerable opposition to calling a constitutional convention was Louisiana. The returns in the referendum held in January, 1898, showed 36,178 for to 7,578 against, a favorable vote of 82.7 per cent.[75] However, this referendum had been preceded two years earlier by rejection of a disfranchising amendment. The election of 1896 was an extremely disorderly one with a Republican-Populist fusion opposing the Democrats. Afterwards the demand for suffrage reform became stronger and the Republican-Populist fusion ended. Many Populists returned to the Democratic fold. Consequently, the convention proposal was approved with little opposition.[76]

Of the five states which revised their suffrage requirements by adopting new constitutions, only Alabama submitted its constitution to the people for their approval. The conventions of the other states proclaimed the adoption of the constitutions. Perhaps they feared that their work would be rejected if exposed to a popular vote.

Opposition to ratification of the Alabama constitution came from the same sections which initially fought the calling of the convention. The principal opposition came from North Alabama. The southeastern wire grass region also tended to vote against the constitution. Although most black belt counties voted heavily in favor of it, five (Autauga, Butler, Choctaw, Lee and Lowndes) cast a majority vote against it. However, the vote was close with the largest opposition being registered in Lee and Butler, 66.9 per cent and 61.7 per cent respectively. The vote on the constitution brought a larger turnout than

73 McDanel, p. 18.
74 *Ibid.*, p. 16. Earlier attempts to call a constitutional convention met with defeat at the polls.
75 White, p. 18.
76 *Ibid.*, pp. 14-18.

that on the convention. The total vote was 190,347; 108,613 favored the constitution while 81,734 opposed. Only 57.1 per cent of those voting approved the new constitution.[77]

The same fear of disfranchisement was prevalent among many North Carolina whites in 1900 when the suffrage constitutional amendment was submitted to the electorate. As in Alabama and Virginia, the contest was largely a sectional one. The chief opposition was in the western, mountainous region where there were many illiterate and poor whites and few Negroes. This was also the section where Republicans were strongest. Of the 97 counties, 32 voted against the amendment. Only three of these counties (Brunswick, Camden and Sampson) were located in the eastern half of the state and only in Sampson was there a sizable opposition vote. The chief support for the amendment came from the eastern black belt. The vote was 182,217 to 128,285; 58.6 per cent of those voting favored the amendment.[78]

There was, then, considerable opposition to the disfranchising movement of the 1890's and early 1900's. Most objections came from sections where whites predominated, and they reflected a fear that whites would be disfranchised along with Negroes. This fact does not positively answer the question of whether there was a desire to disfranchise whites as well as Negroes but it shows an expectation on the part of many whites that they would lose votes. Apparently, the leaders of the movement did not overlook the fact that the permanent suffrage plans would operate to the disadvantage of many whites, especially those of the poorer classes, and they included the poll tax to strike at both poor whites and Negroes. One southerner has written that the leaders in the movement were confronted with two defective classes, unqualified Negroes and unqualified whites. If approval for a constitution were to be gained, both classes could not be dropped simultaneously from the electorate. The Negro could be disposed of immediately but the unqualified white man must first be included

---

[77] For the county-by-county vote, see Heard and Strong, p. 20. See also Mc-Millan, pp. 171-84.

[78] For the county-by-county vote, see Heard and Strong, p. 104.

in the partnership of reorganization and then eliminated by a gradual process.[79]

THE FORCE BILL

Another factor which encouraged the southern states to take steps to revise their suffrage requirements in this period was the threat which came from the national government in the form of a Federal Elections Bill, more commonly called the Force Bill. This measure, introduced in the House of Representatives in 1890 by Henry Cabot Lodge, was designed to provide protection to the Negro voter through national supervision of congressional elections. The proposal never became law although it passed the House.[80] But the threat of a reimposition of national control over elections helped to awaken southern leaders to the fact that they ought to stop the illegal tactics which they were using to regulate the Negro's vote.

The Force Bill had a direct relationship with the disfranchising movement only in those states which adopted suffrage restrictions about the time this measure was before Congress. Since these states pointed the way followed later by the other southern states, the Force Bill had its effect upon the entire movement although it did not directly affect all of the states involved.

The Force Bill exerted its chief influence in Mississippi where the constitutional convention met in 1890. Judge S. S. Calhoon, the president of the convention, advised his fellow citizens:

It will not do to familiarize the federal power with supervision of the ballot in the states. Better to disfranchise one or the other of the races at the South at once. . . .

[79] Murphy, pp. 192-93. Ralph J. Bunche concluded that "the Negro was played up as the major issue in this period of franchise restriction and the literacy qualifications and registration tests, which were clearly aimed directly at the Negro, served to detract attention from the inclusion of poll tax requirements for voting which were destined to affect the white voter even more seriously than the Negro." Bunche, p. 597.

[80] 21 *Congressional Record* 6941, and 22 *Congressional Record* 1746.

The editor of the *Clarion-Ledger* wrote:

If the force bill now pending in Congress passes, it is fortunate for Mississippi that she will be able through her Constitutional Convention soon to assemble to put such restrictions on suffrage as to render it largely nugatory and deprive it of much of its power for evil. Other Southern states are not so favorably situated, but the example set by Mississippi can be followed by them if the measures adopted prove adequate to meet the evil.[81]

The influence of the Force Bill was also felt in Arkansas when adoption of the poll tax was under consideration in 1892. A student of the Arkansas poll tax concluded that the popularity of the tax amendment resulted from fear of measures like the Force Bill as well as the desire to disfranchise the Negro.[82] The state Democratic convention that year supported the tax amendment and also appealed for co-operation in defeating attempts to enact any "force bills." During the election campaign, support was asked for both state and national Democratic candidates in hope that Democratic strength might facilitate the defeat of federal force bills. Simultaneously passage of the poll tax amendment was urged.[83]

In summary, the disfranchising movement of the 1890's and early 1900's was brought about by a combination of factors. One factor was a desire to find a legal basis for Negro disfranchisement, both to secure white supremacy and also ostensibly to purify elections. Another factor of major importance was the Populist party. The movement for suffrage restrictions was greatly affected by the rise of this party which split the whites and led to overtures for the Negro vote; to new fears for white, or more accurately Democratic, supremacy;

---

[81] Both quotations taken from Mabry, "Disfranchisement of the Negro in Mississippi," p. 322. See also Vernon L. Wharton, "The Negro in Mississippi, 1865-1890," *Studies in History and Political Science*, ed. Albert R. Newsome (Chapel Hill, 1947), p. 209. Mr. Wharton believes that the most powerful factor in the desire for legal elimination of the Negro was the change that had occurred in Washington, represented by the Lodge Force Bill and the fact that Republicans were in control of the national government.

[82] Crawford, p. 33.

[83] *Ibid.*, pp. 33-34.

to an increased amount of violence and fraud in elections. It seems evident that the Populist challenge also fostered a wish to eliminate from the voting lists many poor and illiterate whites. Finally, the initiation of the movement was encouraged by the threat of national intervention in elections represented by the Lodge Force Bill. The poll tax was in most instances only one of several disfranchising measures adopted. It was largely overlooked at the time of its adoption, attention being detracted from it by the literacy and registration requirements. Although the tax was primarily portrayed as an additional way to disfranchise the Negro, it appears that the leaders of the movement regarded it mainly as a method of discouraging from voting that class of whites which was beginning to challenge their control of southern politics.

2. THE FORM OF THE TAX

THERE IS A TENDENCY to talk about the poll tax as if it were the same in every state which links it to the suffrage. But it differs greatly from state to state and because of these differences, it varies in its effects on voting. Before the administration of the tax requirement and the effects of the tax upon voting can be significantly discussed, it is necessary to seek answers to the following questions: (1) How much is the tax? (2) Who is liable, and who is exempt? (3) When must the tax be paid if the taxpayer is to be permitted to vote? (4) What proof of payment may be required of voters? (5) What use do the states make of poll tax revenue?

POLL TAX RATES

Supporters of the tax often state that anyone who will not pay $1.00 for the privilege of voting does not deserve to have that privilege. Reiteration of this statement has created the impression that the amount of the poll tax is invariably an insignificant sum. Citation of the annual rate alone tends to confirm this impression. Table 1 shows that the annual rate varies from $1.00 to $2.00. One state (Arkansas) requires an annual payment of $1.00; three states (Alabama, Texas and Virginia), $1.50; and one state (Mississippi), $2.00.

The annual rate, however, does not show the true economic burden of the tax. Three states have cumulative poll tax requirements—i.e., the tax must be paid for each of a series of years. In Alabama and Mississippi, the voter is required to have paid the tax for two years before he is eligible for a ballot and, in Virginia, for three years.

The cumulative feature of the tax is not as severe now in Alabama as it was. Until 1953, Alabama permitted the poll tax to accumulate for a period of 24 years so that a prospective voter might have to pay as much as $36. All poll taxes for each year of residence in the state after age 21 and to age 45 had to be paid. Upon reaching 45, the voter was no longer liable for the tax but he was still required to pay, or to have paid, all taxes for which he had been liable between the ages of 21 and 45.[1] In December, 1953, a constitutional amendment was approved which reduced the period of accumulation to two years and the maximum amount to $3.00.[2] The amendment eased considerably the poll tax requirement not only for those

Table 1. POLL TAX RATES

STATE	ANNUAL RATE	CUMULATIVE PROVISION	MAXIMUM STATE CHARGE[a]	MAXIMUM ADDITIONAL TAX AT OPTION OF LOCAL AUTHORITIES
Alabama	$1.50	Two years preceding election	$3.00[b]	None
Arkansas	$1.00	None	$1.00	None
Mississippi	$2.00	Two years preceding election	$4.00[b]	$1.00, Counties[c]
Texas	$1.50	None	$1.50	$0.25, Counties $1.00, Cities
Virginia	$1.50	Three years preceding election	$4.50[b]	$1.00, Counties, Cities, Towns[c]

[a] Exclusive of penalties.
[b] See textual explanation of Alabama, Mississippi and Virginia.
[c] None actually levied as voting prerequisite.

between the ages of 21 and 45 but also for those 45 and over who had failed to keep up with their payments. Anyone 46 or older on or before October 1 of the year preceding the election does not have to pay any back taxes; anyone who becomes 45

[1] *Constitution,* Art. VIII, sec. 178.
[2] Amendment XCVI.

on or before this date owes that tax for only one year if he is delinquent in payment.[3]

Before 1945, Georgia had a cumulative poll tax which was similar to the Alabama tax between 1901 and 1953. It accumulated for the entire period of liability from ages 21 to 60. Although the annual rate was only $1.00, the maximum liability, including penalties, amounted to $47.47.[4] When in effect, these cumulative provisions of Alabama and Georgia were of considerable significance in reducing voting.

In Virginia, where the tax may accumulate for three years, the maximum liability, exclusive of penalties and local poll taxes, is $4.50.[5] With penalties, the highest possible payment is $5.01.[6]

In Mississippi, the cumulative feature, as applied to the primary election, differs from both the Alabama and Virginia requirements. In Alabama and Virginia, if an individual has not paid his poll tax annually, he may satisfy the cumulative requirement by payment of all poll taxes due in a lump sum.[7] To vote in Mississippi primary elections, the tax must be paid by February 1 of each of the two years preceding the election.[8] Thus, to be eligible for the primary, the significant election in the one-party South, the tax must be paid each year. Otherwise the individual will be disfranchised until he has paid it during two successive years. For the Mississippi general election,

---

[3] See 73 *Quarterly Report of the Attorney General of Alabama* 81 (1953).

[4] Exhibit 28, submitted by Henry H. Collins, Jr., *Hearings on S. 1280*, before a subcommittee of the Committee on Judiciary, U. S. Senate, 77th Cong., 2d. sess., p. 325. Hereafter cited as *Hearings on S. 1280*. Of the other former poll tax states in the South, only Florida had a cumulative tax. Florida's tax was $1.00 per year and had to be paid for two years preceding the election. The annual rate in Louisiana, South Carolina, and Tennessee was $1.00, and in North Carolina the combined state and county tax could not exceed $2.00.

[5] *Constitution*, secs. 20 and 173.

[6] Exhibit 28, *Hearings on S. 1280*, p. 325. Virginians age 21 are not required to pay a poll tax. It is not until age 25 that the full three year payment for delinquents begins. At age 22 a tax is payable for one year only; at 23, also for one year; at 24, for two years if not previously paid.

[7] Virginians may pay their back taxes in installments. A suggested procedure is that payments be made in January, March, and May. There is no method for installment payments in Alabama.

[8] *General Laws of Mississippi, 1936,* Chapter 320, sec. 1, p. 599.

the tax may accumulate for two years to a total of $4.00, exclusive of any county taxes and penalties, and may be paid at one time like the cumulative tax in Alabama and Virginia.[9]

The significance of the Mississippi poll tax requirement for primary elections may be seen by examining tax returns in the other poll tax states. The revenue received from the tax tends to decrease in non-election years, as is shown by the chart of Texas poll tax revenue receipts.[10] In the non-cumulative poll tax states (Arkansas and Texas), failure to pay the tax one year does not endanger the individual's right to vote the following year. In the cumulative poll tax states of Alabama and Virginia, failure to pay the tax in an off-election year can be corrected by a lump sum payment the next year. In Mississippi, failure to pay in an off-election year means the individual cannot vote in the next primary election and cannot again vote until he has paid the tax in each of two consecutive years. Poll tax payment may be easily forgotten when there is no approaching election to serve as a reminder.

Where the tax accumulated for long periods as in Alabama and Georgia, it was considerably more burdensome than where it is paid only for the year preceding the election. The burden of the tax at this time is evident when the per capita annual income of these states is considered. In 1940, Alabama per capita income payments were only $269, although they had risen to $847 by 1950. At this time, the tax could accumulate to $36. In 1940, Georgia per capita income payments were $316 and had risen to $794 by 1945 when the poll tax was

[9] *Constitution,* Art. XII, secs. 241 and 243. The requirement that the poll tax must be paid for two successive years to vote in the primary has been in operation in Mississippi only since 1936. Prior to this time, the cumulative requirement was the same for both the general and primary elections. Before 1935, it was necessary to have paid all taxes, and not just all poll taxes, for the two years preceding a general election. As a result of the depression, many property owners in the thirties were unable to meet their tax payments. Consequently, the constitutional requirement of "all taxes" was altered to "all poll taxes" in 1935. The requirement that all taxes must be paid for two years did not apply to primary elections.

[10] The chart bears out this statement except for the year 1931. The Texas Comptroller of Public Accounts cannot explain why the receipts were so heavy in this non-election year. Letter to author, dated February 27, 1951.

abolished. During this period, the Georgia tax could accumulate to $47.47. In Virginia, the per capita income payments in 1940 were $446 and in 1950, $1,147.[11] Since the maximum cumulation plus penalties is $5.01, a man who has not kept up with his and his wife's payments will owe $10.02. For many Virginia families, this is still a sizable sum of money.[12]

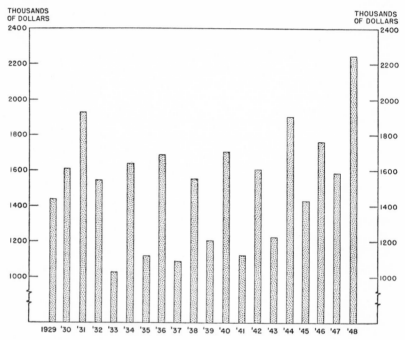

FIGURE 1. Revenue Receipts from Texas Poll Tax: 1929-1948. (Source: Office of Comptroller of Public Accounts, Texas, Revenue and Expenditure Charts, 1929-1948, p. 8.)

In many instances, money which might be used for paying poll taxes is used to purchase more tangible benefits than the privilege of voting. At the time of the 1940 presidential election

---

[11] *Statistical Abstract of the United States, 1954,* p. 304.

[12] See statement of John W. Edelman, Washington Representative, Textile Workers Union of America (CIO), *Hearings on H. R. 29,* etc., before the subcommittee on elections of the Committee on House Administration, H. of R., 80th Cong., 1st sess., p. 136, in which Mr. Edelman discusses the burden of the Virginia tax upon union labo

four farm couples of Green Pond, Alabama, were talking about the AAA farm program and the chance that Speaker of the House Bankhead had of replacing John N. Garner as the vice-presidential candidate on the Democratic ticket.

Only two of the eight voted—or could vote under Alabama's cumulative poll tax law. These two men had paid their $1.50 every year. A third had voted until the drought of 1933. With no election that year he saw no reason for putting out $1.50, he did not have. Next year $3.00 was the price he had to pay to vote, and cotton was selling for 5 cents a pound. He could not spare that much. Now a vote for Bankhead in the Democratic primaries next spring will cost him $11.50. He won't vote . . .

"Lord, that's jus' like me," his wife spoke up. "They drug me out and hauled me down when Bryan [sic] was arunnin' in '24. I hain't voted since. Wonder what they'd charge me now?" We figured it out. It came to $22.50. "That's as much as I give for that cook stove yonder," she answered, "and hit'll last me a heap longer!"[13]

In several states, the burden of the tax levied by the state is increased by a poll tax enacted by local authorities. As Table 1 discloses, Mississippi counties may levy an additional tax up to $1.00;[14] Texas counties may levy an additional tax of 25 cents and Texas cities an additional tax up to $1.00;[15] and Virginia counties, cities and towns may levy an additional tax up to $1.00.[16] No local poll taxes are authorized in Alabama and Arkansas.

Not all local areas in these states have made use of their authority to levy poll taxes. No local poll taxes as voting prerequisites are levied in Mississippi and Virginia. In Texas, all counties levy the tax of 25 cents so the tax per person is $1.75. Some cities require payment of an additional tax of $1.00 but it is a prerequisite for voting only in municipal elections.[17]

[13] George C. Stoney, "Suffrage in the South: The Poll Tax," *Survey Graphic,* XXIX (January, 1940), 7-8.

[14] *Constitution,* Art. XII, sec. 243.

[15] *Vernon's Texas Statutes,* Arts. 7046 and 1030.

[16] *Constitution,* sec. 173.

[17] When Tennessee required poll tax payment, counties and cities were permitted to levy an additional tax up to $1.00. Until 1941, all counties required payment of the additional tax. With the county tax added to the state tax,

The annual rate of the poll tax is, therefore, only from $1.00 to $2.00 but the addition of cumulative provisions increases this rate in Alabama, Mississippi and Virginia. With the repeal of the tax in Georgia and the major reduction of the cumulative period in Alabama, the cumulative feature is no longer as oppressive as it was. Although Virginia now has the tax which accumulates to the greatest sum, the devious requirement of Mississippi applicable to the primary is probably more significant in discouraging prospective voters because it catches them off guard in non-election years. The economic burden of the state tax has been augmented by local poll taxes in Texas. The lowest and least burdensome rate is found in Arkansas.

COVERAGE OF THE TAX

Sizable groups of people are exempt from poll tax payment, as is apparent from a study of Table 2. Such exemptions, of course, lessen the severity of the tax prerequisite and bear upon the suffrage effects of the tax. Some of these exemptions date from the time of the adoption of the tax while others, especially those pertaining to veterans, are of more recent date. The effectiveness of the tax as a disfranchising device has diminished as the number of exemptions has increased.

A common exemption is one based on age. Alabama excuses all persons 45 and over[18] while Mississippi and Texas relieve all those 60 and over. Arkansas and Virginia do not exempt persons because of age.[19]

---

the annual rate was $2.00 throughout the state. When an effort was made to repeal the tax in the early 1940's, it was learned that the county tax could be eliminated independently of the state tax. Beginning in 1941, the tax was repealed by about a third of the counties. A few cities required poll tax payment as a prerequisite in municipal elections. Thus, in some cities, the annual poll tax was $3.00; in some counties, $2.00; and in others, $1.00. Lyndon E. Abbott and Lee S. Greene, *Municipal Government and Administration in Tennessee,* Univ. Tenn. Record Extension Series, XV (Knoxville, 1939), 67 and 90.

[18] The Alabama constitution gives authority to the legislature to raise the age limit to sixty. Such action has never been taken and probably never will be.

[19] When requiring poll tax payment as a suffrage prerequisite, Tennessee and North Carolina exempted all persons 50 and above; Florida, all those 55 and above; Georgia, Louisiana and South Carolina, all those 60 and above.

Another common exemption is that relieving individuals who are incapacitated—the blind, deaf, dumb or maimed from loss of a limb. This exemption is less important than that of age because of the relatively small number of persons involved. Arkansas and Virginia are again exceptions and do not grant immunity for disability.[20]

In recent years, veterans have been included among those groups excused from tax payment. During World War II, all poll tax states, except Alabama, adopted temporary exemptions applicable to members of the armed forces and veterans for the duration of the war and for a short time after its close. Temporary exemptions for service personnel were adopted to answer objections against taxing the voting privileges of persons serving their country and to stave off national control over elections. Only Alabama and Tennessee gave permanent exemptions to veterans. Alabama exempted World War I veterans

Table 2. PERSONS LIABLE FOR POLL TAX PAYMENT

STATE	PERSONS LIABLE	PERSONS EXEMPT[a]
Alabama	Every inhabitant over 21 and under 45, not otherwise exempt	1. All 45 and over[b] 2. Those permanently and totally disabled from following any substantially gainful occupation with reasonable regularity, whose taxable property does not exceed $500 3. Those who are blind or deaf 4. Those with honorable military service between January 1, 1917, and November 11, 1918; between September 16, 1940 and December 8, 1941; or at any time past, present or future, when the United States was, is or shall be engaged in hostilities whether or not as a result of a declared war with any foreign state 5. Members of State Guard during active membership and those who have served 21 years
Arkansas	Men over 21 Women over 21 desiring to vote	1. Women not desiring to vote 2. Any citizen while serving in U. S. armed forces

20 This type of exemption was also common in those southern states which have now abolished the poll tax.

State	Persons Liable	Persons Exempt[a]
		3. Those who become 21 after the time of assessing taxes next preceding an election
Mississippi	Every inhabitant over 21 and under 60, not otherwise exempt	1. All 60 and over[b]
		2. Those who are deaf and dumb, blind or maimed by loss of a hand or foot
		3. Any member or veteran of the U. S. armed forces who, because of such membership, did not have an opportunity to pay
Texas	Every inhabitant over 21 and under 60, not otherwise exempt	1. All 60 and over
		2. Indians not taxed; those insane, blind, deaf or dumb; those who have lost a hand or foot, those permanently disabled and all disabled veterans of foreign wars with 40 per cent or more disability
		3. All members of state militia except for $1.00 tax for schools
		4. Those who, at time of election, are, or within 18 months prior were, members of U. S. armed forces exempt for duration of war or within one year after close of the year in which the war is terminated
		5. Those who become 21 after January 1 and before the following election
Virginia	Every inhabitant over 21, not otherwise exempt	1. Civil war veterans and their wives or widows
		2. Those pensioned by the state for military services
		3. Active members and recently discharged members of U. S. armed forces in time of war
		4. Those who become 21 after January 1 and before the following election

[a] All of these states except Alabama had temporary exemptions applicable to the armed forces and veterans during and at the close of World War II.

[b] Except for the application of the cumulative requirement to those who have just reached the maximum age and are delinquent for the preceding year.

in 1924 and those of World War II in 1944. Preliminary to complete repeal, Tennessee exempted the veterans of both wars in 1949. The Alabama exemption applies also to veterans of any future foreign hostility in which the United States may be involved, whether or not the hostility is the result of a declared war.[21] This last provision was adopted as a result of the Korean War. Alabama veterans who serve in the armed forces during peacetime are not exempt.

Lesser exemptions of service personnel are found in Arkansas, Mississippi, Texas, and Virginia. Arkansas exempts any citizen while serving in the armed forces; Mississippi exempts any member or veteran of the armed forces who, because of such membership, did not have opportunity to pay his poll tax; Texas exempts, in time of war and for one year afterwards, members of the armed forces and those discharged within eighteen months of the election; and Virginia exempts, in time of war, members of the armed forces and those discharged during the calendar year preceding the election. Texas also frees all disabled veterans of foreign wars who have a disability of forty per cent or more.[22]

When South Carolina and Tennessee required poll tax payment as a voting prerequisite, the exemption of women was important. South Carolina never exacted the tax from women while Tennessee relieved them of the tax burden in 1949 when its legislature eased the tax prerequisite.[23] Women are not treated differently from men in any of the present poll tax states. In Arkansas, women who do not desire to vote are not liable for the tax, but this provision is of no significance. Because little effort is made to collect the tax in any of the states, only those men and women who desire to vote pay, although many others are technically liable.[24]

In assessing the full significance of these exemptions, a computation of the persons who are relieved from poll tax payment because of age and sex is illuminating. Table 3 shows the number and the percentage of citizens 21 and over who

21 Alabama *Constitution*, Amendments XLIX (1944) and XC (1951); *Public Acts of Tennessee, 1949*, Chapter III, p. 352.

22 Arkansas *Constitution*, Amendment XXXVI (1944); *General Laws of Mississippi, 1952*, Chapter 397, pp. 601-03; Texas *Constitution*, Art. VI, sec. 2a (1945); Virginia *Constitution*, Art. XVII (1945).

23 *Public Acts of Tennessee, 1949*, Chapter 62, p. 215.

24 Before repeal, Georgia had a somewhat similar provision. Women who were not registered as voters were not liable for the tax; those women who had registered could be relieved of the tax by applying to the county tax collector to have their names removed from the registration book.

were exempt in 1950 from poll tax payment in Mississippi, South Carolina, Tennessee and Texas because of age and in South Carolina and Tennessee because of both age and sex. Although no longer poll tax states, South Carolina and Tennessee have been included to demonstrate the significance of the sex exemption and to show how unimportant as a voting deterrent the tax was in these states before its removal in 1951. In South Carolina 58.6 per cent and in Tennessee 66.9 per cent of the potential voting population were freed from payment because of age and sex. Since Tennessee also excused veterans of World Wars I and II and since neither state demanded payment as a voting prerequisite in primary elections, the tax was even less significant than Table 3 indicates. The South Carolina tax never applied to women nor to primary elections. Tennessee freed women and veterans from payment and removed it as a requirement for primaries in 1949.

The age exemptions alone free large numbers of persons from poll tax payment in Mississippi and Texas. In Mississippi, 18.0 per cent, and in Texas, 16.2 per cent of those persons 21 and over were not required to pay a poll tax in 1950. Because of its former cumulative requirement, Alabama has been omitted from Table 3. Since the reduction of the cumulative period has also benefited those 45 and above who were delinquent, the number relieved because of age may now be computed. Based upon the census of 1950, 695,817 persons are exempt in Alabama because of age. They constitute 39.8 per cent of those persons 21 and above.

Table 3. PERSONS EXEMPT FROM POLL TAX PAYMENT
DUE TO AGE AND SEX, 1950

STATE	EXEMPT FOR AGE[a]		EXEMPT FOR SEX[b]		EXEMPT FOR AGE AND SEX
	Number	Per Cent	Number	Per Cent	Per Cent
Mississippi	217,233	18.0			
South Carolina	78,134[c]	14.1[c]	596,782	51.9	58.6
Tennessee	305,495[c]	31.8[c]	1,017,401	51.4	66.9
Texas	766,592	16.2			

a Those 60 and over, except in Tennessee where exemption began at age 50.
b That is, all women 21 and over.
c Men only, since women were exempt.

The number exempt due to age is important because of the low voter turnout in these states. If exemption from the tax meant that these individuals would then begin to vote, it is possible that the aged would have a weight out of proportion to their number in the total population. However, because individuals are freed from poll tax payment at age 45 or 60, they do not necessarily begin to vote. Habits are not easily changed, especially in later life. Exemption of the aged may provide an opportunity for some to vote who had not done so while liable, but it does not mean that they will vote.

Although the number exempt from poll tax payment because of veteran status cannot be accurately computed, a rough estimate may be made by ascertaining the number of World War II inductees. There were 210,599 persons inducted from Alabama. This number is equivalent to twelve per cent of the voting population as of 1950. Assuming that approximately as many veterans now live in the Cotton State as were inducted during the war and recognizing that additional persons are exempt because of the Korean War,[25] it would appear that at least fifteen per cent of the voting population benefits from the veteran exemption. As a result of the age and veteran exemptions, well over fifty per cent of those persons 21 and over are not liable for a poll tax in Alabama.[26]

The Alabama veteran exemption benefits men more than women since few women have veteran status. Largely as a result of this exemption, women's organizations have taken the lead in recent years to secure repeal of the tax. Their rallying

[25] 62 *Quarterly Report of the Attorney General of Alabama* 15 (1951), and *Constitution,* Amendment XC (1951).

[26] Alabama does not compile statistics on the number of poll taxpayers nor on the number of registered voters. It is, therefore, impossible to compute how many registered voters do not pay a poll tax. The following figures, however, serve as an indication. In 1947, the officials of Madison County reported that there were approximately 12,500 registered voters in the county and that only 2,543 had paid their poll taxes. Birmingham *News,* February 10, 1947. In 1953, it was reported that out of approximately 80,000 qualified voters in Jefferson County, only 19,300 had paid a poll tax in 1952. Birmingham *Post-Herald,* December 12, 1953. These figures do not mean that all persons who did not pay were exempt. Some may have been liable and failed to pay. It may be assumed, however, that a large number of them were exempt.

cry has been that Alabama's tax disfranchises more white women than Negroes.[27]

A veteran exemption is of most importance immediately following a war. However, due to the size of our armed forces in World War II and to the number involved in the Korean War, there will be many veterans in our population for some time and a veteran exemption from poll tax payment will continue to be important.

In Alabama, Mississippi, and Texas, therefore, many citizens are exempt from the poll tax. In the examination of tax rates, it was found that Alabama, Mississippi, and Virginia, the states with the cumulative tax, have the most burdensome rates. These states do not have the most extensive coverage although one, Virginia, is in this group. Arkansas and Virginia have the most extensive poll tax coverage; Mississippi and Texas stand about midway on the scale; while Alabama has the least extensive coverage.

Finally, this inquiry into poll tax liability reveals that the tax tends to bear upon certain groups in a discriminatory fashion. Generally, the young and middle-aged voter must pay it while the aged voter is relieved. The disabled or handicapped person is also freed. In Alabama, non-veterans are discriminated against. The exemptions may encourage the aged, the disabled, and the veteran to vote and give these groups a greater voice in southern politics than their numerical strength justifies.

TIME OF POLL TAX PAYMENT

In those states where the poll tax must be paid a considerable period before the primary and general elections, the monetary burden of the tax is supplemented by the time-of-payment provisions, which also have an effect upon the number of persons qualified to vote. Individuals are called upon to yield their hard-earned cash before knowing who the candidates will be. Since there is frequently little interest in an election to be held some months in the future, many persons neglect to pay the tax before the deadline. When the election draws near and

27 See Chapter 8.

candidates and issues (if any) are known, some persons may desire to vote only to find that they cannot because they failed to pay their poll taxes by the proper time. Thus, citizens may be prevented from voting not solely because they cannot afford to pay the tax but also because they do not pay at the right time. This provision is most effective as a means of disfranchisement with the less educated groups who are frequently unaware of the time when the tax should be paid. It is also used to advantage by professional politicians who see that their followers have paid the tax, or who pay it for them, by the due date.[28]

An analysis of the provisions for time of poll tax payment is presented in Table 4. This analysis establishes the fact that the tax must be paid long before the general election in most poll tax states. For the taxpayer to be qualified to vote in the general election, the tax must be paid approximately nine months before in Alabama, Mississippi, and Texas, and six months before in Virginia. Only in Arkansas may the tax prerequisite be met a relatively short time before the election. Here the tax may be paid as late as one month before the general election.[29]

Since the general election is usually of little significance in the one-party South, it is more important to note how long prior to the primary the poll tax must be paid. In Arkansas, the tax must be paid approximately ten months before the

---

[28] The extent to which the tax is paid for others by politicians is examined in Chapter 4.

[29] Arkansas veterans discharged after the close of the regular poll taxpaying time may pay at any time before an election. *Arkansas Election Laws: Constitutional and Statutory (Simplified), 1954*, p. 8. Florida, South Carolina, and Tennessee also permitted poll tax payment a short time before the general election. In Florida and South Carolina, the tax could be paid as late as thirty days before the election and in Tennessee, sixty days before the election. *Laws of Florida, 1889*, Chapter 3850, p. 13; South Carolina *Constitution*, Art. II, sec. 4 (e); *Michie's Tenn. Code of 1932*, sec. 2027. Since Tennessee also required that the poll tax had to be paid at, or before, the time of payment of property taxes, property owners had to pay well before the sixty-day deadline. Georgia required that the tax be paid six months before an election, while North Carolina demanded payment on or before the first day of May. Georgia *Constitution of 1877*, Art. II, sec. 1, para. 3; *North Carolina Code of 1931*, sec. 5941.

Table 4. TIME OF POLL TAX PAYMENT

STATE	DUE DATE	APPROX. PERIOD DUE BEFORE GENERAL ELECTION	APPROX. PERIOD DUE BEFORE GUB- ERNATORIAL PRIMARY
Alabama	Payable only between Oct. 1 and Feb. 1	9 months	3 months
Arkansas	On or before Oct. 1	1 month	10 months[a]
Mississippi	On or before Feb. 1	9 months	18 months[a]
Texas	Before Feb. 1	9 months	6 months
Virginia	Six months before general election	6 months	3 months

[a] See text for explanation.

gubernatorial primary; in Texas, six months; in Alabama and Virginia, three months; and in Mississippi, eighteen months because of the peculiar cumulative provision for primary elections.[30]

In Arkansas, the poll tax must be paid on or before October 1 to qualify to vote in any election held during the subsequent twelve months. Thus, the tax deadline is only a little more, than a month prior to the general election but it is nearly ten months before the primary.[31] This requirement has been in effect since 1939. Formerly, poll taxes were assessed between the first Monday in January and April 10.[32] Payment was due the following year in a period beginning early in January and running to the early part of July.[33] Payment during this period entitled the person to vote in the last six months of that year, a period which included both the primary and general elections. A result of this procedure was a sharp falling off of tax payments in non-election years. In an effort to raise additional

[30] The gubernatorial primaries are held at the following times: in Mississippi, the early part of August, every other even-numbered year; in Arkansas, the latter part of July, every even-numbered year; in Texas, the latter part of July, every even-numbered year; in Alabama, the early part of May, every other even-numbered year; and in Virginia, the early part of August, every other odd-numbered year.

[31] Except for recently discharged veterans. See footnote 29 above.

[32] *Acts of Arkansas, 1929,* Act 172, sec. 7.

[33] *Pope's Digest of the Statutes of Arkansas, 1937,* sec. 4697.

revenue, the legislature in 1939 changed the collection period to run from the third Monday in February to October 1. Payment at this time entitled the payer to vote in the twelve months period after October 1.[34] Thus, to vote in all primaries and elections, the individual had to pay the tax every year. The change reduced the biennial fluctuations in collections.[35] In addition, it increased the period between tax payment and the primary but reduced the period between tax payment and the general election. In 1947, the Arkansas legislature abolished the assessment procedure and made the tax payable any time throughout the year preceding each October 1 deadline.[36] Therefore, a poll tax paid at any time between October 2, 1955 and October 1, 1956 qualifies the payer for voting from October 2, 1956, to October 1, 1957. These changes suggest that a desire to discourage voting was not the only reason for the selection of the tax payment deadline. In most states, however, it was the principal one.

Alabama has the most restrictive requirement for time of payment since the tax may be paid only from October 1 through February 1. A controversy developed about this requirement during the presidential campaign of 1952. Many citizens who had not paid their poll taxes by February 1, 1952 wanted to vote in this crucial election. A Mobile probate judge ruled that if they paid after October 1, 1952 they could participate. Subsequently, the Attorney General informally advised the county tax collectors and probate judges that this ruling was incorrect and that a person must have paid his tax by February 1, 1952 to vote in November, 1952. The Alabama Supreme

---

34 *Acts of Arkansas, 1939*, Act 82.

35 This effect may be seen in Figure 20.

36 *Acts of Arkansas, 1947*, Act 220, sec. 3. There is now no procedure for collecting delinquent poll taxes. When the time of payment ran from the third Monday of February to October 1, there was such a procedure. If a person paid after the deadline date, he was given a pink, instead of a white, receipt to show that he was not entitled to vote. Some individuals wished to pay even though payment would not qualify them to vote because they had to pay the poll tax before a state or municipal license or permit of any kind could be obtained and before any salary or compensation from public funds could be received.

Court upheld the Attorney General's decision in an advisory opinion.[37]

In Mississippi, the prescribed time of payment is from December 1 through February 1. Payment is accepted after this date (until September 30) although payment after February 1 does not entitle the payer to vote. Neither can the peculiar cumulative requirement applicable to the primary be satisfied by payment after the due date since, to qualify for voting, the tax must be paid annually on or before February 1 for two years preceding the primary. Payment after the February deadline may be made, however, to help the individual qualify himself for a future general election.

In Texas, the tax is normally paid in the period from October 1 to February 1. It may be paid after the due date but the receipt must be stamped to show that the holder is not entitled to vote.[38] Since the Texas tax is non-cumulative, payment after the due date is without significance relative to the suffrage except for instances in which tax officials fail to stamp the receipt. Virginia does not restrict payment to a single period but requires only that the tax be paid six months before the general election.

A further reason for the poll tax payment time requirements is that these times coincide with the calendar of collections for other taxes. A comparison between the time for payment of the poll tax and the time for payment of other taxes indicates that a relationship exists between them.

In Alabama, most taxes become due on October 1 and are delinquent January 1.[39] This period approximates that for the poll tax except that the taxpayer has a month longer to pay the tax on voting. In Arkansas, real estate and personal property taxes are payable from the third Monday in February through October 1.[40] The same period of payment applied to poll taxes

---

[37] Tuscaloosa *News*, October 8, 1952; Birmingham *Post-Herald*, October 9 and 22, 1952; *In re opinion of the Justices*, 60 So. (2d) 686.

[38] *Vernon's Texas Statutes, 1952 Supplement*, Election Code, Arts. 5.09 and 5.12.

[39] *Alabama Code of 1940*, Tit. 51, sec. 23.

[40] *Arkansas Statutes, 1947*, Tit. 84, sec. 1001.

from 1939 to 1947. Mississippi requires the payment of one-half the total amount of most taxes on or before February 1 and the remainder in two equal installments, one by May 1 and the other by August 1.[41] In Texas, the collection of all taxes, including the poll tax, is begun on October 1. All ad valorem taxes become delinquent if not paid by February 1 unless one-half has been paid by November 30.[42]

Virginia levies a penalty of five per cent against anyone who fails to pay income and personal property taxes by December 5.[43] This penalty also applies to the poll tax. As a qualification for voting, the poll tax does not have to be paid until six months before the general election. Therefore, persons may pay after December 5 and still qualify as voters but they must pay the five per cent penalty. As a result, most poll taxes are collected in November, primarily because the poll tax charge is on the personal property tax bill and is paid with other taxes before the delinquent date but also because the first week of December is the payment deadline to vote in city and town elections in June.[44]

Further insight into why particular due dates for poll tax payment were selected may be obtained by examining the reasons given when the tax was adopted. One reason for requiring payment some time before the general election relates to the attempt to purify elections. This factor was particularly evident in Virginia. When a poll tax was required in Virginia from 1876 to 1882, there was no set time for payment before an election. Experience demonstrated that vote-buying through poll tax payment was thereby encouraged. Accordingly, when the tax was again tied to the suffrage, provision was made that it must be paid six months before the general election. The Committee on the Elective Franchise of the 1901-1902 Constitutional Convention explained that "the requirement that this payment shall be made so far in advance is inserted in order to

41 *Mississippi Code, 1942,* sec. 9891.

42 *Vernon's Texas Statutes,* Arts. 7255 and 7336.

43 *Code of Virginia, 1950,* Tit. 58, secs. 117 and 441.

44 Statement of Henry G. Gilmer, Comptroller of Virginia, *Hearings on S. 1280,* p. 430.

prevent the corruption of the franchise by candidates for office on the eve of or during an election. . . ."[45]

A similar argument in favor of requiring poll tax payment by February 1 was advanced in Texas. In answering the claim of tax opponents that it would not purify elections but would have the opposite effect, the editor of the San Antonio *Express* wrote:

This view of the possibilities of the effect of the amendment is far-fetched, as it is unlikely that a vote manipulator would care to run the risk of paying the poll tax of a voter in February [sic], when the general election does not occur until the following November.[46]

The Virginia Committee on the Elective Franchise reported that the six months provision was not only inserted as a means of preventing the corruption of the franchise but also "in order to confine the voting to those persons who value the privilege sufficiently to qualify themselves for it by their own individual and unaided act."[47] This part of the committee report suggests that the time of payment was intentionally set far in advance of the election to decrease the number of voters.

Some members of the Virginia constitutional convention were concerned about the amount of disfranchisement which would be caused by the six months clause. A. P. Thom, a signer of the majority report of the Committee on the Elective Franchise, advised the convention:

Many members of the committee, Mr. Chairman, look with apprehension upon this poll tax requirement. They feel that it is impossible to forecast the result of it. It is no longer a requirement of the prepayment of a poll tax up to the day of election, but the poll tax must be paid six months in advance, which requires the payment to be made before any of the enthusiasm or interest in the individual election has been aroused. Whether that will strike harder on the white suffrage than on the black we do not know, but we know this, that there is danger of it, and we believe further that, if it is done, and the prepayment of the poll tax be made cumulative, if the arrears of the poll tax are piled up upon the white men of the State, it may become a most serious sore upon the body

---

45 *Debates*, p. 600.
46 As quoted in Snow, p. 52.
47 *Debates*, p. 600.

politic, and the source of unending agitation and unending dissatisfaction.[48]

The following comment of a member of the Alabama Constitutional Convention of 1901 reveals the relationship between the time of payment clause and disfranchisement:

I was going to say that the negro and the vicious element will not pay two months ahead of time a dollar and a half in order to exercise this privilege, but if the business man knows he is liable for tax, although he will not give a dollar and a half to vote or exercise the franchise, he will put it on the list of liabilities like he does everything else and tell his clerk to pay it when it is due, and will not wait until the first of February, but will pay it between October and February, along with the balance of his bills, and he will, as a matter of business, qualify himself to vote, and there will be no incentive on the day of election for him to refuse to vote on account of the extra burden; whereas, when the day of election comes, and purchasers come around (and nobody will buy a tramp or a negro ahead of time) or when the politician comes around two weeks before election and wants to buy, lo and behold! the first day of February has passed and he has no vote to sell.[49]

Another member of the Alabama convention reported that he had visited Mississippi recently and had discussed the Mississippi suffrage plan with several delegates, including Judge Calhoon, the convention president. He asked them what provisions gave the most relief in elections.

And from Judge Calhoun [sic] down to the last delegate that I spoke to, told me it was this provision regulating the payment of the poll tax at a particular time and the fact that no legal process could be issued for the collection of it; the fact that it was a voluntary one.[50]

Thus, although there are additional explanations why these times of poll tax payment were chosen, the principal one is that they were selected as further means of reducing the electorate.

In condemning the time requirement of the poll tax, it should not be forgotten that a requirement of registration well in advance of an election may have a similar effect upon voting. The early closing of the registration books in non-poll tax states may operate to discourage voting just as does the requirement

48 *Ibid.*, p. 2979.
49 *Official Proceedings*, p. 3374, Mr. Smith of Mobile.
50 *Ibid.*, p. 3386, Mr. Reese of Selma.

of tax payment several months before the election in poll tax states. In most states, however, the registration closing date is nearer the election than the deadline for poll tax payment. Usually registration does not stop until the third or fourth week before the election.[51]   In Delaware, however, registration closes the last week in June; in Rhode Island, June 30; in Arizona, the fifth Monday before the election; in Kentucky, 59 days before the election; in Pennsylvania, 50 days; in Montana, 45 days; in Nevada and New Jersey, 40 days; and in California, 39 days.[52]   Since these states have a permanent system of registration, the voter is affected by them only when he first registers and not at each election as he is with the poll tax payment provision. Registration requirements are not, therefore, as restrictive upon the suffrage as are the provisions for time of poll tax payment.

PROOF OF PAYMENT REQUIRED OF VOTERS

The requirements to prove that the poll tax has been paid vary considerably. One method of proof is the presentation of the tax receipt to the election officials. Supporters of a federal anti-poll tax bill have charged that this method serves as an additional way to disfranchise prospective voters. Where the tax receipt may be demanded, a person who has lost it could be denied his vote even though he had paid the tax and has met the other suffrage qualifications. Poll tax opponents contend that the provision was designed to strike the uneducated classes, Negro and white, who are unaccustomed to preserving records. There is evidence that proponents of the tax at the time of its adoption felt that the requirement would work primarily to the disadvantage of the Negro.

While the obligation to present a poll tax receipt at the time of offering to vote could result in losing the vote, this provision is not as important as opponents of the tax have indicated. In

[51] *Registration for Voting in the United States* (Rev. ed., Chicago: Council of State Governments, 1946), p. 1. See a similar conclusion in the earlier study by Joseph P. Harris, *Registration of Voters in the United States* (Washington, 1929), p. 195.

[52] *Registration for Voting*, Table III, pp. 9-13.

only one state, Mississippi, is presentation of the receipt the sole means provided for verifying tax payment. To vote in the primary, the individual must have either his poll tax receipts, duplicate receipts or certificates of exemption for the two preceding years.[53] To vote in the general election, the person may be required to produce "satisfactory evidence" of payment of the necessary poll taxes but what the "satisfactory evidence" should be is not specified.[54] An indication of administrative practice may be had from the following notice which appeared before the 1946 election. "Secretary of State Walker Wood said yesterday that voters in Mississippi will not be required to show their poll tax receipts at the special and general elections on Tuesday, November 5."[55]

In Texas and Arkansas, the poll tax receipt may be demanded at the polls but payment may be established by other means. No citizen may vote in Texas unless he first presents to the election judges either his receipt, his certificate of exemption or a sworn affidavit stating that his receipt or certificate has been lost, mislaid or left at home.[56] Authorization of a written affidavit considerably modifies the provision requiring presentation of the receipt.

The Arkansas constitution stipulates that the receipt or other evidence of payment must be exhibited at the time of voting.[57] Another proof is the list of poll taxpayers which is prepared by the county tax collector and filed with the county clerk by October 15. A person with his name on this list may vote by stating that his receipt is not in his immediate possession, that he has not previously used it to vote, and that he does not intend to use it to vote. This statement, unlike the Texas affidavit, need not be made under oath and is necessary only if the election judges ask for it.[58]

---

[53] *General Laws of Mississippi, 1936,* Chapter 320, sec. 1.

[54] *Constitution,* Art. XII, sec. 241.

[55] Jackson *Clarion-Ledger,* October 27, 1946.

[56] *Vernon's Texas Statutes, 1952 Supplement,* Elec. Code Art. 8.07; *Constitution,* Art. VI, sec. 2.

[57] Amendment No. VI.

[58] *Arkansas Statutes, 1947,* Tit. 3, sec. 122. In connection with these requirements in Texas and Arkansas, it should be noted that the poll tax serves as a

In Alabama and Virginia, virtually no reliance is placed upon the use of the receipt as a method of establishing poll tax payment. In both, the official list of voters is used to ascertain whether the tax has been paid. The Alabama statute states specifically that the receipt need not be shown at the polls.[59] Election judges in Virginia use as conclusive evidence of payment the lists of poll taxpayers which are prepared by the county and city treasurers. Further evidence of payment may be prescribed by law but has not been except in the case of a voter who has moved. If a voter has moved from one county or city to another, or from one ward to another, he may show the election judges his receipt as proof of payment.[60] This procedure is aimed at protecting the suffrage of persons who have changed their residence rather than at trying to keep them from voting.

The analysis of the provisions for proof of payment leads to the conclusion that the requirement of presentation of the tax receipt is less important than the foes of the tax have argued. Since there are alternative methods of proving payment, loss of the receipt is not necessarily accompanied by loss of the vote. The primary significance of the requirement lies in the way in which it may be used by election officials. Some voters may be required to present a receipt before voting while others are not.

---

substitute for a system of voter registration there. In Texas, the receipt, exemption certificate or sworn affidavit takes the place of a list of qualified voters which is ordinarily prepared where a registration system is in effect. Persons exempt from payment and residing in cities of 10,000 or more must secure an exemption certificate but those living in smaller communities need not. At the time of voting, election officials stamp the receipt or exemption certificate to indicate that it has been used in voting and retain the affidavit. In Arkansas, the receipt or the list of poll taxpayers is used also in place of a list of registered voters.

[59] *Alabama Code of 1940*, Tit. 17, sec. 136. A list of poll taxpayers is prepared by the county tax collector by March 15 and filed with the probate judge who furnishes it to the election officials.

[60] *Constitution*, sec. 38; *Code of Virginia, 1950*, Tit. 24, secs. 120, 124 and 128. See also *Stokes* v. *Hatchett*, 18 Va. Law Reg. 251 (1912).

DISPOSITION OF PROCEEDS FROM THE TAX

One final question remains to be answered in sketching the form of the poll tax. How is the revenue from the tax used? In each state where the tax is a suffrage prerequisite, all or a part of the revenue is used for the public schools. Texas and Virginia are the only states that allow part of the proceeds to be used for some other purpose. In Texas, fifty cents of the $1.50 state tax is set aside for general revenue needs of the state, while in Virginia the same amount is paid by the state into the treasury of the county or city where collected to be used as the local authorities desire.[61]

The use of poll tax revenue for educational purposes has been cited repeatedly as a justification for the tax. The financial needs of the school systems in the South are well known. When repeal of the tax is urged, a stock reply is that the tax is essential for the support of the schools. The argument confuses the poll tax as a source of revenue with the poll tax as a voting prerequisite. In the South, the tax is first a suffrage measure and only incidentally a means of raising revenue. In justifying the tax as a source of school funds, its supporters fail to compare poll tax revenue with the total amount spent for education. They also neglect to discuss why there could not be a poll tax only for revenue without any relation to the suffrage. A number of states levy a poll tax which is not connected with voting.

An examination of state finances shows clearly that the poll tax is insignificant as a source of revenue and contributes but a small proportion to the total amount spent for education. For example, in the fiscal year ending September 30, 1954, Alabama spent $94,391,213 for schools. In the same year, $548,543 was collected from the poll tax. Thus, in an important election year the tax produced only 0.58 per cent of the

---

61 *Vernon's Texas Statutes*, Art. 7046; Virginia *Constitution*, sec. 173. Of the former southern poll tax states, only North Carolina permitted part of the revenue to be used for a purpose other than education. Not more than 25 per cent of the revenue could go to the support of the poor. *Constitution*, Art. V, sec. 2.

amount spent for the schools that year.[62]   For fiscal 1953,
Alabama spent $86,877,318 for schools and collected $312,320
from the poll tax.[63]   The tax raised only 0.36 per cent of the
school expenditures that year.   In 1954, the poll tax yielded
slightly more than it cost the state to operate the schools for one
day and in 1953, the amount equaled the state's contribution to
keep the schools open for about four and one-half hours.

The Arkansas poll tax yielded in 1953 about 1.66 per cent of
the amount spent by the state for education and public schools
in the fiscal year ending June 30, 1954.[64]   In Mississippi, the
tax produced for the fiscal year ending September 30, 1953,
slightly less than two per cent of the amount spent by the state
for common schools in the fiscal year ending June 30, 1954.[65]
For the fiscal year ending August 31, 1954, the Texas poll tax
raised about 0.66 per cent of the amount expended by the state
for free schools and vocational education and slightly less than
0.50 per cent of the amount received from all taxes and
licenses.[66]   The state's share of Virginia poll tax revenue for
the fiscal year ending June 30, 1954, was equivalent to 1.44 per
cent of state expenditures for public free schools.   The total

[62] Department of Finance, *Annual Report,* Fiscal Year Ending September 30,
1954, pp. 87 and 82.   The poll tax yielded more than usual this year because
of the reduction of the cumulative period.   As a result of this reduction and
an approaching gubernatorial primary, many persons paid the tax for the
first time.   The above figures and subsequent ones have been converted to the
nearest dollar.

[63] *Ibid.,* Fiscal Year Ending September 30, 1953, pp. 81 and 76.

[64] In 1953, 532,162 poll tax receipts ($1.00 each) were sold and $32,250,154
was spent for education and public schools.   List of 1953 poll tax receipts sold
obtained from Arkansas Department of Finance and Administration; State of
Arkansas, *Biennial Report of the State Department of Finance and Adminis-*
tration, covering fiscal years 1950-51, 1951-52, 1952-53, 1953-54 (Little Rock,
1954), p. 3.

[65] Mississippi collected $514,608 from the poll tax and spent $26,433,161 for
common schools.   Letter to author from Alex McKeigney, Chairman, Mississippi
State Tax Commission, dated July 7, 1955.

[66] Texas spent $205,420,083 for free schools and vocational education;
$2,085,388 was obtained from the poll tax and $498,041,114 from all taxes and
licenses.   Of the poll tax revenue, only $1,391,898 was available for the schools.
Letters to author from Robert S. Calvert, Comptroller of Public Accounts,
dated June 27 and July 5, 1955.

poll tax revenue was only 0.86 per cent of the total tax receipts.[67]

With reference to the tax as a source of school funds, a former Alabama superintendent of schools said:

The poll tax costs our schools many times more than the meager revenue it brings in. If our poll tax was repealed, a group of people would gain the ballot who would insist on more adequate expenditures for public education. . . .[68]

In summary, the annual rates of the poll tax are not excessive but the cumulative feature in Alabama, Mississippi, and Virginia makes the tax more burdensome there. In any consideration of its burden upon the suffrage, note must be taken of the large number of persons who have been freed from payment. The exemptions not only lessen the burden of the tax but also give a special advantage to those groups who have been relieved. The requirement that the tax must be paid long before an election is another feature aimed at depressing the turnout of voters. Most of these states require payment several months before either the primary or general election. The provisions specifying the proof of payment are not as important as tax opponents have attempted to establish although, in some cases, the necessity of proving payment before voting may be a troublesome feature for the prospective voter. Finally, the tax revenues are used for school purposes. This use serves as a justification for continuance of the tax but the amount raised is so small that it is of little importance for the state school

[67] Virginia spent $67,653,976 for public free schools; total tax receipts were $170,224,490 with $1,458,161 coming from the poll tax. Of the poll tax money, $972,107 was available for schools. In the computation, only the amount spent for "public free schools" has been used since two-thirds of the poll tax receipts go to the public schools. Total state expenditures for education were $112,-881,184. Poll tax receipts represent only 0.86 per cent of this amount. Total state revenues for this year were $403,915,301. The poll tax produced only 0.36 per cent of this total. *Report of Comptroller to the Governor of Virginia,* Fiscal Year Ended June 30, 1954, chart at end of report.

[68] Albert H. Collins, as quoted in George C. Stoney, "Who Is Fit to Vote in a Democracy?" *Proceedings of the National Conference of Social Work, 1941,* p. 176. See also "The Poll Tax—A Burden upon Education," *The Southern Planter,* January, 1938.

systems. This use also confuses the tax as a device to restrict
the suffrage with the tax as a revenue measure. Where the poll
tax is tied to the suffrage, its purpose is to limit the electorate
and not to raise revenue. The most burdensome poll taxes are
found in Virginia, Mississippi and Alabama; those of Arkansas
and Texas are less severe.

3. ADMINISTRATION OF POLL TAX COLLECTION

SOUTHERN METHODS of collecting the poll tax, and the attitudes toward collection, vary as widely as the amounts of the tax, the scope of liability, and other matters discussed in Chapter 2. Although in some non-southern states the poll tax is a bona fide device for raising revenue, where it is a prerequisite for voting, it is not. An examination of relevant legal provisions and of methods of collection reveals that large scale payment is not desired. The tax is nominally a revenue measure and it does provide some revenue, but primarily it restricts voting. To the extent that this purpose is achieved, the revenue aspect of the tax suffers. Payment of bona fide taxes is not only invited but, wherever possible, enforced. Payment of poll taxes by large segments of the population, on the other hand, is discouraged.

In most poll tax states, the statutory provisions concerning collection of the tax are designed to discourage, rather than encourage, its collection. The Alabama constitution provides that no legal process nor any fee or commission shall be allowed for poll tax collection. Payment is left on a voluntary basis.[1] There are no penalties for delinquency. No bills are sent out, and in most places, no effort is made by the tax collector to notify the taxpayers when the tax should be paid. The tax is not collected with property taxes and no special reminders are sent out to property owners. In a few cases, when a man is

---

[1] *Constitution*, Art. VIII, sec. 194.

paying his property taxes, it might be suggested that he pay his poll tax also, but this depends upon the tax collector. Before 1901, when the tax was not a suffrage prerequisite in Alabama, payment could be enforced. It was when the tax became a voting requirement that its payment was placed on a voluntary basis.[2]

Although constitutionally poll tax payment is purely voluntary in Alabama, some efforts have been made in recent years to make payment easier. Jefferson County, the home of Birmingham, is the outstanding example. The tax collector has established booths at approximately 25 places throughout the county to make payment more convenient. These booths have been set up in department stores, the YMCA, CIO locals, drug stores, restaurants and municipal buildings. Assistance in manning them has come from the County PTA Council, and publicity as to their location has been given through the local newspapers. In connection with these booths, the county tax collector said in 1953: "I don't want anybody to lose their vote for failure to pay poll tax."[3]

Early in 1949, the tax collector of Tuscaloosa County moved to make poll tax payment easier for some citizens. Until this time, all poll taxes had to be paid at the courthouse, either by taking or mailing the money to the collector's office. In January, 1949 the tax collector authorized two members of the Central Labor Union to accept payment of poll taxes.[4] These men were appointed as deputy collectors on their own request because they were anxious for union members to become qualified voters. They knew that many members would not leave work to go to the courthouse to pay the tax. Each deputy was given a receipt book. He could collect from union men at their place of work, at home, at the union hall or at any place where he met them.

---

[2] In relation to voluntary payment of the tax, the following exchange occurred during the constitutional convention of 1901: "MR. CUNNINGHAM—Is it not a fact that this is not a tax but a voluntary contribution to the State? MR. REESE—Yes, sir." *Official Proceedings*, p. 3333.

[3] Birmingham *Post-Herald*, January 24, 1953. See also Birmingham *News*, January 4, 24, 30, and February 1, 1947; January 24 and 25, 1949.

[4] Editorial, Tuscaloosa *News*, January 31, 1949.

Appointment of these labor leaders as deputy poll tax collectors discloses an awareness of the growing political importance of labor in the South and shows the type of efforts being put forth to make labor politically conscious in this region. In subsequent years, members of the Tuscaloosa League of Women Voters have also been authorized to collect poll taxes. In 1950, the League established two booths in the downtown area for this purpose.[5] In January, 1954, the League collected the tax in super-markets and in city and county schools.

Payment of the tax is also voluntary in Arkansas. The only stipulation tending to encourage payment is one to the effect that the tax must be paid to secure a state or municipal license or permit of any kind and to receive any salary or other compensation from public funds.[6] Individuals who are looking to the state for employment or favors are compelled to pay the tax and to qualify to vote to this extent. No legal encouragement is given to other groups. This requirement helps slightly to enforce the collection of the poll tax. It also may help to increase the number of qualified Negro voters since Negro school teachers and Negro recipients of public funds must pay.

Until 1947, Arkansas required assessment of the tax prior to payment. The poll tax was assessed at the same time as personal property taxes, i.e., between the first Monday in January and April 10. Since assessment is no longer necessary, individuals now go directly to the tax collector to pay their poll taxes. This has made it easier for those who do not pay real property taxes to avoid the assessment of personal property taxes. Tax officials have objected to the abolition of poll tax assessment because it has made it more difficult to enforce the personal property tax requirement. With reference to poll tax administration, there has been no criticism.

The Arkansas assessment law was adopted as another obstacle to Negro voting. The tax did not have to be assessed during the regular time for assessment to qualify for voting, but if it was not, a penalty of $1.00 was levied. Therefore, all assessment delinquents owed $2.00 instead of $1.00 when the time

5 *Ibid.*, January 25, 26, and 30, 1949; January 10, 12, and 29, 1950.
6 *Arkansas Statutes, 1947*, Tit. 3, secs. 127-29.

for tax payment arrived. The principal effect of the assessment procedure was to double the tax for delinquents. Spokesmen for eastern Arkansas, the area with the largest Negro population, have admitted that they "never assessed Negroes." If tax officials overlooked the assessment of Negroes and Negroes themselves failed to assess the tax at the proper time, the penalty for late assessment aided in deterring them from becoming qualified voters. In 1941, the legislature provided that no further penalties were to be imposed upon delinquent assessments. With the discontinuance of the penalty, the assessment procedure was no longer of any particular significance. By 1947, it was regarded as a nuisance and was abolished without great opposition. About the only objection came from representatives of eastern Arkansas.[7]

Although poll taxes do not have to be paid at the same time property or other taxes are paid in Arkansas, county tax collectors have in some instances refused to accept poll tax money until property and other taxes have been paid. In other cases, tax officials have given the impression that the poll tax should be paid along with the payment of personal property taxes. They have no means of enforcing such payment. This action illustrates the fact that administrative officials frequently take considerable liberties with the law in carrying out the functions of their offices.

No instances were found in Arkansas of any special procedures used by tax officials to encourage poll tax payment. Tax collectors who were contacted stated that payment was made at their offices in the courthouse and that deputies were not sent into the counties to collect the tax. Formerly, deputies had occasionally gone out but the collectors believed that it is no longer necessary due to improved methods of transportation.

Arkansas formerly permitted an individual to authorize in writing an agent to pay his poll tax. Various partisan groups used the authorization procedure as a means of paying the poll taxes of their supporters. Because this manner of paying the tax was associated so frequently with corrupt election practices, it was repealed in 1949.[8]

[7] *Acts of Arkansas, 1941,* Act 37, sec. 2; *Acts of Arkansas, 1947,* Act 220.
[8] *Arkansas Statutes, 1947, 1953 Cumulative Supplement,* Tit. 3, sec. 103.

Various local newspapers in Arkansas have directed attention to the necessity of poll tax payment by a specified time to qualify for voting. Special groups have also waged poll tax payment campaigns. One such campaign was carried on by a number of organizations in 1947. The Young Democratic Club, the Amvets, the Junior Chamber of Commerce, and the East Arkansas Business League were among the civic and veterans' organizations that participated. These groups wished to increase the potential electorate to augment the chances of electing Sidney S. McMath to the governorship. Such drives tend to be sporadic. While they may be effective occasionally, they do not take the place of regularized procedures for the encouragement of tax payment. No such procedures exist in Arkansas. An organization like the NAACP has not engaged in any statewide campaign to urge poll tax payment although some individual branches, like the one at Pine Bluff, have undertaken local campaigns.

In Mississippi payment is voluntary and no bills are sent out. In most cases, no efforts are made by the county sheriffs, the officials charged with poll tax collection, to remind the taxpayers to pay it. The constitution stipulates that no criminal proceedings to enforce collection are to be allowed, but it does make the tax a lien upon taxable property.[9] This provision may indicate a desire on the part of the drafters of the Constitution of 1890 to encourage property owners to become voters. At one time, however, Mississippi law specifically provided that poll taxes could be paid independently of property taxes.[10] Although this law is no longer in effect, the statutes provide that those persons liable must volunteer payment and that the county tax assessor must not list their names on the personal roll of the county.[11] Thus, poll taxes are assessed separately from personal property and real estate taxes.

Further examples of liberal interpretations of the laws by administrative officials were found in Mississippi. The sheriff as tax collector is permitted to levy a fee of $1.00 upon the

9 *Constitution,* Art. XII, sec. 243.
10 *General Laws of Mississippi, 1934,* Chapter 192, p. 445.
11 *Mississippi Code of 1942,* sec. 9919.5.

payment of delinquent poll taxes. However, none of those interviewed did so and the general opinion was that this fee was not collected anywhere. The sheriff is also directed to compile by March 1 a list of persons delinquent in poll tax payment. This list is for the use of election commissioners in checking those who are ineligible to vote because of poll tax delinquency. Some sheriffs compile the list while others do not.

Special groups have undertaken campaigns to encourage poll tax payment in Mississippi but these efforts appear to have been even more scattered and ineffective than in the other states. In Hinds County, for instance, the League of Women Voters has reminded voters through the local newspaper when the tax should be paid. In 1947, the governor, Fielding L. Wright, took the unusual step of appealing to the citizens to pay their poll taxes. He did so as the titular head of the State Democratic party.[12] Perhaps Governor Wright acted because of a fear of increased voter participation by Negroes. Luther P. Jackson found that this fear existed in Mississippi and that some city officials were using the newspapers to warn fellow whites to pay their poll taxes so that white supremacy would not be endangered.[13]

In Virginia, collection of the poll tax is enforceable but not until the tax has become three years past due.[14] Since it is necessary to have paid the tax for three years preceding an election, this provision relative to tax collection dovetails with the cumulative feature. Its collection may not be enforced until after the tax has ceased to relate to the suffrage.

During the constitutional convention of 1901-1902, the provision for the collection of the tax was discussed thoroughly. The debate focused on whether or not tax collection should be enforced. One delegate observed that the object of the poll tax was either to raise revenue or to serve as a restriction upon the suffrage.

[12] New Orleans *Times-Picayune*, February 1, 1947.
[13] "Race and Suffrage in the South Since 1940," *New South*, III (June-July, 1948), 8. Relative to increased poll tax payment and registration by Negroes, see New York *Times*, February 2, 7 and 9, 1947.
[14] *Constitution*, sec. 22.

If you are anxious to collect revenue you could do it by having the payment of it compulsory without any prerequisite as to the right to vote. But having adopted the plan that you shall have it as a prerequisite to the right to vote, you must have the idea of keeping certain people from voting. . . . We all know that if you make the collection of this tax compulsory you will simply defeat the real object you have in view.[15]

Since the purpose of the tax was to restrict the suffrage, the convention decided not to allow the enforcement of its collection until its payment ceased to relate to voting.[16]

Assessment is also necessary in Virginia. Tax assessment for poll and other taxes takes place on January 1 with the bills being sent out in October and November. The deadline for payment of the general tax bill is December 5. A five per cent penalty is charged if taxes are paid after this time. Since the poll tax does not have to be paid until six months before the general election, the individual's voting status is not affected by failure to pay by December 5, but the annual amount that he owes is increased to $1.58 from $1.50. If the tax is still delinquent after June 30 of the year following its assessment, interest at six per cent is added.[17] As noted previously, most poll tax collections are made in November because of these administrative procedures.

Assessing the poll tax in Virginia at the same time as other taxes encourages payment by property owners but not by non-property owners. The poll tax is treated as one item in the general tax bill. Property owners are assessed for the poll tax along with assessment of their property. However, those non-property holders who are not assessed for the poll tax alone often fail to pay it. In this way, administration of the

15 *Debates*, pp. 2864-65, Mr. Meredith.

16 In 1924, a law was adopted which required that the poll tax for the preceding year must have been paid as a condition of issuing a license, permit or authorization of any kind, except a marriage license. This law was similar to the one in Arkansas but it had less effect upon encouraging citizens to qualify themselves to vote because of Virginia's cumulative feature. In 1939, the Supreme Court of Appeals declared the act unconstitutional on the basis of section 22 of the constitution which provides that the collection of the poll tax shall not be enforced by legal process until it has become three years past due. *Campbell* v. *Goode*, 172 Va. 463, 2 S.E. (2d) 456.

17 *Code of Virginia, 1950*, Tit. 58, secs. 4, 960-64.

assessment procedure gives little encouragement to non-property holders to pay the tax but does work to secure payment from property owners. This is not, however, the situation on a state-wide basis. Some county officials make an effort to assess all who are liable. Another result of this system is that some citizens pay the poll tax as an item of the general tax bill without realizing that they have done so and without bothering to qualify themselves further for voting.

The Virginia poll tax may be paid without having been assessed at the regular time for assessment. The taxpayer may assess it immediately before paying it by going first to the assessor's office and then to the collector's office.[18]

Virginia tax collectors oftentimes try to discourage members of low income groups from paying the tax by telling them that they are not compelled to pay. Luther P. Jackson reported that some treasurers always greet the Negro taxpayer with this type of "pay-if-you-wish-to" message.[19] Many of them, white as well as Negro, are easy to persuade and voluntarily tell the treasurers that they do not care to pay the poll tax item in their tax bill.

In his studies of the voting status of Negroes in Virginia, Dr. Jackson noted the variations by counties and cities in poll tax payment by Negroes. In his opinion, these variations did not necessarily indicate a greater desire to vote in one county or city than in another. In most cases, they showed the difference between local officials in assessing and collecting the tax. He found that, in each of the counties having a low percentage of poll tax payment, the "pay-if-you-wish-to" policy was a factor in producing the low rating.[20]

---

[18] Luther P. Jackson, *The Voting Status of Negroes in Virginia, 1947-1948,* Eighth Annual Report (Virginia Voters League, Petersburg, 1948), p. 13.

[19] "Race and Suffrage in the South Since 1940," p. 7.

[20] Jackson, 1946, p. 6. Dr. Jackson published these reports annually from 1940 to his death in 1950. For figures by selected counties and cities showing failure to assess and collect the tax for 1935, see "The Poll Tax—A Burden Upon Education," *The Southern Planter,* January, 1938. The figures show (1) that from one-fifth to one-third of all persons assessable with poll taxes was not assessed and (2) that from one-third to one-half of the assessments made was not collected.

An effort by administrative officials to aid individuals in paying their poll taxes occurred in Richmond in 1947. During 1947-48, there was a virtual landslide of Negro applicants for registration as voters. This demand arose as the result of an intensive campaign by the Richmond branch of the NAACP. It was further stimulated by the candidacy of a Negro, first, for a seat in the House of Delegates and, later, for membership in the city council. On May 1, the city treasurer and the commissioner of revenue announced that they would keep their offices open on Saturday morning, May 3, thereby extending the poll tax deadline by another half-day. Since these offices were normally closed on Saturdays, this action was a concession on the part of the officials. The request that it be done came from the president of the Richmond NAACP, Dr. J. M. Tinsley. The decision not only indicated the willingness of the tax officials to co-operate in poll tax payment but also disclosed the rising political power of the Negroes in this area. In Henrico and Chesterfield counties, the tax officials also announced that their offices would be open on Saturday although normally they were closed. The Chesterfield office was to be open all day Saturday "as a special courtesy."[21]

The above incident reveals that Negro organizations in Virginia have been active in urging poll tax payment by members of their race. In addition to local branches of the NAACP, the Virginia Voters League has taken the lead. Until his death in 1950, this league was headed by Luther P. Jackson. The results of the activity of these organizations are disclosed in Dr. Jackson's annual reports which show a steady increase in the number of Negroes qualified by virtue of poll tax payment. Poll tax and registration drives on a smaller scale have been conducted among Negroes in Charlottesville, Danville, Fredericksburg, Hampton, Lynchburg, Newport News, Norfolk, Petersburg, Portsmouth and Roanoke.[22]

Besides the Negro organizations, white groups in Virginia have urged payment of poll taxes. A one-time leading, but now

---

21 Richmond *News-Leader*, May 1, 1947; Richmond *Times-Dispatch*, May 2, 1947.
22 Jackson, 1947-1948, p. 10.

inactive, organization was the Virginia Electoral Reform
League.[23] Its primary interest was in poll tax abolition but it
also worked to encourage poll tax payment in order to swell
the ranks of voters demanding a change in Virginia's suffrage
laws. Various newspapers also aided in such campaigns,
especially the Richmond *Times-Dispatch*.

According to its laws, Texas provides more adequately for
the enforcement of poll tax payment than do the states
previously examined. However, these laws are frequently not
enforced or at best are poorly enforced.

One such statute is that poll tax delinquents are subject to
three additional days of road work over the five days normally
required or to the payment of a fine of $3.00.[24] No instances
of the enforcement of this statute were discovered. Provision
has been made for levying penalties upon late poll tax payment.
These penalties are the same as for other delinquent taxes.
Beginning with February, the penalty is one per cent, increasing
each month by an additional one per cent until July when it
becomes an eight per cent penalty. After July 1, delinquent
poll and ad valorem taxes bear interest at six per cent from
the date of delinquency. As far as could be ascertained, this
law is not carried out with reference to the poll tax since its
collection is not enforced.[25]

Texas procedures for poll tax collection have tended to
encourage payment by property owners with little encouragement for non-property holders. However, within recent years,
these procedures have been altered in the direction of making
poll tax payment a purely voluntary matter with no more
assistance being given to property owners than to non-property

[23] This league is discussed in connection with the movement to repeal the
tax. See Chapter 8.

[24] *Vernon's Texas Statutes, 1948*, Art. 6758.

[25] *Ibid.*, Art. 7336. Another minor provision requires that an individual must
have paid his poll tax to act as a judge, clerk or supervisor of any election,
or as chairman or member of any district, county or city executive committee
of a political party. *Vernon's Texas Statutes, 1952 Supplement*, Elec. Code,
Art. 3.04. Not enough individuals are affected by this law for it to be of great
significance with reference to tax collection. Although a similar law is not
found in the other states, this requirement is undoubtedly a part of their
unwritten laws.

owners. Negro informants report that this action was taken to prevent Negro property owners from being encouraged to pay their poll taxes. Although no significant new voting restrictions were added in Texas following abolition of the white primary by the United States Supreme Court in *Smith* v. *Allwright*,[26] this minor step was taken to prevent giving any aid to Negroes in qualifying as voters.

A recent change in the assessment procedure indicates this attempt to divorce poll tax collection from collection of other taxes. A long-standing rule was that the county tax assessor-collector had to assess all poll taxes at the same time as he assessed other property. Under this rule, poll taxes were assessed during the period from January 1 to April 30 and were charged on the tax roll with the ad valorem taxes. Since 1947, by authority of the attorney general, poll taxes have not been charged on the tax roll and have not been assessed until the time of collection, i.e., in the period from October 1 to February 1.[27] Thus, neither property nor non-property tax-payers receive notices pertaining to poll tax payment now.

According to an early opinion of the Texas attorney general, poll taxes may be paid without the payment of property taxes but, except in the case of a homestead, property taxes cannot be paid without payment of poll taxes.[28] This opinion ties payment of poll taxes with payment of property taxes but it applies only to payment of taxes on property which is not the residence of the taxpayer. A 1945 opinion of the attorney general further indicates the trend to separate poll tax payment from property tax payment. The opinion relates to collection of delinquent taxes on real estate and personal property. The attorney general ruled that these delinquent taxes could be accepted without at the same time exacting payment of any delinquent poll taxes.[29]

Several instances in which administrative officials made it easier to pay the poll tax were noted in Texas. If anything, tax

26 321 U.S. 649. See Donald S. Strong, "The Rise of Negro Voting in Texas," *American Political Science Review*, XLII (June, 1948), 510-22.

27 *Opinions of the Attorney-General, Texas*, No. V-95, March 20, 1947.

28 *Report of the Attorney-General, Texas, 1906-1908*, p. 380.

29 *Opinions of the Attorney-General, Texas*, No. O-6596, June 11, 1945.

officials have been more co-operative in encouraging payment
than in the other states, especially within recent years.   The
principal method is that of authorizing deputies to collect the
tax.   An act of 1951 requires that in all counties containing a
city of 10,000 or more people, other than the county seat, the
tax collector shall appoint a deputy poll tax collector.   This
deputy must maintain his office at some convenient place
during January.   Four weeks notice of the deputy's authority
and of the location of his office must be given.[30]   Thus, in
many places, prospective voters do not have to go to the
courthouse to pay their poll taxes.

Both Negro and white deputies have been commissioned.
They represent civic and labor organizations.   In connection
with the annual poll tax drive of the Dallas Junior Chamber of
Commerce, members were appointed as deputies to assist the
tax collector in the final rush of payment.[31]   Representatives of
the Federation of Women's Clubs were also among those
selected.   In some places, special booths have been set up in
factories to enable union members to satisfy the tax requirement easily.   According to a CIO member, two booths have
been provided in some plants during January.   At one, the
employee received a $3.50 advance in wages which he took to
the adjacent booth to pay the poll taxes of his wife and himself.
The recent appointment of Negro poll tax deputies indicates
the rising importance of the Negro in Texas politics.   Negroes
have been appointed in Dallas, Tarrant, Harris, and Travis
counties.[32]   As many as 28 Negro poll tax deputies were
appointed in Houston in 1947 and 18 were commissioned in
Dallas.   Some of these deputies went from door to door urging
members of their race to pay the tax.   Others operated from
booths in retail stores.

The same groups who have provided deputy poll tax collectors have been in the forefront in conducting tax payment
campaigns.   The Dallas Junior Chamber of Commerce directs
an annual poll tax payment campaign.   Women's organizations

[30] *Vernon's Texas Statutes, 1952 Supplement*, Elec. Code, Art. 5.19.
[31] Dallas *Morning News*, January 14, 1947.
[32] Strong, p. 512.

through the Federation of Women's Clubs have also urged payment as a means of becoming qualified to vote. Some CIO and AF of L unions have worked to get their members to pay the tax. This union activity has stimulated tax payment by both whites and Negroes. For instance, the Longshoreman's Union, which includes members of both races, requires that every member pay his poll tax to maintain membership.

A poll tax payment campaign by Negro organizations in Dallas had surprising results. It aroused so much response in nearby Waxahachie that more Negroes than whites were qualified to vote in the 1947 city election.[33] One Negro organization which encourages poll tax payment is the state-wide Progressive Voters League, established within the past few years. In cities like San Antonio, Houston, and Austin, local Negro political organizations include pay-your-poll-tax campaigns among their activities. Branches of the NAACP assist the movement as they do in other states. All of these groups work through the churches in urging poll tax payment and the importance of qualifying to vote.

When South Carolina required poll tax payment as a prerequisite for voting, payment of the tax was mandatory. It was a misdemeanor to fail or to refuse to pay and, on conviction of having done so, the individual could be fined as much as $10 plus costs or imprisoned at hard labor on the public works of the county for a maximum of twenty days.[34] Rarely was payment of the tax forced, however. When Governor R. M. Jefferies was asked by a United States Senate Judiciary subcommittee in 1942 about enforcement of the criminal liability provisions, he first tried to avoid a direct answer and finally replied:

. . . I will say this: sometimes there is laxity in enforcing it, Senator—I will be absolutely fair. Some counties do not bother

33 *Ibid.*, p. 513. Many whites had neglected to pay their poll taxes since this was an off-election year when only city officials were to be elected. Both whites and Negroes were taken by surprise. The whites handled the situation through the city officials, who told the Negroes that they would not be permitted to vote.

34 *South Carolina Code of 1942,* sec. 1720.

with it much. . . . We have tried to collect it, but like any other law, sometimes enforcement is lax. . . .[35]

In 1948, the comptroller general of South Carolina stated that poll tax collections were prosecuted like those for other taxes and then added that the poll tax was difficult to collect. He indicated that many persons of low income might have changed their residence during the eighteen to twenty month period between assessment and delinquency collection, making it virtually impossible to locate them. He also said that the practice of pressing for poll tax collection was very uneven over the state.

Investigators on the staff of the Myrdal study found few instances in which collection of the poll tax was forced in South Carolina. The treasurer of Sumter County knew of no cases where a person had been jailed or fined for non-payment of the tax in his county. The treasurers of Pickens and Greenville counties made similar statements. In Charleston County, delinquent tax collectors collected from about two per cent of the delinquents sent to them. Beaufort was the only county where any significant effort was made to collect the tax. The treasurer stated that poll tax collection was forced because it made general tax collection easier. He also advised that, from 1932 to 1940, approximately ten people had been put on the road to work out their road and poll taxes and that about a half-dozen persons were forced to pay the $10 fine each year.[36]

When Tennessee had a voter poll tax, it, like South Carolina, had fairly stringent provisions relative to its payment. Payment was tied to payment of property taxes. Penalties were charged for delinquent payment and delinquent taxes were turned over to a deputy to collect. If delinquent, the taxpayer was subject to the sale of his personal property and to garnishment proceedings.[37]

As in South Carolina, enforcement of these provisions was often lax and varied from county to county. In 1940, the assistant trustee of Hamilton County stated:

---

[35] *Hearings on S. 1280*, p. 485. See also p. 480.
[36] Bunche, pp. 688-90, 649-51, and 666-68.
[37] *Williams Tennessee Code, 1934*, secs. 1559, 1547, 1574 and 1577.

You see we're supposed to collect it, but you always can't. . . . Of course, he can't vote unless he's paid his last year's poll tax. He knows that already without us telling him. But, that don't mean much to a lot of people.[38]

With reference to the requirement that a receipt for property taxes should not be issued until the poll tax had been paid, the same official said:

Well, we're not supposed to, but most of the times we do, especially when they argue about it or when we're right busy like in February or March. Some people, they kick about paying poll tax because they think it's just something the politicians get, but when they find out it's for schools, they generally pay up. . . .[39]

Few efforts by administrative officials to make tax payment easier were found in Tennessee. The trustee of Davidson County reported that all payments had to be made in his office at the courthouse. He believed that at one time deputies and constables in some rural counties had gone into the county to collect taxes, including poll taxes, but that this practice had been discontinued.

Some attempts to aid labor union members were discovered. In 1947, a Tennessee CIO representative stated that the manner in which tax payment was handled depended upon the attitude of the trustee in each county. Some trustees allowed union men to take poll tax receipt books and sell the receipts to anyone they wished. Another procedure was to deputize a man and send him to the plant to collect the tax. Another method was to require a union representative to bring a list of names and addresses with the money to the trustee's office. The receipts were mailed to each individual.

In Memphis, the Crump machine permitted AF of L members to take poll tax receipt books to plants and homes to facilitate payment by fellow members. This practice was permitted because the AF of L co-operated with the Crump organization in return for the organization's assistance in fighting the CIO. A CIO member reported that the Crump

[38] Bunche, p. 665.

[39] *Ibid.* In 1949, when Tennessee greatly modified its poll tax prerequisite, an act was approved which established a one-year statute of limitations on the collection of delinquent poll taxes. *Public Acts of Tennessee, 1949,* Chapter 236, p. 790.

machine had a card file on all CIO members. When deputies took poll tax receipt books from door to door in Memphis selling receipts to faithful Crump supporters, they skipped the houses of CIO men. One CIO member was visiting his neighbor when a deputy poll tax collector called. The neighbor received a receipt and the CIO man asked for one. The deputy refused to issue it to him and said that he would have to go to the courthouse to pay his tax.

No effective provisions are on the statute books relative to the enforcement of poll tax collection. The law makers wished to make payment a voluntary, and not an obligatory, matter. Even where there are statutes directed toward enforcing its payment, these laws are more often honored in the breach than in the observance. The examination into administrative procedures showed that few officials have acted to make tax payment easier. Since it is usually necessary to go to the courthouse to pay the tax, many individuals fail to pay, simply because it is too much trouble and not because they cannot afford to do so. Also they may not want to take time off from their jobs to journey to the courthouse. Others may miss paying on time because they are unaware of when the tax should be paid, or because the deadline slipped past unnoticed. This is possible since administrative officials do little to advise citizens when the tax should be paid. In many instances, officials specifically discourage payment. About the only persons to whom encouragement is given by the laws and their administration are property owners. In this fashion, administration of the poll tax helps to keep political power in these states in the hands of conservative, propertied interests.

Although the data obtained indicate that most administrative officials have not acted to stimulate poll tax payment, some instances of such action were discovered. Tax administrators have been more co-operative in recent years in assisting citizens to pay their poll taxes. This change may be a result of the national attention devoted to the tax within recent years. Because of the charges made about the tax, some state and local officials appear to have been moved to improve their administration of the poll tax laws. Perhaps another reason is the growing voting strength of Negroes which resulted largely from the invalidation of the white primary. Because of increased Negro participation, whites are encouraging greater participation on the part of fellow whites and are urging and making easier poll tax payment.

Administration of poll tax collection may operate to discourage and deprive as many individuals from voting as the cost of the tax. Those people whom the tax helps to keep among the disfranchised are not cut off from the suffrage simply because of the fiscal aspects of the tax. In view of the lessened value of the dollar and the rising money income of the South, more and more people are able to pay the tax but many fail to do so because of the manner in which its collection is administered.

A special comment is in order regarding the relation between Negroes and administration of the poll tax. Specific attention is given in Chapter 6 to the effect of the tax upon Negro disfranchisement. Reference is made here only to the way in which administration of tax collection from Negroes is carried out. In most places, tax collectors have not been opposed to accepting payment by Negroes. Negro leaders have reported that they have not experienced any difficulty in getting officials to accept poll tax payments. While this is the general pattern, exceptions exist, particularly in Mississippi. Luther P. Jackson reported that "on more than one occasion recently in certain cities in Mississippi officials have refused to accept payment from Negroes on the ground that too many of them were seeking to pay and vote."[40] It was feared that white supremacy might be endangered. This threat to white supremacy was brought to the attention of the inhabitants of Hinds and Jackson counties in an impassioned front page editorial in January, 1947. They were called to awake because white supremacy was in peril.

Negroes in large numbers are paying their poll taxes down at the county courthouse—the first step essential to suffrage.

Almost any hour of the day Negroes waiting at the tax windows outnumber the whites 10 to one and 20 to one.[41]

40 "Race and Suffrage in the South Since 1940," pp. 7-8.
41 As quoted in Birmingham *News,* January 30, 1947.

In Virginia, Dr. Jackson found that most of the traditional practices of racial discrimination by public officials were diminishing. Only a few officials who practiced discrimination remained. In poll tax assessment and collection, some officials were more lax in their dealings with Negroes than they were with whites since they did not want the Negroes to be qualified to vote. In counties where the Negroes constituted from 25 to 50 per cent of the population, they experienced no racial difficulties in paying their poll taxes or in registering.[42]

An instance was found in Alabama of restraining tactics used by collection officials against a Negro. The man had been an agricultural extension agent and because of some of his activities was not regarded highly by either whites or Negroes. When he first went to pay his poll tax, he was told that no receipts were on hand and that consequently his money could not be accepted. The next time he took his check for the correct amount but the officials would not accept a check. Finally, he went with the exact amount of money, laid it on the counter and told the officials that when they got the receipts and were ready to accept payment of taxes he would appreciate receiving his receipt. In the end, the officials were forced to accept his money and to mail him a receipt.

The above instances are significant because they are so few. They reveal that there is not any general attempt to discriminate against Negroes in the payment of poll taxes. This fact is contrary to generally accepted belief.

[42] Jackson, 1947-1948, p. 12.

4. THE POLL TAX AND
CORRUPTION IN ELECTIONS

AN ARGUMENT FOR POLL TAX adoption was that this requirement would help to purify elections. Disfranchisement leaders contended that the South must exclude Negroes from exercising political power and that methods other than violence, intimidation, and corrupt practices must be found to protect public morals. But opponents of the tax now charge that, instead of purifying elections, the poll tax has caused considerable political corruption. Investigation of poll tax administration discloses that several corrupt practices have been associated with this tax.

VOTE BUYING THROUGH POLL TAX PAYMENT

Payment by politicians and others as a means of buying votes is one of the abuses most frequently attributed to the poll tax. This practice occurs in varying degrees in all present poll tax states, and it occurred in other southern states prior to abandonment of the tax requirement. Its extent fluctuates with the intensity of election contests, but it seems less serious than advocates of poll tax abolition claim, and less common and less serious than it was in earlier years.

All of the states but Mississippi[1] have laws which forbid payment of another's tax as a means of influencing his vote, but

[1] South Carolina also had no laws which forbade the payment of another's tax. Since poll tax payment was not a prerequisite for primary elections, the practice of purchasing votes through tax payment was not widespread and the necessity for such legislation was apparently not felt. In 1940, the treasurer

such measures are difficult to enforce and little effort is expended on their enforcement.

The practice of vote buying through poll tax payment is not as widespread in Mississippi as it was formerly. When the two-year cumulative requirement could be met by one payment in the year of the primary election, there was considerable purchasing of poll taxes by politicians. This action was discouraged when, in 1936, the requirement was adopted that the tax must be paid annually for each of two years preceding the primary. Most candidates do not know eighteen months ahead of time whether they will be running and, thus, do not contribute money for tax payment. Considerable work is involved in following up and in seeing that the same persons have the tax paid for them the second year as had it paid the first. Such a system requires more advanced planning than where the tax may be paid retroactively or where only annual payments are necessary. This law appears to be more effective in preventing vote buying through poll tax payment than the specific prohibitions in the other states. Even so, vote buying is reported to exist on a large scale in a few Mississippi counties.

The Alabama constitution provides that if anyone pays the poll tax of another or advances him money for that purpose to influence his vote, he shall be guilty of bribery and upon conviction may be imprisoned for a period up to five years.[2] The effectiveness of this prohibition is greatly weakened by the clause "to influence his vote," because to convict anyone it must be proved that he paid the tax of another or gave him the money to pay it specifically to influence that person's vote. Since this is difficult to prove, the constitutional interdiction against paying another's tax has not been effective in preventing the practice.

A major political figure in most Alabama counties is the probate judge. His office maintains the records of qualified voters. In most counties a separate card record is kept which shows the years that a person has paid his poll tax. If the

of Greenville County stated that the only election which caused candidates to pay the taxes of prospective supporters was the election for school trustees in rural districts. Bunche, p. 652.

[2] *Constitution*, Art. VIII, sec. 195.

individual is exempt, the card is so marked. Since the probate judge is an elected official and has ready access to poll tax records, he may use them to his own advantage. He may remind delinquents who will vote for him to pay their taxes. His opponent may also check these cards and do likewise, since they are public records, but in a particularly close race, the opposing candidate might find access to them difficult.

There is nothing illegal in reminding your friends to pay their taxes, but incumbent probate judges seeking re-election have not always stopped there. They may put up money for payment of poll taxes to secure votes. They may also have tax payment records marked paid when the taxes have not been paid. The latter action has occurred in the office of the Tuscaloosa County probate judge although not within recent years. In Bibb and Etowah counties, probate judges have engaged in all of these practices.[3]

In Cullman County in 1940, an election official, who was also a county Democratic executive committeeman, claimed to know personally at least fifty persons who had back taxes paid during the previous payment period by the different candidates for probate judge. One man entered his office and told him a candidate had offered to pay half of his back poll taxes of $36 if he would pay the other half. The man wanted to accept but felt he would be obligated to this candidate. He asked the election official for advice since he wanted to vote for the other candidate.

. . . I told him to wait a minute. I went back and phoned up .... and told him about it because I knew he was paying them up, too. .... said "You send him up here and we'll fix him up." And he went up there and .... paid the $18.[4]

Another election official estimated that at least 2,000 voters

---

[3] Bunche, pp. 132-33, and 679. A member of a UMWA local in Bibb County reported an instance when poll tax records were "fixed" by the probate judge. By the 1939-1940 collection period, he owed $15 in poll taxes. Another union member approached the judge for him. The judge brought his tax payments up to date for $10.50 and marked "out of state" on the card for the three years for which no tax was paid. Similar arrangements were made for at least eight other union members. *Ibid.*, p. 681.

[4] *Ibid.*, pp. 713-14.

had their poll taxes paid by both sides in this election. He told how his son got his tax paid.

My boy, there, got his tax paid up by .... I'm ashamed to say it, but he did. He's 23 and he hadn't paid his tax to vote, and I was after him about it one night when another fellow was over here. He said, if he'd go home with him, his daddy could fix it up. Well, my boy went home with this friend and they went up to the courthouse together, and got right. I told my boy he ought to be ashamed of hisself . . . but he swore he didn't promise nobody how he was going to vote, but he knowed the man was aworkin' for .... and you know, yourself, if a man puts out for you, you're bound to feel obligated.[5]

At this same time, the Cullman County probate judge, who was a candidate for re-election, stated that $15,000 had been put up that year for paying poll taxes and that this money came out of two candidates' pockets.[6] George Stoney, a member of the Myrdal study staff, found that politicians used three methods in paying the tax for voters in Cullman County. One method was for an agent of the candidate to give the money directly to one member of a family who paid the tax for several members. Another was to give the money directly to each individual who was to bring the receipt to show that he had paid the tax. A third was for a lawyer, acting on behalf of the candidate, to solicit permission to pay the tax for prospective voters.[7]

In Table 5, annual poll tax receipts for Clarke County, Alabama, from 1940 to 1949 are listed. This table shows clearly that whenever there is an election for probate judge in this county, tax payments shoot up significantly.[8]

A Superintendent of Education of Macon County, Alabama, said in reference to the payment of poll taxes by political leaders:

Money buys everything in this world. . . . It has bought elections in this county for the last thirty years, I know; I've been in them,

---

[5] *Ibid.*, p. 714.

[6] *Ibid.*, p. 716.

[7] *Ibid.*, p. 713. See also George C. Stoney, "Tool of State Machines," *The Poll Tax* (American Council on Public Affairs, 1940), p. 11, and Allan A. Fletcher, "Poll Tax Politics," *New Republic*, CII (May 20, 1940), 664.

[8] *Alabama*, XIV (June 24, 1949), 8.

but I suppose it buys elections all over the country. . . . The politicians pay back poll taxes. . . . I've seen them pay as high as $36 for one voter. . . .[9]

Table 5. POLL TAX COLLECTIONS IN CLARKE COUNTY[a]

1939-1940	$17,302.50
1940-1941	2,094.00
1941-1942	5,842.50
1942-1943	2,376.00
1943-1944	5,761.50
1944-1945	2,665.50
1945-1946	16,389.00
1946-1947	2,235.00
1947-1948	6,072.00
1948-1949	2,127.00

[a]Probate judgeship election years are italicized.

The Macon County probate judge estimated in 1940 that twenty per cent of the total poll tax collected each year was paid by candidates. Examples of this practice were also given by an election official of Owens Cross Roads in Madison County and by a clerk in the Coffee County tax collector's office. The tax collector of Madison County reported that on February 1, 1940, he kept his office open until midnight and that the corridors were filled with people "hanging around, waiting for some candidate to pay their poll tax." Every candidate for re-election was absent from the courthouse all day.[10]

In Montgomery County, a tax collector observed that few men dare to announce their candidacy for office before the close of the poll tax season and that those who are rumored to be candidates "get worried to death by people after them to get their poll taxes paid." A federal district judge stated that in this county candidates for probate judge often ride out into the county and arrange for persons to vote for them by getting them to sign up to have their poll taxes paid. He pointed out that the law permits a man to pay the tax for another if he does it without intending to influence his vote. He concluded that

9 Bunche, pp. 151-52.
10 *Ibid.*, pp. 152, 717-19.

the law obviously is almost impossible of enforcement or even of interpretation.[11]

Poll tax payment by mail is permitted in Alabama. In this way, candidates or their agents may readily pay the taxes of prospective voters since little effort is made to determine whether payment comes from the person for whom the receipt is written. The tax collectors of Montgomery and Bibb counties both reported that this was the case in their counties.[12] This practice is also permitted in Tuscaloosa County. If an individual comes into the collector's office in this county to pay the tax for others as well as for himself, he is not questioned about who gave him the money. The money is accepted and the receipts are handed to him for delivery to the individuals whose tax has been paid. The collector recognizes that there may be considerable payment of poll taxes as a means of winning votes but does not consider it his responsibility to inquire into this practice.[13]

During an Alabama legislative committee hearing concerned with repeal or modification of the poll tax, one legislator favored abolition because of the cost of the tax to candidates. He stated that they had to pay $200 to $300 each election in poll taxes and that they were forced to do so whether they wished to or not.

Often where particularly keen bidding for votes has occurred in an Alabama election contest, individuals who have paid poll taxes openly have been cheated by some of their supposed supporters. Persons who have had their taxes paid have taken money from both sides. One man in Cullman County was reported in 1940 to have collected $12 from both sides and to have shown the same receipt to both paymasters.[14]

11 *Ibid.*, pp. 719 and 617.
12 *Ibid.*, pp. 679-80.
13 An interesting incident occurred one year in Montevallo, Alabama. A faculty member of Alabama State College for Women, which is located there, went to pay his poll tax prior to February 1. He was informed that it had already been paid. A few days after the election, the defeated candidate appeared on his doorstep and informed the faculty member that he had paid the tax. Since the teacher had not voted for him, the candidate thought that he should be reimbursed!
14 Bunche, p. 715.

In Arkansas, the only persons who may pay the poll tax for another are the husband, wife, son, daughter, sister, brother, father or mother. It is a felony for any official responsible for issuing poll tax receipts willfully or corruptly to permit any person not entitled to pay a poll tax to do so. It is a misdemeanor for any person to purchase a poll tax receipt to which he is not entitled.[15] Formerly a non-relative could pay the tax for another person if he had a written authorization. Because of corruption associated with this practice, it was abolished in 1949.

When payment by an agent was allowed, Arkansas law provided for several safeguards against vote buying, but they were not effective. The authorized agent was not to pay the tax for the purpose of influencing someone's vote. He was forbidden to give the receipt to anyone other than the person to whom it was issued and also forbidden to give it to him without repayment of the tax. It was unlawful for any person to vote on a poll tax receipt unless he had actually paid the amount of the tax to the collector or to the person who paid it. It was also unlawful to be in possession of a poll tax receipt other than your own after five days following the date of issuance and to deliver or receive a receipt after such time.[16]

A 1937 inquiry into political practices in Hot Springs disclosed the ineffectiveness of these laws. A legislative committee investigated how the lax and corrupt public officials in this resort city kept themselves in office. The records of the Garland County tax collector showed that 11,800 poll tax receipts were issued out of a population of about 44,000. More than 2,000 of these receipts were issued upon written authorizations. Many of the judges and clerks of election were found to be employees of gambling houses; others were employees of the city or county. Witnesses testified that the mayor, Leo P. McLaughlin, called in various city employees and gave them lists of persons from whom they were to obtain authorizations to pay their poll taxes. After the authorizations were obtained,

15 *Arkansas Statutes, 1947, 1953 Cumulative Supplement*, Tit. 3, secs. 104.1, 1522, and 1529.

16 See *Pope's Digest, 1937*, secs. 4899, 4901, and 4695; *Acts of Arkansas, 1939*, Acts 82 and 46.

the receipts were issued by the tax collector and delivered to the mayor. Mayor McLaughlin then sent the purchaser of the receipts to the city clerk who reimbursed him. At the proper time, the receipts were delivered to the voters whose names appeared on them if they could be counted upon to vote the McLaughlin ticket. The tax collector's records also showed that several policemen and officers of Hot Springs bought large blocks of receipts. Among them was George McLaughlin, brother of the mayor and clerk of the police court. Large lists were also purchased by operators of gambling houses.[17]

The state legislative investigation of 1937 did not stop the corrupt practices of the McLaughlin machine, as a group of World War II veterans disclosed in July, 1946 when they revolted against Mayor McLaughlin. Sidney S. McMath, at that time a candidate for prosecuting attorney of Garland County and later governor, headed the group. The veterans sued nineteen of the mayor's closest followers plus the county tax collector, the county clerk, and the county election commissioners. They charged that 3,768 void, fraudulent, and fictitious poll tax receipts had been issued and that of this total 3,026 names had been certified in the poll book as those of qualified voters.

Judge John E. Miller of the United States District Court for the Western District of Arkansas heard the case, since a congressional primary election was involved. Following a three-day hearing, Judge Miller voided 1,607 receipts. As in 1937, the mayor's clique was composed of city and county employees and gamblers. The group had acted as agents in obtaining authorizations to pay the poll tax for others. It was proved that the authorizations were not written by the individuals to whom the receipts were issued. The defendants claimed that they had obtained oral authorizations but the Court ruled that oral authorizations were not permitted by law. The Court also expressed grave doubts that the receipts were delivered within the five-day period and that the amount of the tax was repaid by the persons to whom the receipts were issued.

[17] Exhibit 7, "Arkansas, the Poll Tax and Corruption," submitted by Henry H. Collins, Jr., *Hearings on S. 1280*, pp. 277-78.

About half of the voided receipts were issued to names from a list furnished by Will Page, a Negro owner of a gambling house. It was proved that his list was a copy of a former poll tax list. Sidney McMath and J. O. Campbell, candidate for tax assessor, won the case when they solved the skip method employed in issuing receipts from this list. Starting with the A's and continuing in alphabetical order, three receipts were issued to names on Page's list. Then, there was a skip of one number in the receipt book. That receipt went to any applicant. Three more receipts were issued to names on Page's list, then a skip, and so on. The veterans group proved that many "persons" on all lists were dead, fictitious or transients. In other instances, the addresses that had been given were fictitious.[18]

When Arkansas permitted an agent to pay a person's poll tax, authorization forms were provided. Beer and liquor interests made considerable use of them. In many places, liquor stores had them available so that their customers could authorize the owners to pay their poll taxes. One newcomer to Arkansas signed an authorization slip for himself and his wife in a liquor store, paid the $1.00 tax for both and in a few days received the receipts through the mail. No questions were asked; the individual did not have to take an oath; he had only to sign his and his wife's names and give their address. Since he was unknown to the liquor store manager, his experience illustrates how informal and how open to laxity and corruption

[18] *Brad O. Smith, Jr., et al* v. *Will Page, et al,* Memorandum Opinion (Mss.), United States District Court, Western District of Arkansas, Hot Springs Division, July 11, 1946. See also John L. Fletcher, *Arkansas Gazette,* November 3, 1946. A member of the McMath group advised that this decision made it possible for them to win the 1946 election in Garland County. He stated that it would have been impossible for the veterans to have won had a large number of fraudulent receipts been held valid. He also said that, in subsequent elections, persons holding invalid poll tax receipts or inclined to secure fraudulent receipts were afraid of court action. In March, 1947, Mayor McLaughlin was indicted on further charges involving poll tax receipts and the 1946 campaign, the case being prosecuted by Sidney S. McMath. The trial resulted in the acquittal of Mr. McLaughlin in November, 1948, and no appeal was taken. Memphis *Commercial Appeal,* October 24, 1948; and letter to author from Clyde H. Brown, Circuit Judge, 18th Judicial Circuit, Hot Springs, Arkansas, dated July 22, 1949.

poll tax payment was in Arkansas when payment by an agent was permitted. Liquor and beer interests provided this service on the theory that a person who got his receipt through them was unlikely to vote for prohibition. In 1947, approximately 3,000 poll taxes were paid in this manner in Little Rock.

According to the sheriff of Jefferson County, who was also the tax collector, the American Legion also used the blank authorization forms. When authorizations were brought in, the sheriff accepted them with the money and delivered the receipts to the persons who brought them. He was not required to mail the receipts to the persons in whose order they were written.

In October, 1948, it was charged that authorization forms were used to influence an election to decide whether Arkadelphia should purchase the municipal water works. The proposal lost by some 32 votes; a total of 1,116 votes were cast. Before the election, some 200 poll tax receipts were issued on presentation of authorization forms. Three employees of the Arkadelphia Water Company were charged with having procured these receipts to influence votes. A circuit judge acquitted them and ruled that:

> The mere purchase of a poll tax receipt for another is not a violation of the law, nor is it a violation of the law for one to undertake to persuade another to vote for or against a particular question.
> Before any of these defendants can be convicted of this charge, the evidence must show beyond a reasonable doubt not only that the poll tax was purchased by the defendant and that the defendant undertook to influence the holder of such poll tax receipt to vote for the water company, but it must also show beyond a reasonable doubt that said poll tax receipt was given or promised to the elector as a consideration for his voting for the water company. . . .

This interpretation of Arkansas' election law made it virtually impossible to prevent poll tax payments as a means of influencing votes. Following the decision, the *Arkansas Gazette* editorialized that under the decision the purchaser of a poll tax receipt would violate the law only if he refused to hand over the receipt except in return for a specific promise to "vote right." Such a violation would be all but impossible to prove in court.[19]

19 *Arkansas Gazette*, October 31, 1948.

Authorization forms were not, of course, used only for questionable purposes. Various civic clubs made considerable use of them to increase voting. However, since the written authorization procedure was so frequently associated with corrupt election practices, it was stopped.

The efforts of the Good Government League of Crittenden County provide an additional illustration of poll tax payment by Arkansas political leaders. Veterans organized this league in 1946 in an effort to defeat the machine of County Judge Bond, popularly known as "Sly Cy" Bond. The league had purposes similar to those of the organization headed by Sidney McMath in Garland County. Its leaders realized that they could accomplish nothing until they had some qualified voters on their side and that, to get them, they would have to stage a poll tax payment campaign. They conducted a drive for the payment period which ended on October 1, 1946, and increased the number of payments from nearly 4,000 to more than 6,500. They led a similar drive the following year and got over 4,000 persons to pay. The league had about thirty workers going around with blank authorizations. As far as possible, league workers had persons pay for their own receipts. If anyone said that he could not afford it, they gave him a receipt anyway. The league estimates that it paid for about 1,000 of the 4,000 receipts purchased through its efforts.

The organization of "Sly Cy" is said to have followed the practice of shaking down liquor and beer licensees on the basis that money was needed to buy poll tax receipts for people who would vote to keep the county wet. In 1947, $25 was collected from each of these licensees. Since there were some 300 of them, approximately $7,500 was obtained. It was estimated that only 1,500 receipts were controlled by the machine. If so, most of the money collected did not go for poll tax purposes.

Another example of the use of the poll tax for political advantage was found in Washington County, Arkansas. A retired chancery court judge reported that the only time the county came close to having a "boss" was when the sheriff and the tax collector teamed up. The sheriff bought several hundred poll tax receipts for some actual persons and some fictitious persons. On election eve, he put a number of marked ballots in each ballot box. He also entered the names of his fictitious poll taxpayers in the poll books so that the election records would be in order. The tax collector had previously reported their names as having paid the tax and these names appeared on the printed list of qualified voters. The liquor people were also involved. Subsequently, the individuals concerned were exposed and prosecution and penitentiary sentences followed.

A procedural change by the county audit division of the Arkansas comptroller's office also indicated that political leaders paid the poll taxes of others. Formerly, this division required county tax collectors to certify immediately after the October 1 deadline the amount of poll taxes collected. The figures received were unsatisfactory because of duplication in poll tax sales. Sometimes two persons would pay the same person's tax. When a political leader came in with a long list of persons for whom he wished to pay, it was usually impossible for the tax collector to check every name at that time. After the period for payment had passed, a check might reveal 100 or 150 duplications. Thus, a later time for certifying poll tax collections was authorized.

A full page political advertisement in the *Northwest Arkansas Times* in August, 1940 revealed that politicians had purchased poll tax receipts. The names of the persons to whom receipts were issued in four townships were listed with the names of purchasers of the receipts. The majority of the receipts had been purchased by supporters of the winning candidate for sheriff.[20]

A state official commented that the buying of poll tax receipts in Arkansas is primarily a county matter. Because the payment deadline, October 1, is long before the primary election, it does not pay state political forces to put up money for poll taxes. Most state candidates are not certain so far in advance that they will run. Occasionally, the state administration will send $1,000 or so into a county to cover poll taxes already arranged. The official remarked that this is a foolish

[20] The advertisement was inserted by an opponent of the sheriff. Exhibit 7, *Hearings on S. 1280*, pp. 279-81.

practice since the votes usually have to be bought again the following year.

Texas has several laws designed to prevent poll tax payment by candidates and others as a means of buying votes. Although the practice has not been stopped, it has not been as widespread as in Alabama and Arkansas. Any candidate for office, anyone on his behalf and anyone interested in any question to be voted on is forbidden to pay the poll tax for another person. Anyone convicted of so doing may be imprisoned for a period of from two to five years. Candidates and their supporters are forbidden to pay poll taxes for any reason and not just for the purpose of influencing votes as in Alabama. An exception is made for husbands and wives who may pay the tax for one another.[21]

Since 1951 Texas has permitted an authorized agent to pay the poll tax, as Arkansas used to do. Before this time, the Texas tax could be paid by an authorized agent only if the payer lived in a city of less than 10,000 persons or, if he lived in a city of 10,000 or more persons, if he was absent from his precinct at the time for payment.[22] There is no evidence that the type of corruption which was associated with payment by an agent in Arkansas has been connected with the Texas method. The fact that candidates and their supporters are forbidden to pay poll taxes in Texas undoubtedly accounts for the difference between the two states.

Several penalties have been provided in Texas. Anyone who knowingly becomes an agent to obtain a poll tax receipt or certificate of exemption except as provided by law, or who gives or loans money to another to induce him to pay the tax, may be fined as much as $500. A tax collector may be fined a maximum of $1,000 and removed from office if he delivers a receipt or exemption certificate to anyone except the one entitled to it and at any other time than the time when the tax is paid or the certificate applied for. If any tax collector issues

21 *Vernon's Texas Statutes, 1952 Supplement,* Elec. Code, Art. 5.13 and Penal Code, Art. 203; *Constitution,* Art. VI, sec. 2.

22 *Vernon's Texas Statutes, 1952 Supplement,* Elec. Code, Art. 5.11 and *General Laws of Texas, 1941,* Chapter 132, secs. 1 and 2.

a blank poll tax receipt or exemption certificate or knowingly
delivers either to a fictitious person, he may be judged guilty
of a felony and imprisoned for from three to five years. Any
taxpayer who makes any false statement to procure a poll tax
receipt may be imprisoned for from one to three years.[23]

Concerning actual practices, a San Antonio political observer
said:

They [the politicians] buy up as many poll tax receipts as they can
before the books close, keep them on file and pass them out to their
'owners' on election day—with instructions of course, and an extra
dollar or so for sweetnin'. There is a law about no person being
allowed to pay anybody else's poll tax; but that, like the one about
people who don't pay being given road work or a fine, is enforced
only when it's convenient.[24]

Poll taxes of Mexicans and Negroes in Texas have frequently
been paid for them as a means of controlling their votes. In
some areas, the practice has been to gather together a truckload
of Mexicans and to take them to the county courthouse. Each
one is given $1.75 with which to pay the tax. After receiving
the receipt, the Mexican is told that it belongs to the politician
who gave him the money. If the Mexican is considered
reliable, he may be allowed to retain the receipt. If not, it is
collected and held until election day. For his trouble in going
to pay the tax, the Mexican may receive a bottle of beer. Since
Mexicans are migratory, they are frequently given blank
receipts so that someone else may use them at election time. In
some places, particularly in Laredo, blocks of blank receipts
may be bought. Donald S. Strong found that the purchasing
of receipts by politicians was most prevalent in South Texas
and the Rio Grande Valley, the section where the percentage
of Mexicans in the population is the greatest.[25]

[23] *Vernon's Texas Statutes*, Penal Code, Arts. 201, 204, 205, 199, 200, and
200a-02.

[24] As quoted by Stoney, "Suffrage in the South," p. 5.

[25] "The Poll Tax: The Case of Texas," *American Political Science Review*,
XXXVIII (August, 1944), 698. Dr. Strong also reports that this type of corruption was aired by a Texas senatorial investigating committee and by a
committee of the United States House of Representatives in 1919 and 1929
respectively and that these investigations did not have any apparent effect in
lessening the practice.

During congressional hearings on anti-poll tax bills, Hoyt S. Haddock of the CIO Maritime Committee reported on poll tax payment practices in Texas as follows:

... during an election that took place while I lived in Port Arthur, I saw Negroes herded together and taken to the polls where they were forced to vote on poll-tax receipts which were handed to them by the political machine. Those engaged in illegal occupations were required to vote for the right people or be run out of town.

Another example of poll-tax abuse exists at Port Isabel, Tex. At this port, dealers pay the fishermen's taxes, and force them to vote their ticket, or see that their livelihood as fishermen ceases.[26]

In San Antonio, a Negro political boss, the late Charlie Bellinger, was reported to "own" 3,000 poll tax receipts. At poll tax payment time, he would have $3,000 or $4,000 which probably had come from white candidates who were interested in securing his aid. Bellinger would round up a sufficiently large number of Negroes and give them money to pay the tax. After having done so, they would turn their receipts over to Bellinger who would hold them until election day. On election day, the receipts would be distributed to individuals whom Bellinger regarded as reliable. Hence, he "owned" the receipts.

Maury Maverick, a former congressman and mayor of San Antonio, has stated that in one Texas town some 4,000 or 5,000 wholly fictitious names were added to the roll of poll taxpayers. The custom was to hold the receipts until election day and, then give them to persons meeting the description on the receipts fairly closely.[27] Maverick was himself indicted for violating the law forbidding the payment of another's poll tax. According to his account, he made a contribution of $250 to a local union with a membership of about 2,000. This money was part of a $1,000 contribution made by Maverick to the national union, the International Ladies Garment Workers Union. He told the union to use it for a poll tax campaign—for advertising, for transporting members to the tax collector's office and so on but not for the actual payment of taxes. He

---

26 *Hearings on S. 1280*, p. 249.

27 The poll tax receipt in Texas carries a description of the taxpayer. Information pertaining to his age, sex, residence, race, birthplace, and occupation is included. It is used as an identification card when the individual votes.

was indicted for paying the poll tax of others but was found not guilty.[28]

In Virginia, the constitution provides that the poll tax must be paid personally by the payer. When Virginia had a poll tax suffrage prerequisite from 1876-1882, there was considerable vote buying through poll tax payment. Consequently, when the tax was again tied to the suffrage, the word "personally" was used to try to prevent this practice.[29] Virginia law further provides that an individual may not pay nor offer to pay the poll tax of another with the intent of having that person's name placed on the list of qualified voters except that he may pay the tax of a close relative. Anyone who violates this provision is guilty of a misdemeanor.[30]

Despite these preventive efforts in the Old Dominion, the practice persists. In January, 1940, Governor James H. Price advised the General Assembly that:

Information has reached my office that large amounts of poll taxes have been paid in bulk in certain sections of the State during the past year and not by the individual voter, as the law contemplates and provides. Many thousands of dollars have been invested in this practice. . . . The poll tax has become . . . an instrument of fraud and of vicious practices. . . .[31]

In 1941, a subcommittee of the Virginia Advisory Legislative Council, in reporting on a study of the suffrage provisions of the constitution, stated:

In Virginia, the comptroller prepared a report for this committee showing the payment of poll taxes throughout the State, and that report is enough to shock anyone who believes in the democratic processes, because it shows the block payment of poll taxes; that is, it is a rather common tactic, particularly in the Ninth District of Virginia, and the voting in the last election would demonstrate that beyond question.[32]

[28] Maury Maverick, "Let's Join the U.S.," *Nation,* CL (May 11, 1940), 592-93. See also "Trial of a Tax," *Newsweek,* XIV (December 11, 1939), 20; New York *Times,* October 17, December 3 and 9, 1939.

[29] *Constitution,* Art. II, sec. 20. See also Tipton R. Snavely, "The Taxation of Negroes in Virginia," *Phelps-Stokes Fellowship Papers* (University of Virginia, 1916), No. 3, p. 31.

[30] *Code of Virginia,* 1950, Tit. 24, sec. 129.

[31] Virginia General Assembly, Senate Document No. 1, 1940 sess.

[32] As quoted in statement of Moss A. Plunkett, *Hearings on S. 1280,* p. 75.

The state comptroller, LeRoy Hodges, studied poll tax collections for the ten year period 1931-1940. He found that the bulk of collections is made in November, before the December 5 delinquency deadline. He also discovered that collections jump up in April and May, prior to the six-months-before-election deadline for the November election. At this time, heavy payments are made on "omitted" taxes, i.e., poll taxes paid by or for people not assessed on the regular tax rolls. Mr. Hodges reported: "There is ample evidence that these capitation taxes are frequently paid en bloc, and not 'personally' as required by the State constitution."[33] His statement was later refuted, although not effectively, by his successor as comptroller, Henry G. Gilmer. To his predecessor's comment concerning block payments, Mr. Gilmer's only answer was: "There is no record of any information in the comptroller's office that would justify a statement of this kind by the State comptroller."[34] Since he did not answer Mr. Hodges more tellingly, it seems evident that there is considerable substance to Mr. Hodges' statement.

David G. George, a director of the Southern Electoral Reform League, testified before a United States Senate subcommittee in 1942 that over the previous decade at least 56 county treasurers in Virginia were found short in their accounts. When some of those treasurers were brought to trial, it was found that they were short because they had marked poll tax receipts paid, but failed to get the money from the organizations or individuals who had promised it.[35]

The Virginia Auditor of Public Accounts, L. McCarthy Downs, took sharp issue with Mr. George's testimony. According to him, there were only 44, and not 56, instances where treasurers had failed to meet their accountability. Only four treasurers had been tried for misappropriation of public funds in the preceding twelve years, and poll tax receipts were not involved in their trials. He concluded:

The vast majority of the so-called shortages were simply technical in nature and no person is justified in making the statement that

---

[33] Included with statement of David G. George, *Hearings on S. 1280*, p. 92.
[34] *Hearings on S. 1280*, p. 430.
[35] *Ibid.*, p. 91.

Virginia county treasurers were short because they had marked poll
tax tickets 'Paid' and had not received the money therefor.[36]
The statement of the auditor seems based upon more solid
ground than that of Mr. George, but even if the county
treasurers have not engaged in marking receipts "paid" before
receiving the money, the charge of block payments has not been
answered.

In connection with block payments of poll taxes, Mr. George
informed the Senate subcommittee of a contested election
brought to trial in 1939. The case resulted from a corrupt
Democratic primary in Accomack County. Evidence was submitted at the trial that at one precinct the majority of the poll
taxes were paid in block. Out of 1,100 votes, 400 were cast by
absentee ballot and most of the absentees were at home and
were not ill. Paying the poll tax for someone else and procuring
an absentee ballot for him have been combined frequently.
Mr. George stated that often the person whose tax was paid did
not know it until the local "heeler" called and gave him an
application for an absentee ballot. When the mail ballot was
received, the voter took it to the local politician who marked
and mailed it and gave him whatever sum had been agreed
upon. Mr. George testified that this practice regularly occurs
in a large part of the state.[37]

In 1947, Mr. George said that block payment of poll taxes
had decreased in Virginia. He believed that the increase in
union membership helps to explain the decline. Many of the
new union members are persons who formerly permitted their
taxes to be paid by political bosses. Now that they are
organized, they are not under the influence of the machine as
they were. Other contributing factors are the increase in
income levels in recent years and the effect of anti-poll tax
agitation in making the electorate more sensitive to abuses in
its administration.

Moss A. Plunkett, a leader of the liberal faction of the
Virginia Democratic party, stated in reference to his 1941
candidacy for lieutenant governor:

36 *Ibid.*, p. 429.
37 *Ibid.*, pp. 91-92.

In connection with that candidacy, I met with the liberal people of Virginia in the various counties and learned from them, first-hand, the working of the poll tax, particularly in the districts in Virginia where the practice is more widespread than it is in other sections, and I was told, frankly, that there would be no possibility of my matching the 85,000 votes which the poll-tax crowd has in its vest pocket in Virginia, except by a corresponding expenditure, and that it would take over $100,000 to finance the necessary campaign in the State.[38]

He testified further that "there has not been and there never will be any attempt on the part of the politicians of Virginia to refute the statements that block payment of poll taxes is a recognized practice in Virginia."[39] According to him, candidates for county office carry the burden of these payments rather than the state headquarters.

The practice of block payment has been reported not only by poll tax opponents but also by the Virginia State Democratic organization. In 1945, a subcommittee of the Democratic State Central Committee recommended a revision of the election laws. With reference to the poll tax, the subcommittee reported:

The serious abuse of the laws relating to payment of poll taxes is the recognized practice of what is called the block payment of poll taxes. The practice has not been prevented by the existing statutes and it is believed that it can be prevented only by amending these statutes so as to make it more difficult for block payments to occur without detection and also to impose more serious penalties upon persons who pay the poll taxes of others and upon officers who receive such payments.

The report pointed out that poll tax payment by one person for another was unlawful only if proved to have been made under circumstances indicating an intent to have the person's name placed upon the list of qualified voters. The subcommittee made suggestions directed toward correcting this condition but no action has been taken.[40]

Similar practices were associated with poll tax payment in

38 *Ibid.,* p. 78.
39 *Ibid.,* p. 81.
40 Democratic State Central Committee of Virginia, *Recommendations for Revision of Election Laws,* report of subcommittee appointed under resolution of September 22, 1945, December 1, 1945, p. 14.

Georgia and Tennessee when the tax was a voting prerequisite there. In 1940, the tax collector of Ware County, Georgia, stated that the poll tax was "so crooked . . . why . . . this last time—hell, everytime as far as that goes—they'll come in here with a list of 75 or 100 names and pay up their taxes. I've seen them pay as high as 350 at a trip."[41] A Burke County official estimated that forty per cent of the people registered for the 1936 election had their poll taxes paid by candidates.[42]

When revision of Georgia's constitution was under consideration in 1943 and 1944, a member of the Constitutional Revision Commission stated that his sole reason for supporting poll tax repeal was the corruption connected with it. His experience had been that those persons who could be controlled by the machines had their poll taxes paid for them but that those who thought for themselves did not and many forgot to pay their tax on time.[43] In 1945, Roy V. Harris, veteran politician and legislator, stated that many local, county, and state officers paid the poll tax of their supporters and that this custom was not confined to any one section but applied to a majority of the counties and was a severe burden on all candidates.[44]

In 1940, a Chattanooga labor leader and campaign manager in local politics stated:

Anything they tell you up at that county courthouse about not selling poll taxes to these ward heelers is bare-faced lying. They buy up back dated poll taxes after the books are supposed to be closed. . . . They never keep a record of receipt books. . . . I've seen them erase names and have people vote—two and three of them— on the same receipt. . . . In some of the wards, the Republican is bought off or he's so drunk it don't make any difference to him. . . . What they do is, they take a whole book of extra receipts and put down the money for it. If they have to show an account of it, the money is there, if they don't after the election they get it back. . . . I've seen men with whole fist fulls of poll tax slips and registration certificates handing them out at the door of the polling places and taking them up when the people come out. . . .[45]

[41] Bunche, p. 724.
[42] Ibid., p. 141.
[43] James V. Carmichael, in Records of the Commission of 1943-1944, To Revise the Constitution of Georgia, ed. by Albert B. Saye (1946), p. 100.
[44] Atlanta Banner Herald, January 12, 1945.
[45] Bunche, p. 732.

Racketeers, bootleggers, number and policy barons were said to purchase large blocks of receipts before each election in Chattanooga as partial payment for the protection given their illicit enterprises by the city administration. These interests provided fleets of automobiles for the political machine so that floating voters could be carried from one polling place to another to use the receipts.[46]

A Republican and former member of the County Board of Elections in Hamilton County, Tennessee, stated that the most common use of the poll tax was to control elections either through block purchase or bogus receipts. Although it would seem difficult to use bogus receipts when there was a certified list of poll taxpayers, there were actually two lists prepared. The certified list was not used at the polls but was replaced by a special list which included more than 6,000 names of persons who had not paid their poll taxes. The Democratic party or some of its candidates put up enough money to cover the improper receipts in case anyone should discover that the tax had not been collected from everyone whose name appeared on the special list. In most cases, the party's "pot" was returned. When on the Board, this Republican acquired one of these lists and locked it with a certified list in his safe. The County Democratic Committee offered precinct officers $50 for its return and threatened discharge if they did not find it. The party's pot was turned over to the county. The Republican reported that three men in his own party would not speak to him afterwards since about $2,000 of the money came from them. Following this incident, the Democratic party organization adopted a new method. They bought the unused portions of receipt books on the last day for payment. Receipts were supposed to be issued consecutively, but in the last rush of payment, several books were used simultaneously, and the parts left over were the ones bought by the organization.[47]

In Greene County, Tennessee, a group of about six Republicans put up $12,000 in the 1930's with which they bought 6,000 poll tax receipts. With these receipts, they ousted the

[46] *Ibid.,* p. 616.
[47] *Ibid.,* pp. 733-34.

Democrats. One of the group stated that block buying of
receipts was common there. Some politicians gave the receipts
to reliable voters while others held them until election day.
They might have a place near the polling booth where they
passed out a receipt, plus a card guide of voting instructions
and possibly a dollar bill to each voter. The politician said
that, in raising a pool for poll tax payments, office holders
would contribute from $1,000 to $2,500 depending upon how
wealthy they were and what office they desired.

The famous Crump machine in Shelby County used the poll
tax to advantage in retaining its control. Machine representatives would register a large number of fictitious persons, usually
giving addresses in sections of Memphis where many Negroes
and lower class whites lived. They also bought large numbers
of receipts. On election day, the machine sent trucks to Oseolo,
Arkansas, and loaded them with anyone available. The trucks
returned to a polling place. On arrival, each person was given
a registration slip and a poll tax receipt. He presented the
receipt and registration certificate to the election official and
was given a marked ballot which he deposited in the ballot box.
On leaving, he surrendered his registration certificate and
receipt and in return received $1.00. These individuals were
then taken to another polling place and the process continued
as long as there was time.

A politician in McMinn County, Tennessee, reported that it
was customary for candidates there to collect funds, one for
each party, for the purpose of buying poll tax receipts. Block
buying of receipts also occurred in neighboring Polk County
where machine leaders held the receipts and distributed them
on election day.

Additional evidence of block buying of poll tax receipts and
of purchasing votes through tax payment in Tennessee was
brought out in congressional hearings on the various federal
anti-poll tax bills. Homer Wilson, a self-styled amateur politician from Strawberry Plains, testified that politicians kept a
record of the number who voted in each precinct and of the
number of poll taxes bought by their opponents. They then
attempted to buy a greater number of receipts. He stated
further:

. . . in a lot of counties where they are politically organized, what they do is go down and buy the poll taxes, get the receipts, and then take those receipts and see that they do the work. They go out and pick their men, and they tell them "Now, here is a poll-tax receipt and you go in there and vote. Use it, that is all right."[48]

Bernard Borah, a United Mine Workers representative and a resident of Knoxville, reported that, in 1936, a politician approached him and asked how many votes he could furnish for the machine candidate.

I told him I was not so much interested in it, and then he drew out of his pocket a sheaf of poll-tax receipts, with no name filled in, simply signed receipts for poll taxes, and gave them to me and told me, "Now, if you know of a fellow who is reliable, here are about 50 of them, and fill them out and give them to the men that you want to vote" and he told me it would be all right, and to give a certain sign at the polling booth, because they would then know the receipts were coming from the right place, and everything was all right.[49]

The practice of block buying of poll tax receipts appeared less widespread in the late forties. An informant advised that this practice was not as frequent in Memphis then as formerly. The Crump machine maintained control by keeping a close tab on registration and poll tax payment and by ascertaining that its supporters registered and paid their poll taxes. The organization did not want to use methods like block buying of receipts when unnecessary. A Nashville newspaper man believed that the practice was declining although he admitted it still existed in many counties. A politician in Smith County reported that little block buying of receipts occurred there. Some receipts were paid for by politicians but not on a wholesale basis.

Candidates for public office and members of political machines are not the only ones who pay poll taxes to secure votes although they are the chief offenders. Both labor unions and employers have engaged in the practice.

48 *Hearings on S. 1280*, pp. 171-72.
49 *Ibid.*, pp. 173-74. See also testimony of Mrs. Kate Bradford Stockton, pp. 89-90; and statement by George W. Hardin, *Hearings on H. R. 29*, before the Committee on Rules and Administration, U. S. Senate, 80th Cong., 2d sess., p. 321.

With increase in unionism in the South has come an increase in political activity by labor groups. Union leaders realize that they must increase labor's political participation to win advancements for union members through political action. Consequently, they encourage their members to become qualified voters and to vote. They have seen entrenched political machines buying votes through poll tax payment; they have also witnessed employers requiring their employees to pay their poll taxes and to vote as management desired. To fight fire with fire, the unions have instituted poll tax payment programs of their own. Not all programs have remained within the letter of the law. In some cases, union leaders have gone beyond merely urging their members to pay the tax and have actually arranged for its payment for them.

In a north Alabama city, the CIO Industrial Council undertook a poll tax payment program. The council printed cards which were similar to those used in the office of the probate judge. A tax payment record was kept for each union member and the cards were filed in the desk of the council head. He saw that members kept up-to-date in their payments. If necessary, the council loaned money to its members to pay back and current taxes. The council head also collected from union members for payment of their poll taxes. He then took a list of taxpayers to the tax collector and wrote a check on a CIO account to cover the amount due. In December, 1945, and January, 1946, more than $4,500 was delivered to the tax collector. With reference to the legality of the program, the council head advised county officials that he would expose other abuses if they prosecuted him. No action was taken against him. Plans were discussed to push this system in other CIO unions in Alabama.

In a textile plant in Cordova, Alabama, the union paid the tax for its members and was reimbursed by funds withheld by the company. Before the workers were organized, the company withheld the money for the tax. After unionization, the union asked the company to continue the check-off procedure and the management agreed. A similar procedure was proposed to industrial plants in Jefferson County but the managers refused to adopt it on the excuse that they doubted its legality.

In 1937, a United Mine Workers local in Walker County, Alabama, borrowed $1,100 from a Jasper bank and advanced money to whites and Negroes for poll tax payment. As a result, 485 persons became qualified voters; 267 were Negroes. Seven other Alabama locals later adopted the same program.[50]

The CIO established a poll tax payment system for its members in Virginia. Card forms were provided for them to sign in authorizing the union to pay their poll taxes. After signing these authorizations, the union paid the tax en bloc for them. The CIO contended that it was within the law since the money was loaned by the union. However, according to a CIO representative, repayment was not always expected. This method of block payment by the CIO was accepted in counties where labor had a significant vote but refused where labor was weak. It was used especially in Richmond and Roanoke.

When Tennessee had a voter poll tax, the chairman of the Board of Elections in Hamilton County, discussing the buying of poll tax receipts by labor unions, said:

They're not supposed to, but I know they do. I guess the labor unions are guilty just like the rest when it's in the politicians interest to allow it. . . . They've done it for years. Why, they just put down the money and buy up a whole book of them.[51]

However, a labor organizer in Chattanooga stated:

. . . Most unions can't afford to play around with poll tax receipts. I know of only one local in the last few years that paid poll taxes out of the treasury; that was a small, but very active local of the movie operators. . . .[52]

Management is not as active in arranging for payment of employees' poll taxes as formerly. With the growth of unionism in the South, employers have largely ceased tax payment programs. Before unions came, they wanted their employees to be qualified voters because they could influence their votes. With the advent of unions, they lost control over the vote of their workers. Therefore, most employers are no longer interested in encouraging their workers to vote.

Where employers arranged for payment of their employees'

50 Bunche, p. 467.
51 *Ibid.*, pp. 730-31.
52 *Ibid.*, p. 764.

poll taxes, the usual practice was to deduct them from wages. In 1940, the tax collector of Lee County, Alabama, said that representatives of the Opelika Mills Company and the Pepperel Manufacturing Company brought him long lists of employees' names accompanied by the money for the tax. He thought that the money was deducted from wages and that the companies had the workers "sign slips of paper" so they would not be accused of forcing the employees to pay the tax.[53] The Opelika registrar advised that, as the mill workers registered, the book-keeper of the Opelika Mills Company was present and asked each one if he wanted to pay the tax personally or have the mill take it out of his wages.[54] The president of a Huntsville union stated that fewer workmen paid the tax than formerly because the mills used to make them pay it but no longer did so. The union asked management to deduct the tax from wages but management refused.[55] In 1940, a mill superintendent of Enterprise, Alabama, brought the poll taxes for fifty employees into the collector's office. He explained that he had taken the money out of wages.[56] The Montgomery tax collector reported that the telephone and power companies had someone bring in poll taxes for their employees and he assumed that the money was deducted from wages.[57]

An Alabama CIO representative testified in 1942 that many voters would not be qualified if their employers had not helped them to pay their poll taxes. He stated that large corporations had advanced money to carefully chosen employee representatives with instructions to pay employees' taxes; that at least three persons employed by the Republic Steel Corporation, Raibel Cooperage Company, and the Alabama Fuel and Iron Company knew about this practice; that it was done despite the law.[58] In 1946, a CIO leader in Huntsville stated that before 1933 a condition of employment in some mills was the up-to-

53 *Ibid.*, p. 645.
54 *Ibid.*, p. 325.
55 *Ibid.*, p. 124.
56 *Ibid.*, p. 718.
57 *Ibid.*, p. 680.
58 Statement of Yelverton Cowherd, Regional Director, CIO, *Hearings on S. 1280*, p. 119.

date payment of the poll tax. When the companies could no longer control the labor vote, they stopped insisting on its payment.

A Tennessee labor representative testified in 1942 that he knew some workmen who had their poll taxes paid by the company for which they worked.[59] A United Mine Workers representative from Tennessee reported that employers deducted money for the tax from employees' pay and purchased receipts for them, holding the receipts until election day. On election day, the employers gave the receipts to the men with instructions on how to vote.[60]

Evidence of poll tax payment by liquor interests was also discovered. Use of the authorization system of tax payment by liquor and beer interests in Arkansas was previously discussed. Apparently these interests did not actually contribute money for tax payment. However, a municipal court judge in Greenville, Mississippi, stated that bootleggers there did most of the paying of poll taxes for other people. It was rumored in 1947 that the taxes of 2,500 persons were paid in this way. The sheriff, who is also the tax collector, and the bootleggers collaborated. Sometimes the sheriff held out a block of receipts after the payment deadline to permit bootleggers to pay the tax for their delinquent supporters.[61]

59 Statement of William D. Berry, *ibid.*, p. 98.

60 Statement of Bernard Borah, *ibid.*, p. 176.

61 For an earlier instance of poll tax payment by brewers in Texas, see Peter H. Odegard, *Pressure Politics: The Story of the Anti-saloon League* (New York, 1928), p. 252. In 1942, the Farm Security Administration was charged with paying poll taxes in Alabama in violation of the Alabama constitution. It was accused of paying the poll taxes of its rehabilitation borrowers so that they would constitute a pressure group to appeal to Congress for large appropriations for it. The charges were made by Edward A. O'Neal, president of the American Farm Bureau Federation, and Robert K. Greene, probate judge of Hale County. The FSA categorically denied that it had ever paid the poll taxes of any of its clients. It admitted that, in checking indebtedness, a check was made on the amount of poll taxes owed by prospective borrowers. This was done to discover the borrower's total indebtedness. The Administration also admitted that, as a part of its rehabilitation program, it had urged its clients to qualify as voters. The agency had not, however, paid any poll taxes. The individuals concerned had to pay their own taxes although they might use money loaned to them by FSA. See *Hearings on Agriculture Department*

From the preceding account, it is evident that the poll tax has frequently been paid for individuals as a means of influencing votes and that laws designed to prevent this practice have been ineffective. In most cases, these laws are difficult to enforce, but in any case, little effort has been expended in trying to execute them. The extent to which the tax is paid for political "hangers-on" and machine supporters makes a mockery of one of the classic arguments for it. This is the argument that the tax keeps government in the hands of the politically élite and that it excludes from the electorate corrupt, illiterate, disinterested, and ignorant voters. The poll tax is no guarantee that such persons will be prevented from voting but, on the contrary, they often become qualified by having their taxes paid for them. The principal violators of the laws forbidding tax payment as a means of obtaining votes are candidates for office and other political figures. Other groups resort to this practice when desiring to achieve certain ends through political action. Employers have seen that their employees' poll taxes were paid when they could control their votes. Since most employers have lost this control, few of them now encourage tax payment by their workers. Labor unions have taken over the practice to increase the voice of labor in Dixieland. Although the custom of paying another's poll tax to secure his vote is far from moribund, it is not as prevalent now as formerly. The attention directed to this practice through publicity used in the fight against the tax undoubtedly accounts for much of this decline.

ADDITIONAL ABUSES IN POLL TAX ADMINISTRATION

Although the chief abuse connected with the poll tax as a suffrage measure is its payment by groups and individuals as a means of buying votes, there are additional violations of poll

---

Appropriation Bill for 1943, before the subcommittee of the Committee on Appropriations, H. of R., 77th Cong., 2d sess., Pt. 2, pp. 322-29, 737-38, and 751-53; *Hearings* before the Joint Committee on Reduction of Nonessential Federal Expenditures, 77th Cong., 2d sess., Pt. 3, pp. 699-742, 862, and 887-90; and New York *Times,* January 24, February 7, 11, and 14, 1942.

tax laws. Some of these violations were referred to incidentally in discussing tax payment by others. For instance, reference was made to the purchase of receipts after the payment deadline. That each state has a set time for payment and that this time is ordinarily long before the general and primary elections was demonstrated in Chapter 2. When it is in the interest of the tax collector, time of payment requirements are often overlooked.

In 1940, the tax collector of Jefferson County, Alabama, admitted that he was not strict about observing the deadline for payment. He said: "When people tell me they honestly forget it and when I know every penny of it goes to the school, I don't see hardly how I can refuse to take their money." Apparently, however, he did not oblige all taxpayers since his clerk refused the money of several persons who offered it after the deadline. Perhaps these were individuals who could not be counted on to vote "right."[62]

At Montevallo, a faculty member at Alabama College for Women failed to pay his poll tax by February 1 one year. He told a local politician that he could not vote because of this failure. The politician replied that he would handle the matter if the faculty member would write a check for the amount due. According to a Negro professor at Montgomery State Teachers College, some poll tax receipts dated later than February 1 were accepted and some were turned down in the November, 1946, election in Montgomery.

In allowing an individual to pay the poll tax after the deadline, the usual practice is to back-date the receipts. A Mississippi politician stated that back-dating of receipts was practiced in only six or seven counties there. He believed that the practice is so corrupt that the local government would have to be very crooked to do it. However, a State Democratic Executive Committee member said in 1947 that the greatest difficulty with poll tax administration was that some sheriffs allow payments after the deadline.

There is not the same possibility for fraudulent administration of the rate provisions as there is for the laws pertaining to

---

[62] Bunche, p. 677.

tax payment by another and for those relating to the time of payment. Since revenue records must be kept, it is more difficult to cover up non-payment or partial payment than either block purchasing or back-dating of receipts. Where the tax is non-cumulative, little need exists for allowing a person to pay only a part of the tax. Since the amount is small, the tax-payer can pay all if he can pay a part. The situation differed when Georgia and Alabama had a poll tax which accumulated over the entire period of liability. In these states, an individual may have been unable, or may not have wanted, to pay the full amount of his back taxes but he may have been able and willing to pay part of them. To secure his vote, administrative officials excused him from paying some or all of his back taxes.

The practice of excusing an individual from paying back poll taxes has occurred in Alabama. Reference was made earlier to the fact that probate judges have canceled part of back taxes by marking "pd" on their records. Considerable looseness in administration of the cumulative provision has occurred in connection with an individual's change of residence. When persons have transferred their voter registration to a new county, they have been given a clean poll tax record simply on their word that they were not in arrears. Some probate judges have marked poll tax records fully paid at the time individuals move to another county. In other instances, when a person registered in a new county, he claimed that he was over-age or exempt for some other reason. Such claims were seldom checked. The Montgomery County probate judge stated in 1940 that there were numerous cases where people moved from that county owing from one to twenty years back poll taxes and voted in another county without procuring a transfer.[63]

In Georgia, the cumulative provision was not applied uniformly. The tax was supposed to be cumulative over the entire period of liability from ages 21 to 60 with the maximum amount being $47.47. However, in Atlanta, the tax was reported to accumulate only for seven years. In many counties, individuals were required to pay only up to $4.00 or $6.00, depending on whatever the local political group decided was a

[63] *Ibid.,* pp. 676-77.

convenient sum. In 1939, one county ring, anxious to win a district office, charged no poll tax at all and put every white person on the poll books.[64] The Ware County Board of Registrars ruled in 1940 that anyone who paid $5.00 could become eligible no matter how much he owed in back taxes. The board chairman stated that this was done because "so many people got behind during the depression—good people . . . and they couldn't pay up."[65]

A Tennessee representative of the United Mine Workers testified in 1942 that many persons in his state had voted without having poll tax receipts.

I know of a situation in La Follette and other counties in Tennessee where we have actually pledged to vote large groups of men without poll-tax receipts, a system which was worked out where we had a certain sign that we would make in going in to vote, and the person handling the vote would know not to make any charge, and would pass that man as a member of the machine.[66]

A subcommittee of the Virginia Democratic State Central Committee reported in 1945 that sometimes election judges permitted persons to vote when the treasurer's list failed to show that their poll taxes were paid. The subcommittee concluded that this was "probably" not a widespread practice.[67] An Arkansas newspaper man pointed out that in some counties in his state occasionally more votes were returned than poll tax receipts issued. This excess of votes over receipts cannot be explained entirely by exemptions because of the few exemptions in Arkansas, so some individuals must have voted without having paid the tax.

Exemptions from poll tax payment provide another opening for partisan administration. In 1940, Ralph Bunche concluded that "the administration of the exemption clause is, to put it mildly, 'liberal'."[68] The disability exemption has been particularly abused in Alabama. The Madison County probate judge reported that the exemption list was always high there, usually

64 Stoney, "Who Is Fit to Vote in a Democracy?" p. 175.
65 Bunche, p. 704.
66 Statement of Bernard Borah, *Hearings on S. 1280*, p. 175.
67 Democratic State Central Committee of Virginia, p. 14.
68 Bunche, p. 671.

numbering about 400. In 1936, extra votes were sought because of an approaching election for county commissioner. Candidates began bringing in supporters who "had bad coughs, broken fingers, lumbago, or were hard-of-hearing." On their affidavit that they were disabled, they were exempted. The number of exemptions doubled in this election. The incident occurred under the former law which provided that all permanently disabled persons whose taxable property did not exceed $500 were exempt from the poll tax. The new requirement, that the individual must be "permanently and totally disabled from following any substantially gainful occupation with reasonable regularity," cut the total exemptions in Madison County to 150.[69]

Differences in administration of the disability exemption also existed in South Carolina when the poll tax was in effect. A treasurer of Pickens County interpreted the exemption to mean that if a person were fifty per cent disabled, he was exempt. Under this interpretation, about 1,000 persons were exempt in this county. In Greenville County, few persons were exempt since the law was construed to require total disability before an exemption was allowed.[70] Actually the law did not state the amount of disability but exempted "those incapable of earning a support from being maimed or from any other cause."[71] The exemptions were also handled loosely in Sumter County. If a man appeared to be totally disabled or unable to support himself, the treasurer granted him an exemption without requiring a doctor's certificate. In 1940, the treasurer estimated that 200 exemptions were granted in this way.[72]

Proof of payment provisions may also be administered in a partisan manner. Where the receipt may be demanded at the polls, election officials may or may not ask that it be shown. This requirement may be enforced rigidly when it is desired to exclude certain individuals and loosely when it is desired to

69 *Ibid.*, pp. 671-72. See *Alabama Code of 1928,* sec. 3022 (7) and *General Laws of Alabama, Extra Session 1936-37,* Act. 84, p. 96.

70 Bunche, p. 674.

71 *Code of South Carolina, 1942,* sec. 2565.

72 Bunche, p. 674.

include certain persons. In 1948, a Tennessee CIO official testified that he had observed elections in Nashville where officials asked for the receipts of only some individuals. The last time that he had voted he was asked for his receipt but the preceding eight or ten voters were not. He concluded: "Of course, the election officers knew my identity and the slate they favored was the anti-labor slate."[73] The treasurer of Greenville County, South Carolina, stated in 1940 that election officials did not enforce the requirements about showing receipts except in special elections for school trustees.[74]

There is, therefore, not only considerable corruption associated with the poll tax but also the tax laws are loosely administered. A lax administration is generally characteristic of political processes in the South. Largely due to the discretion vested in local officials, there is often no uniformity of practice even within a given state. Little supervision by state agencies occurs. The county official tends to be a law unto himself. This fact is especially true of poll tax administration.

This inspection into practices associated with poll tax payment and into some of the abuses connected with its administration raises the question whether the tax breeds political corruption. A reason given for its adoption was that it would purify elections. The analysis of the operation of the tax shows that it has not increased the honesty of elections below the Mason-Dixon line. Has the poll tax, instead of purifying elections, caused greater corruption in the electoral process?

This question is difficult to answer. Many corrupt practices have been associated with the poll tax. The principal ones have been illustrated at some length. It cannot be validly maintained, however, that the tax causes general political corruption because fraudulent procedures have been connected with it. The tax may lend itself to distinctive dishonest practices but it is not the cause of them. The cause is more

73 Statement by Harold S. Marthenke, Executive Secretary-Treasurer, Tennessee State CIO Council, Nashville, Tenn., *Hearings on H. R. 29*, pp. 327-28.
74 Bunche, p. 652.

deep-seated and exists within the society which permits such conduct to continue. All corrupt election practices in the South are not associated with the poll tax. The tax gives corruption a peculiar form. Its repeal does not mean the end of corrupt elections for corruption exists in the states which formerly had a poll tax. As long as society condones corrupt methods, repeal simply means that other dishonest election procedures are used. It is doubtful whether the poll tax is as instrumental in causing political corruption as its opponents would have us believe. The root cause lies in the general laxness and looseness of political processes in the South.

5. VOTING: BEFORE AND AFTER ANALYSES

OUT OF THE POLL TAX REPEAL movement of recent years have come charges that the tax is the chief cause for the disfranchisement of southern citizens, white as well as Negro. In fact, propaganda against the tax seems designed to leave the impression that the tax alone causes the low voter participation in southern states. These charges have been made before congressional committees and in congressional debates. They have been circulated throughout the nation by newspaper and magazine articles. Sweeping allegations—like the one that the poll tax disfranchises ten million southerners, six million whites and four million Negroes,[1]—from repetition have become accepted as fact.

An illustration of the extent to which such charges have been accepted may be seen in an important government document, *The Report of the President's Committee on Civil Rights.* The committee quotes an estimate made during a debate in the House of Representatives in July, 1947 that only ten per cent of the potential voters in the then seven poll tax states participated in the 1944 presidential election as against 49 per cent in non-poll tax states. It is implied that the tax accounts for the 39 percentage point difference in participation. A chart presents similar information graphically and gives the reader the distinct impression that the tax alone causes the low voting

[1] Southern Electoral Reform League, *Plain Facts About the Poll Tax* (Atlanta, Ga.), undated pamphlet.

rate.[2] From the literature and arguments used in support of federal anti-poll tax bills, the investigator is led to believe that the southern suffrage system has but one fault—the poll tax.

Charges made about the disfranchising effects of the poll tax have been mainly generalized statements. Few attempts have been undertaken to examine its effects critically. Where statistical methods have been used to demonstrate the number of voters disfranchised by the tax, the usual procedure has been to compare voting turnout in poll tax states with that in non-poll tax states, the method used in *The Report of the President's Committee on Civil Rights.* Users of this method conclude that the tax causes the lower voter turnout in the poll tax states. They give little consideration to other factors which in part explain the low voting record of the South—for instance, the one-party system, the former white primary, registration procedures, the presence of a large Negro population, inertia and a custom of non-voting.[3] Because of many interrelated factors, it is difficult to ascertain the effect of one of them. It is easy to prove that the voting record of southern states is considerably lower than that of non-southern states but it is difficult to show how much of the burden for this difference must be borne by the poll tax. An attempt is made here to arrive at an estimate of the effect of the poll tax upon electoral participation and to test the charges placed against it by its opponents.

BEFORE AND AFTER ADOPTION ANALYSES

One possible way to discover the disfranchising effects of the poll tax is to compare the turnout of voters before and after its adoption as a suffrage prerequisite. Since other suffrage

[2] *To Secure These Rights, The Report of the President's Committee on Civil Rights* (Washington, 1947), pp. 38-39. Hereafter cited as the *Report of The President's Committee.*

[3] See V. O. Key, Jr., *Southern Politics in State and Nation* (New York, 1949), pp. 504-08. Professor Key's study contains a chapter in which the disfranchising effects of the poll tax are examined. A similarity between the conclusions of Professor Key and the writer will be observed. The writer began his study of the poll tax under Professor Key's supervision and in connection with the preparation of *Southern Politics.*

restrictions were adopted in most southern states at the same time as the tax, this method cannot be applied to all present and former poll tax states. It may be used for Arkansas, Florida, Tennessee, and Texas because they did not adopt a battery of suffrage restrictions at the time that they imposed the poll tax.

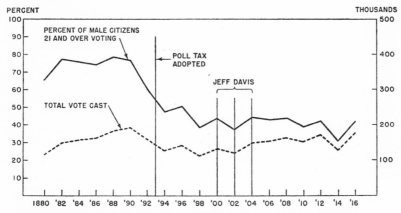

FIGURE 2. Vote in Arkansas General Elections for Governor, 1880-1916.

Figure 2 shows the trends in voting in Arkansas' general elections for governor from 1880 through 1916.[4] Participation began to decline before the poll tax was adopted in 1893. The number of votes cast rose steadily through 1890 and then dropped precipitously in the elections of 1892 and 1894. The reduction in turnout was greater in 1892, the year before the tax was adopted, than in 1894, the year after. Between 1890 and 1892, there was a reduction of nearly seventeen percentage points while between 1892 and 1894, there was a further reduction of just over thirteen percentage points. Following the election of 1898, the turnout rate hovered around the forty per cent mark, except for 1914 when it dropped to approximately thirty per cent. From 1890 to 1898, the turnout in Arkansas

[4] The percentage rates of participation were computed on the basis of the number of all citizens 21 and over as shown by census reports. Figures pertaining to the total vote for governor were supplied by the Arkansas Secretary of State.

gubernatorial elections dropped more than 38 percentage points. Inasmuch as nearly half of this decrease occurred before the poll tax was adopted, other factors must have produced some of the reduction. It appears that the tax served to accelerate a movement already underway. A liberal estimate of the effect of its adoption is that the tax was responsible for no more than one-fourth of the total decrease in voting participation, i.e., for no more than eight to ten percentage points of the total decrease. But this amount of decrease is significant in elections where only thirty to forty per cent of the eligible voters participate.

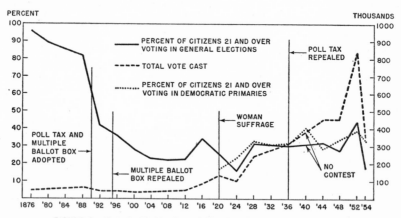

FIGURE 3. Vote in Florida General Elections for Governor, 1876-1954.

Voting trends in Florida general elections for governor from 1876 to 1954 are shown in Figure 3.[5] Florida provides a unique opportunity to study the effect of the poll tax upon voting. This state did not adopt a number of suffrage restrictions when the tax requirement was enacted. It has since repealed the tax. Thus, the effects of both adoption and abolition may be examined. Figure 3 presents the trends in Florida guberna-

[5] Percentage rates were computed in the same manner as those for Arkansas. Election returns were obtained from the following sources: 1876—William T. Cash, *History of the Democratic Party in Florida* (Tallahassee, 1936), p. 69; 1880-1896—*Appleton's Annual Cyclopedia* (New York); 1900-1916—*World Almanac* (New York); 1920-1948—Heard and Strong, *Southern Primaries and Elections;* 1952-1954—*Report of the Secretary of State, Florida, 1951-52* and *1953-54.*

torial elections from a date preceding poll tax adoption in 1889 to one following its repeal in 1937.

A cursory examination of this figure leads to the conclusion that the poll tax had a considerable effect upon reducing the Florida electorate following its adoption. But it must be noted that, although a general disfranchisement plan was not adopted, the poll tax was not the sole restrictive measure enacted in 1889. The legislature also passed a multiple ballot box law which was patterned after a similar South Carolina statute of 1882. It required county commissioners to provide at each polling place as many as nine ballot boxes, labeled according to specified categories of offices or propositions. Ballots were valid only if in the proper ballot box. The act, therefore, struck directly at voters who could not read.[6] The poll tax requirement was moderate in comparison with those of later acts of other states. The amount was $1.00; it accumulated for two years and could be paid as late as thirty days before the election.

Figure 3 shows a drop of approximately forty percentage points in the voting rate for governor from 1888 to 1892. The actual number of ballots cast also declined. More than 26,000 fewer ballots were cast in 1892 than in 1888 despite an increase in the potential electorate of over 14,000. Since the multiple ballot box law went into effect at the same time as the poll tax, the tax was not responsible for all of this drop. The percentage rate of participation was gradually declining in preceding years although the actual number of voters was increasing slightly. This gradual reduction indicates that the poll tax and multiple ballot box acts served as important accelerators of a movement already underway.

Before estimating the effect of the poll tax, it must be noted further that the multiple ballot box law was replaced in 1895 with a statute that inaugurated the Australian ballot system.[7] Figure 3 shows that the participation rate continued to decline following repeal of the multiple ballot box act. Not only did

---

6 Charles D. Farris, "Effects of Negro Voting Upon the Politics of a Southern City: An Intensive Study, 1946-48" (Mss., Ph. D. Dissertation, University of Chicago, 1953), pp. 43-44.

7 *Ibid.*, p. 51.

the rate decline further but also the actual turnout was less in 1900 and 1904 after having remained about the same in 1896. These facts indicate that either the poll tax or some "hard to identify" factor, like inertia, was having a significant effect upon the number of people voting in Florida.

The great 1892 decrease resulted primarily from the failure of the Republican party to run a candidate. In 1888, the Republicans had polled more than 26,000 votes, a figure which corresponds closely with the 1892 decrease. In 1892, the Democratic candidate was opposed by a nominee of the Farmers' Alliance. The vote polled by him when added to the vote polled by the Democratic candidate was approximately equivalent to that polled by the Democratic nominee in 1888. The Farmers' Alliance probably secured most of its support from dissatisfied Democrats. Thus, it appears that the immediate effect of the poll tax and multiple ballot box provisions was to bring about the disfranchisement of those voters who had been supporting the Republican ticket, i.e., the Negroes. Beginning with 1896, the Republicans again placed a ticket on the ballot but they polled a considerably smaller vote than they had before 1892. In 1876, 1880 and 1888, the Republican vote was well over 20,000 but following 1892, it did not again reach this mark until 1920.[8]

What effect, then, did poll tax adoption have in reducing voter participation in Florida? Although it is impossible to state exactly what its effect was, it is significant that by 1904 only 23 per cent of the potential voters were participating in the general election for governor while as many as 95 per cent had voted in 1876. From 1888 to 1904, the rate of participation declined by more than 58 percentage points. A fair estimate is that not more than one-fourth to one-half of the reduction resulted from the tax requirement, but this reduction is significant. Poll tax adoption appears to have had a more positive effect upon reducing the electorate in Florida than it had in Arkansas.

[8] Republicans as such did not run a candidate in 1884. An independent candidate was endorsed by the Republican State Convention. He received a vote slightly larger than Republican candidates had been polling. *Appleton's Annual Cyclopedia, 1884*, p. 333.

Figure 3 shows a slight increase in voting in the first gubernatorial election after poll tax repeal in Florida in 1937. Since the 1940 election was uncontested, the 1944 election was the first one following repeal. The increase in participation over that of 1936 was two percentage points. Voting was generally lower throughout the country in 1944 because of wartime conditions. But for the war, the turnout might have been considerably greater. However, turnout declined in 1948 and was below that for the pre-repeal years of 1936, 1932 and 1928. In 1952, it shot up to 43.7 per cent, the highest rate reached since the 1880's. That poll tax repeal cannot be assigned full credit for this increase is evident from the results of the next election. In 1954, the rate of participation declined just as rapidly as it had risen in 1952 and reached the second lowest point of any election during the period analyzed. The great increase in the 1952 gubernatorial election reflects the intense interest aroused by the Eisenhower-Stevenson campaign. The 1954 special election to fill the vacancy created by the death of Governor Dan McCarty is not a fair one for comparative purposes. It was not associated with presidential elections as gubernatorial elections in Florida usually are. Greatest interest was aroused by the Democratic primary. The fact that the Republican candidate, J. Tom Watson, died shortly before election day further accounts for the poor turnout. Poll tax repeal may have made it easier for more Florida citizens to vote in 1952 than otherwise would have voted. The results of the 1954 election warn against assigning too much significance to a single factor and show that, even though the tax has been lifted, turnout will be low in unexciting elections.

In a predominantly one-party state, a more accurate method of estimating the effects of poll tax repeal upon voting is to examine the trends in primary elections. The turnout in gubernatorial primaries from 1920 through 1954 is also shown in Figure 3.[9] Voting behavior in these primaries generally compares with that in the gubernatorial general elections. The

[9] Voting behavior in primaries for the entire period could not be examined because primaries were not begun in Florida until the early 1900's. See Cash, pp. 106-08. Figures for primary elections before 1920 are not readily available.

turnout tended to increase before the tax was removed. Following abolition, the rate went up by nearly nine percentage points in 1940 but fell back in the war year of 1944 to less than in the pre-repeal year of 1936. It climbed again in both 1948 and 1952 but did not reach the 1940 high. Another drop occurred in the special election in 1954. Except for 1944, the turnout rate has been generally higher since repeal. The violent fluctuations which occurred in the 1952 and 1954 general elections were not present in the primaries for these years.

This post-repeal analysis of voting in Florida gubernatorial primary and general elections indicates that poll tax repeal has had a slight effect upon increasing the turnout rate in general elections and a somewhat greater effect upon increasing participation in primary elections. Repeal has not, however, brought a stupendous increase. The analysis further reveals the difficulty of discovering the effect of a single factor upon voting behavior.[10]

Figure 4 presents the trends in Tennessee gubernatorial elections from 1874 through 1918.[11] It shows an immediate sizable drop in voting following poll tax adoption in 1890, the turnout declining from a high 80.3 per cent in 1888 to 51.3 per cent. The poll tax was not, however, the only suffrage law which took effect at this time. In 1889, the so-called "Myer's" and "Dortch" laws were adopted. The Myer's law required voters in more populous centers to register in their voting precincts and to present registration certificates to the election

---

Therefore, only the percentages of participation from 1920 are shown. Returns for primaries through 1948 are available in Heard and Strong, pp. 36-44. The returns for 1952 and 1954 may be found in the reports of the Florida Secretary of State.

[10] A more complete examination of voting trends before and after repeal using primary election returns may be found below, pp. 126-29.

[11] Participation rates were computed in the same way as those for Arkansas. Gubernatorial election returns were obtained from the Tennessee Secretary of State. Since Tennessee's poll tax ceased to affect the suffrage in 1951, an analysis for the period before adoption and after repeal could have been made as in the case of Florida. It was not because only two gubernatorial elections have occurred since poll tax elimination. The effect of poll tax removal upon Tennessee primary elections is examined below, pp. 132-33.

officials.   The Dortch Act applied the Australian secret ballot
to the more populous counties and cities and required voters

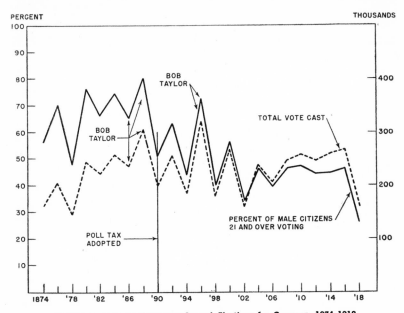

FIGURE 4.   Vote in Tennessee General Elections for Governor, 1874-1918.

to mark their own ballots in secret, unless blind or otherwise
physically disabled. All three laws were regarded as "obnoxious"
by Republicans because they believed that the laws would
prevent hundreds of Republican Negroes from voting.[12]   In
estimating the effect of the poll tax upon voting in Tennessee,
consideration must be given to the fact that the Myer's and
Dortch laws had a simultaneous influence.

Figure 4 reveals that participation in Tennessee gubernatorial elections fluctuated; the percentage tended to be higher
in presidential election years than in non-presidential election
years.   The full amount of the 29 percentage point decline in
the 1890 election cannot be attributed to the Myer's, Dortch

12 J. S. Sharp, "The Entrance of the Farmer's Alliance into Tennessee Poli-
tics," The East Tennessee Historical Society's *Publications,* No. 9 (1937), p. 85.
See also Sharp, "The Farmer's Alliance and the People's Party in Tennessee,"
No. 10 (1938), p. 106.

and poll tax laws because 1890 was not a presidential election year and a lower turnout would have undoubtedly occurred even without these measures. The participation rate rose again in 1892 and went still higher in 1896, coming within eight points of the 1888 high. Campaigns during these years were highly exciting; interest in their outcome was intense and voters poured from the hills and the valleys to register their choice. The picturesque and highly popular "Bob" Taylor, the possessor of great vote appeal, won the governorship both years as he had in 1886. An approximation of the effect of the three suffrage laws may be obtained by examining the difference in turnout between 1888 and 1892. The rate in the latter year was 17.5 percentage points less than in 1888. Certainly this comparison is nearer the truth than one between 1888 and 1890. The voting rate did not again reach the height attained in 1896 and in a number of years preceding the adoption of the three election laws. Beginning with 1904, participation tended to stabilize within the forty per cent range except for the wartime year of 1918.

What can be concluded about the effect of poll tax adoption upon turnout in Tennessee gubernatorial elections? Following adoption of the tax, turnout was lower than it had been previously. Without doubt some of this reduction was caused by the Myer's, Dortch and poll tax laws. But the high turnout in some years following enactment of these laws indicates that still other factors influenced participation. An intelligent guess is that the tax accounts for not more than five to ten percentage points of the average reduction that occurred.

Figure 5, which shows voting trends in Texas gubernatorial elections from 1880 to 1916, lends support to some of the preceding conclusions.[13] This figure reveals more clearly than have those for the other states the danger of claiming that the poll tax alone caused the disfranchisement of southern voters. In Arkansas, a decline in voting began before the tax took effect. This tendency is considerably more apparent in Texas

---

[13] Participation rates were computed in the same way as those for Arkansas. Gubernatorial election returns were obtained from *Texas Almanac and State Industrial Guide, 1947-1948.*

where the tax was adopted more than ten years after it was imposed in Arkansas, Florida, and Tennessee. The peak in the gubernatorial vote was reached in 1896, a significant election

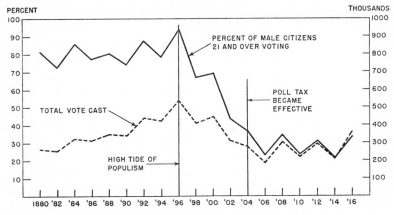

FIGURE 5. Vote in Texas Elections for Governor, 1880-1916.

year in the nation and the year when the Populist party was at its zenith in Texas. After 1896, participation declined precipitously, dropping by fifty percentage points between 1896 and 1902, the election before the poll tax became effective. Following poll tax adoption, the rate was only seven points lower than in the preceding election. After 1904, participation tended to fluctuate with presidential elections. The rapid decline in voting following 1896 shows conclusively that the poll tax was not the primary factor causing the low voter participation in the Lone Star State. The tax cannot be charged with producing more than five percentage points of the total decrease.[14]

The tendency for voting to decline before poll tax adoption raises a query about the real causes for this drop. It is doubtful if a complete or final answer could ever be given, but the question calls for speculation.

Poll tax adoption occurred some time after the South was restored to southerners and, in particular, to white Democratic

14 See also Key, pp. 534-35.

southerners.   As shown in Chapter 1, the Negro's vote was controlled in some manner.   The chief support of southern Republicans came from the recently liberated Negro.   By hints, threats and shotguns, Republican Negroes were discouraged from voting.   By the time of poll tax adoption, inter-party conflict was largely suppressed and non-Democrats appear to have abandoned the fight.   Cessation of party conflict results in reduced interest in elections and in fewer votes.   The Populist party brought a renaissance of political interest, but this party was not especially strong in Arkansas, Florida or Tennessee.   In Texas, it was of little consequence after 1896. Perhaps by the time Texas adopted the poll tax, the general movement for a reduced electorate had already progressed farther here than in the other states.   Inasmuch as tax adoption followed more closely upon the beginning of the voting decline in Arkansas, Florida and Tennessee, the fact that a reduction would have occurred in them, poll tax or not, does not stand out as clearly.   In Florida, the first of these states to enact a tax prerequisite, the tax may appear to have had a greater influence upon reducing the electorate than it actually had.   It seems valid to conclude that the poll tax helped in a minor way to achieve disfranchisement but it primarily reflected in law a trend already begun.[15]

BEFORE AND AFTER REPEAL ANALYSES

Another way to measure the effect of the poll tax upon voting is to apply the before and after method to a study of voting in those states which have abolished it. North Carolina, Louisiana, Florida, Georgia, South Carolina, and Tennessee have done so. Significant analyses cannot be made of North Carolina's and South Carolina's voting records before and after repeal.   In North Carolina, poll tax abolition coincided with the granting of woman suffrage in 1920.   The addition of so many potential voters and the simultaneous repeal of the tax make an analysis

15 An analysis was also made of participation in presidential elections from 1880 through 1916 in Arkansas, Tennessee, and Texas and from 1872 through 1952 in Florida. Since the results were comparable to those of gubernatorial elections, they have been omitted.

of the effect of repeal meaningless. In South Carolina, the poll tax never applied to primary elections. Since few Republican candidates have run for either governor or United States senator and since, when they have, they provided very weak opposition for Democratic candidates, the turnout in South Carolina general elections is not a good indication of the size of its electorate. Therefore, an estimation of the suffrage effect of the poll tax by comparing voter turnout in South Carolina general elections before and after repeal is of no worth. But before and after repeal analyses can be made for Louisiana, Florida, Georgia, and Tennessee.

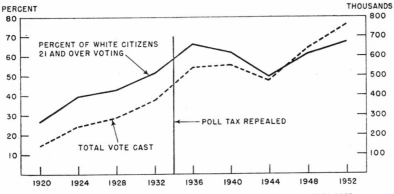

FIGURE 6. Vote in Louisiana Democratic Primaries for Governor, 1920-1952.

Louisiana repealed the poll tax in 1934 under the leadership of Huey Long. Figures 6 and 7 show the voting trends in Louisiana Democratic primary elections for governor from 1920 to 1952 and for United States senator from 1920 to 1954. Both the per cent of white citizens 21 and over voting and the total vote cast are charted.[16] These figures show electoral participation increasing before poll tax repeal became effective. They also disclose that the increase has not been constant in

[16] Percentages are based upon census reports of white citizens 21 and over rather than all citizens 21 and over on the assumption that for most of this period the Negro vote was insignificant in Louisiana Democratic primaries. The election data upon which these figures and those which follow were based may be found through 1948 in Heard and Strong. Election returns for recent years were obtained from the various secretaries of state. In each instance, the vote used was that of the first primary.

both total vote and in percentage of voting since tax elimination. They substantiate the earlier conclusion that many factors affect voting participation and that just one factor, such as the poll tax, may not startlingly affect the number of voters.

Examination of Louisiana gubernatorial elections reveals that Huey Long's political career marked an increase in

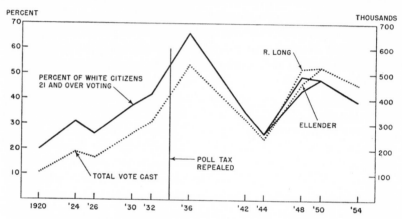

FIGURE 7. Vote in Louisiana Democratic Primaries for United States Senator, 1920-1954.

political interest. He first ran for governor in 1924 and by 1928 had captured enough support to win the Democratic nomination. By 1932, the Kingfish had moved on to the United States Senate but his machine controlled the state and a lively contest increased the vote in both gubernatorial and senatorial primaries. Following poll tax repeal in 1934, the vote rose again in the 1936 primaries. By this time, Long had been felled by an assassin's bullet but his organization was striving to win without him. After 1936, a slight decrease in the turnout rate occurred in the 1940 gubernatorial primary and a greater decrease in the 1944 race. Participation was generally lower in 1944 because of war conditions. Voter participation climbed again in 1948 when several strong candidates competed for the governor's chair, including former Governor Sam Jones and Earl K. Long, Huey's brother. The apex for this period was reached in 1952. Nine candidates participated, four of whom were particularly strong. One was backed by Governor Earl K. Long. Because of bitter opposition to Long, interest was high.[17]

After 1936, interest in the senatorial race decreased more sharply than interest in the gubernatorial one. John H. Overton was unopposed in 1938. By 1944, participation was lower than it was immediately preceding poll tax repeal. However, it soared in 1948 when Russell Long, Huey's son, ran to fill the vacancy caused by Overton's death and Allen Ellender asked for renomination. Turnout was again high in 1950 when Russell Long was nominated for a full term, but it declined in 1954 when Ellender was nominated for his fourth term.

Abolition, then, has not been followed by a greatly increased rate of voting in the Pelican State. A rise began before tax removal. Much of this rise was due to the interest aroused by Huey Long and his program. Undoubtedly the increase from 1932 to 1936 was greater, but it is impossible to saw how much greater. Although poll tax repeal occurred in 1934, other restrictive requirements were in effect until 1940.[18] Removal of the tax did not open the sluice gates so that voters could pour forth. Estimating the effects of repeal is further complicated by World War II when voting turnout was lower throughout the nation. The 1948 elections were the first in which a fair test could be made. Figures 6 and 7 indicate that participation will continue at a higher rate than in the twenties. For the Democratic gubernatorial primaries, the average rate of participation by adult white citizens was 40.2 per cent before repeal and 61.1 per cent since repeal. For the senatorial primaries, it was 31.2 per cent and 46.5 per cent respectively. A fair estimate appears to be that poll tax abolition increased the per cent voting by about five percentage points.[19]

The effects of poll tax repeal in Louisiana can also be estimated by inspecting registration figures. Following repeal

17 Due to increased voting by Negroes in recent years, the percentages for 1948 and 1952, based upon only white citizens 21 and over, overestimate white participation rates. In 1946, there were 7,561 Negro registrants; in 1952, 97,101. See reports of Secretary of State for relevant years.

18 See Chapter 7.

19 See Key, pp. 604-05.

in 1934, the number of registered voters had increased by more than 240,000 by March, 1936. This increase exceeded sixty per cent of the number of registered voters as of October, 1934, just before the repeal amendment was ratified. However, more voters were registered in October, 1932 than in October, 1934. The increase between October, 1932 and October, 1936 was more than 160,000, an increase of approximately one-third. Since repeal, the number of registrants has consistently been well above the number before repeal. The lowest number was reported in October, 1938 when only 45,000 more voters were registered than in October, 1932. The greatest increase occurred immediately following poll tax repeal. A conservative estimate is that tax removal resulted in an immediate increase of at least 100,000 in the number of registered voters.

Poll tax repeal in Louisiana appears to have benefited white women more than any other group. Between October, 1934 and March, 1936, 123,000 white women were added to the rolls while just over 120,000 white men became voters. In October, 1934, 66 per cent of the registrants were white men while only 33.7 per cent were white women. By March, 1936, the proportions had been changed to 59.6 per cent and 40 per cent respectively. The proportion of white men has continued to decline and the proportion of white women to increase but the most significant increase in the proportion of white women occurred immediately following poll tax repeal. The number of Negro registrants did not rise significantly following repeal. A very slight numerical gain occurred in 1936 for both Negro men and women. However, in 1940, fewer Negroes were registered than in 1930. Negro registration did not expand until after the end of the white primary.[20]

The Florida poll tax ceased to be a suffrage prerequisite in 1937. Figures 8 and 9 show the voting trends in Florida gubernatorial and senatorial Democratic primaries from 1920 to 1954 and from 1920 to 1952 respectively.[21] They disclose a

[20] Information pertaining to registered voters may be found in reports of the Secretary of State.

[21] Since Negroes have participated more freely in Florida Democratic primaries than in those of Louisiana, the percentages were computed on the basis of all citizens 21 and over.

similarity with the Louisiana trends, especially in the gubernatorial primaries. In Florida gubernatorial primaries, the participation rate rose steadily in the twenties, leveled off in the thirties, climbed again in 1940 following the 1937 repeal of the tax, fell back in the wartime election of 1944, rose again in 1948 and 1952 and declined slightly in the special election of 1954. The chart indicates that poll tax removal had a decided effect in increasing the turnout in the 1940 election. However, eleven candidates competed in this election and an increase would probably have occurred whether or not the tax was repealed.

An even sharper rise took place in the 1938 senatorial

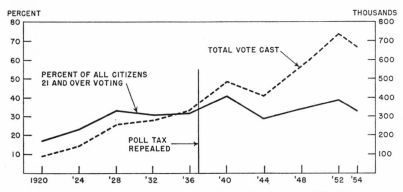

FIGURE 8. Vote in Florida Democratic Primaries for Governor, 1920-1954.

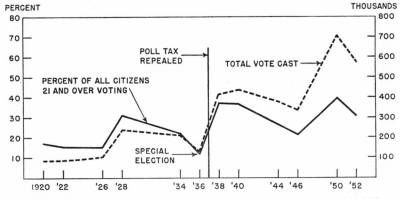

FIGURE 9. Vote in Florida Democratic Primaries for United States Senator, 1920-1952.

primary. The 1936 primary was a special one which did not stimulate much interest.[22] Turnout in senatorial primaries and elections is often erratic due to fluctuations in interest. When an election is virtually uncontested, little interest is aroused and turnout is low. On the other hand, two strong candidates bring many voters to the polls. Since little interest was shown in the 1936 primary, it is fairer to compare the 1938 rate of participation with that in 1934. Claude Pepper contested both of these primaries; he lost in the run-off in 1934 but won in the first primary in 1938. In 1938, Pepper ran for re-election since he had been elected without opposition in 1936 to fill an unexpired term. The 1938 primary was a particularly keen contest. Pepper had four opponents, two of whom were of first rank. During his two years in the Senate, Pepper had consistently supported President Roosevelt and his New Deal program. He received the President's blessing in the campaign. One of his chief opponents, ex-Governor Sholtz, campaigned as a friend of the President while the other, Representative Wilcox, called himself an "independent thinking" candidate.[23] The participation rate in 1938 increased by approximately fifteen percentage points over that of 1934. The greater intensity of the 1938 contest undoubtedly accounts for much of this increase.

Since 1938, participation has not been consistently high in Florida Democratic senatorial primaries. In 1940, turnout was large; the number of voters exceeded the number who participated in the 1938 primary but the percentage rate was slightly smaller. During the wartime year of 1944 and the immediate post-war year of 1946, participation declined but the hotly fought Pepper-Smathers race in 1950 more than doubled the number of voters and nearly doubled the rate of turnout. Voting decreased again in 1952. In this primary, Spessard Holland, running for nomination for his second full term, was offered little opposition by William A. Gaston.

---

[22] Charles O. Andrews and Doyle E. Carlton competed for the nomination, which Andrews won. Florida's other Senate seat was also vacant at this time but Claude Pepper was unopposed in both the primary and general elections.

[23] J. B. Shannon, "Presidential Politics in the South," *Journal of Politics*, I (August, 1939), 151-52.

Poll tax repeal appears to have aided in increasing voter turnout in Florida. That it had less effect than poll tax opponents would have us believe is evident. As in Louisiana, other factors, such as the sharpening of the political conflict, the resurgence of the southern conservative because of threats to his position and the personalities of the candidates, brought an increased turnout. However, it is significant that the average rate of participation in the Democratic gubernatorial primaries before repeal was 27 per cent and since repeal has been 34.8 per cent. For the Democratic senatorial primaries, it was 20.1 per cent before repeal (if the special primary of 1936 is omitted) and 32 per cent since repeal. Although no specific amount of increase can be attributed solely to repeal, it seems fair to estimate that poll tax abolition increased the participation rate of all adult citizens by not more than five percentage points.[24]

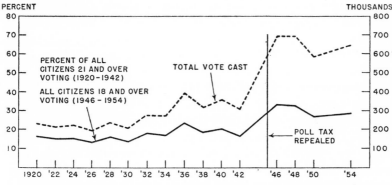

FIGURE 10. Vote in Georgia Democratic Primaries for Governor, 1920-1954.

The most spectacular increase in voter turnout following poll tax repeal occurred in Georgia. Figure 10 shows the voting trends in the Democratic gubernatorial primaries from 1920 through 1954. The tax was abolished in 1945. The number of people who voted in 1946 more than doubled the number of voters in 1942 and was by far the largest turnout up to this time. It has not since been exceeded. Although participation

[24] See Key, pp. 605-06. An analysis of voter registration cannot be made for Florida. Although Florida now publishes registration figures, this information does not go back to the time of poll tax repeal.

tended to climb before the forties, this trend was not as strong as in Louisiana and Florida. How much of the great increase that occurred in 1946 can be attributed to poll tax repeal?

Other factors affected the 1946 turnout besides elimination of the poll tax. One was the invalidation of the white primary by the United States Supreme Court in 1944. As a result, politicians courted Negroes for their votes in 1946.[25] Probably more Negroes voted because of poll tax repeal than would have otherwise but, without the fall of the white primary, few would have voted even though the tax was abolished.

Another factor affecting the turnout was the lowering of the voting age to eighteen by a 1943 constitutional amendment. The 1946 contest was the first gubernatorial primary in which the 18 to 21 year old group voted.

The 1946 race was also a highly exciting one. Eugene Talmadge bid for a return to the governor's chair against J. V. Carmichael. He based his campaign upon the preservation of white supremacy and cited the attempt by Carmichael supporters to secure Negro votes as his justification. Thus, participation in 1946 was influenced by collapse of the white primary, lowering of the voting age, and the excitement of the campaign as well as by poll tax repeal. Fall of the white primary and interest in the election worked to increase the participation rate while lowering of the voting age probably had the opposite effect.

Voting has continued high in Georgia gubernatorial primaries since 1946 although the turnout of that year has not been exceeded. All recent campaigns have aroused great interest. In each, the Talmadge organization played the leading role. In 1948 and 1950, the principal contestants were Herman Talmadge, Old Gene's heir, and Melvin E. Thompson. The 1948 primary was a special one necessitated by the death of Old Gene in 1946 shortly before his inauguration. Subsequently a bitter contest over the governorship developed between the lieutenant governor-elect, Thompson,

[25] For this reason, Georgia's participation rates were computed on the basis of all citizens 21 and over for the years 1920-1942 and all citizens 18 and over for the years 1946-1954.

and Herman Talmadge, a write-in candidate in 1946. The contest was first settled in Thompson's favor by a decision of the State Supreme Court and in 1948 in Talmadge's favor by the voters. The feud continued in 1950 and again "Hummon" won. In 1954, Thompson was opposed by several Talmadge lieutenants—Marvin Griffin, lieutenant governor; Fred Hand, speaker of the House; and Tom Linder, commissioner of agriculture—as well as by five lesser candidates. Griffin, apparently the favorite of the Talmadge organization, won.

In connection with voting turnout since repeal, note must be taken of the fact that the legislature enacted a Voters' Registration Act in 1949.[26] According to Governor Talmadge, its purpose was to end block voting by Negroes. It probably helped somewhat to counteract the effects of removal of the poll tax and the white primary.

Since poll tax repeal, the number of voters in Georgia gubernatorial primaries has been about double what it was before repeal. The average rate of turnout has also approximately doubled—16.9 per cent before repeal and 30.3 per cent after repeal. From the preceding account, it is clear that this increase was influenced by a number of factors. However, poll tax removal appears to have had a greater effect upon raising voter participation in the Cracker State than it had in Louisiana or Florida. The fact that Georgia had a tax which accumulated over the entire period of liability accounts for this difference. Because of the cumulative feature, the Georgia tax bore more heavily upon the voters than either the Louisiana or Florida taxes. Repeal in Georgia was probably responsible for five to ten percentage points of the turnout increase in the gubernatorial primaries.[27]

26 No. 297, *Georgia Laws, 1949.*

27 See Key, pp. 607-08. A worthwhile analysis of Georgia senatorial primary elections cannot be made because no significant ones occurred between 1945 and 1954. In 1948 and 1954, Richard Russell was unopposed for re-nomination. In 1950, Walter F. George was opposed by Alex McLennan, an Atlanta attorney, and won by a landslide. Even without a spirited contest, more than twice as many votes were cast in 1950 as in an equally dull contest in 1944 which George also dominated. Russell polled some 225,000 more votes without an opponent in 1954, than were cast in 1936 when he was opposed by Gene Talmadge. These figures indicate that an increase has occurred in senatorial

The Tennessee poll tax was not formally repealed until 1953 but it ceased to apply to primary elections in 1949.[28]   Figure 11 charts the voting trends in the Democratic gubernatorial

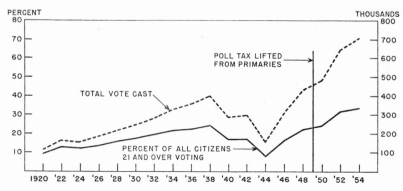

FIGURE 11.   Vote in Tennessee Democratic Primaries for Governor, 1920-1954.

primaries from 1920 through 1954.   The chart shows a gradual growth in participation through 1938, a decline during the war years and a rapid upsurge in the post-war period.   Voting participation was on the increase before the tax was lifted. The number of voters in 1948 was in excess of the number for 1938, the preceding year of highest turnout, although the percentage rate of turnout was not as high.   Since tax removal, participation has been higher both in absolute numbers and in rate.   By 1954, the number of voters had increased by nearly 300,000 over the 1948 figure.   The turnout rate had risen by nearly twelve percentage points.   Interest in the four primaries from 1948 to 1954 was high.   Gordon Browning was a candidate in each one, emerging as the winner in 1948 and 1950 but losing to Frank Clement in 1952 and 1954.

The period since removal of the Tennessee tax is insufficient to make any positive estimate as to the effects of abolition, but

primaries similar to that in gubernatorial primaries. However, since George and Russell dominated Georgia senatorial primaries for more than twenty years, these primaries do not serve as satisfactory indicators of the size of the electorate.

28 See Chapter 7.

the situation appears similar to that in the states previously analyzed. Participation was rising even before the tax was eliminated; exciting elections stimulated a greater turnout. Lifting the tax undoubtedly encouraged more persons to vote, but probably caused less than five percentage points of the total increase.[29]

ALABAMA: EFFECTS OF A CUMULATIVE TAX

The Alabama poll tax has not been repealed but in December, 1953 the cumulative period was reduced from the entire 24 year period of liability to two years. This reduction lowered the maximum sum that any person would have to pay at one time from $36 to $3.00. The change occurred in time for individuals to qualify under it for the 1954 primary elections. Alabama provides an excellent opportunity to analyze the effects of a cumulative tax upon voting.

A major increase in the number of registered voters occurred immediately following ratification of the constitutional amendment which altered the cumulative period. Since accurate figures on the number of registered voters in Alabama are not available, an exact statement of how large the increase was cannot be made. Based upon a survey of 24 of the 67 counties, LeRoy Simms of the Associated Press estimated that 202,000 new voters were added statewide by April 1, 1954, an increase of one-third in the total number of registrants. He judged that approximately 608,000 persons were registered in 1952 and 810,000 by April, 1954.[30] This writer attempted to find out by questionnaire how many new voters registered in January, 1954. Usable replies were received from only fifteen counties. Based upon these returns and the difference in turnout between the 1952 presidential election and the 1954 Democratic gubernatorial primary, it appears that Simms' estimate is

29 Democratic primary elections for United States senator were also analyzed. The analysis yielded comparable results. Since voting behavior in senatorial primaries is more erratic than in gubernatorial primaries, no analysis of them is included.

30 Birmingham *News*, April 7, 1954 and Birmingham *Post-Herald*, April 16, 1954.

approximately correct. In 1954, 168,261 more votes were cast
than in 1952.

Figure 12 shows the trends in Alabama Democratic gubernatorial primaries from 1920 through 1954. The significantly
increased turnout in 1954 is graphically portrayed. The voters

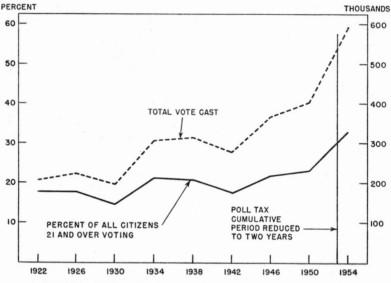

FIGURE 12.   Vote in Alabama Democratic Primaries for Governor, 1922-1954.

increased by more than 190,000 over the number who turned
out in 1950 and the participation rate was raised by nearly ten
percentage points. The increase was equal to about half the
number of voters in 1950. As stated above, the turnout was
also well above the previous high recorded in the Eisenhower-
Stevenson race of 1952. The 1954 gubernatorial campaign
aroused great interest. "Big Jim" Folsom, a proved vote
stimulator, led a field of seven candidates. However, the 1946
and 1950 campaigns also stirred the voters. In 1946, Folsom
competed against four candidates, while in 1950, the race was
between his lieutenant, Phillip Hamm, and Gordon Persons,
plus thirteen additional candidates. Folsom emerged victorious
in 1946 and Persons in 1950. It is significant that "Big Jim"
received 228,868 more votes in 1954 after reduction of the

cumulative period than in 1946 when the tax could accumulate for 24 years.

Analysis of voting in Democratic primaries for United States senator yields comparable results. In the Sparkman-Battle race of 1954, 214,804 more votes were cast than in the Hill-McNeil contest of 1950. The per cent of all adult citizens voting in 1954 was 30.6 compared with 19.6 per cent in 1950. Until 1954, the highest turnout in senatorial primaries was recorded in 1950. In both gubernatorial and senatorial primaries, the participation rate increased by approximately ten percentage points following the cutting of the cumulative period. The significance of this increase stands out when it is noted that the average participation rate in gubernatorial primaries from 1920 through 1950 was about twenty per cent and that the turnout rate in senatorial primaries during the same period never exceeded twenty per cent.

Reduction of the cumulative period, therefore, resulted in a major increase in registered voters and in voting participation in Alabama. Was the increase general throughout the voting population or did some groups benefit more than others? As in Louisiana, white women were the chief beneficiaries. Of the total newly registered voters in eleven counties replying to the questionnaire, 57.2 per cent were women, 51.9 per cent white women. Simms estimated that 102,000 of the 202,000 new voters were women. He judged that the proportion of women voters had increased from 30.9 per cent in 1952 to 35.8 per cent in 1954 and further estimated that the number of women registered in 1954 was about 55 per cent higher than in 1952 while the number of men registered increased by about 24 per cent.[31] Figures for specific counties illustrate the effect of the 1953 amendment in encouraging white women to become voters. In Coosa, 420 of the 842 new registrants were white women; in Dale, 652 of 1171; in Elmore, 986 of 1561; in Marengo, 470 of 679; and in Madison, 1087 of 1763. A large proportion of both white and Negro women were exempt from paying any poll tax because of age. Approximately sixty per

31 Birmingham *Post-Herald*, April 16, 1954 and Tuscaloosa *News*, April 16, 1954.

cent of the newly registered women in ten counties were so exempt.[32] An even greater proportion of the men were exempt due to age—over 71 per cent.

The change in the cumulative requirement did not result in hordes of Negroes registering in Alabama. More Negroes registered but apparently not in much greater proportion than had occurred in the recent past. In eleven counties, 12.2 per cent of the total new registrants were Negroes. In 1950, the per cent of non-whites in the population of the state was 32.1 and the median non-white percentage for these counties was 33.4. Lowndes County with 82.2 per cent non-whites registered no Negroes during January, 1954 while Franklin County with 5.2 per cent non-whites registered 400 Negroes in a total of 2,900 and Madison County with 27.2 per cent non-whites enrolled 196 Negroes in a total of 1,763. The Associated Press also found that new Negro voters were about in the usual proportions.[33] Slightly more Negro men registered than Negro women. Of the 12.2 per cent Negro registration in the eleven counties, 6.9 per cent were men.

The increase in voters was fairly well distributed throughout the state except that Black Belt counties generally did not register as many voters as did northern counties. Simms estimated that the 34 northernmost counties increased the number of voters by 130,000 while the 33 southern counties enlarged their rolls by 72,000. Major increases took place in Jefferson, Etowah, Mobile, Tuscaloosa, DeKalb, Walker, Calhoun, Montgomery, Baldwin, and Talladega while Lowndes and Greene, both with a Negro population in excess of eighty per cent, had slight gains.[34]

Reduction of the cumulative period had, therefore, a significant effect upon increasing the number of voters in the Cotton State. The period since this reduction is insufficient to make any final estimate of its effect in raising voter participation.

[32] One chairman of a registration board commented that it was surprising how many wives of politicians in the county were just registering. In doing so, they referred to Mrs. Persons' registration. The wife of the Alabama governor did not become a registered voter until after reduction of the cumulative period.
[33] Birmingham *News*, January 17, 1954.
[34] *Ibid.*, April 7, 1954.

However, it appears that between five and eight percentage points of the 1954 increase resulted from the relaxation in the poll tax requirement. Probably more than 150,000 persons were added to the poll lists as a result of this change. Because of the past low level of voting in Alabama, these increases are extremely important ones. Lowering of the cumulative period not only encouraged many non-voters to register but also resulted in many registered voters, disqualified through failure to pay the tax, becoming requalified. The 1953 amendment particularly encouraged white women to become voters. A significant proportion of the new voters, men as well as women, were persons freed from tax payment because of their age. The number of Negro registrants increased but not startlingly.

CONCLUSIONS

What conclusions about the effect of the poll tax upon voting result from this examination of voting both before and after adoption and repeal? An obvious one is that no single factor affects voting but that turnout is influenced by many inter-related causes. Because of this fact, it is extremely difficult to isolate any one factor and assign a definite weight to it. The investigation also showed that voting tended to decline before adoption and to increase prior to repeal. Thus, in both instances, the action taken with respect to the tax seemed to aid a movement already underway. The tax did not initiate the trend. Poll tax adoption did not cause a permanent decrease in voting; similarly, tax repeal did not produce a steady increase in participation.

Following its adoption, the poll tax apparently caused the greatest voting reduction in Florida and the least decrease in Texas. In Florida, the tax may have caused as much as fifteen percentage points of the reduction that occurred in the 1890's whereas in Texas, it was not responsible for more than five percentage points of the total decrease. The disfranchisement caused by the tax in Arkansas and Tennessee was closer to the Texas decrease than to that in Florida. These estimates, especially that for Florida, are liberal ones.

Poll tax repeal did not increase voting by more than five percentage points in Louisiana, Florida, and Tennessee. In

Georgia, where the tax accumulated for several years, a rise of five to ten percentage points may have been due to abolition. A similar increase resulted in Alabama after reduction of its cumulative period. Since the change in the Alabama tax was not accompanied by several other suffrage alterations, the effect of the tax upon voting stands out more clearly than it did in Georgia. In both instances, the burdensome effect of a long cumulative period is revealed.

The Louisiana and Alabama analyses indicated that their poll taxes bore particularly heavily upon women. Following repeal in Louisiana and alteration of the cumulative feature in Alabama, white women registered in greater numbers than any other group. Large numbers of Negroes did not register although many were added to the rolls in several Alabama counties.

These effects of poll tax repeal are mainly short-term ones. The long-run effects may be of more consequence. Habits are not changed easily, especially those of long standing. Many southerners have acquired a habit of non-voting. This practice does not alter overnight simply because of poll tax repeal. Removal of the tax should encourage more persons to vote but does not mean that they will. Over a longer period, repeal may have more significant effects upon increasing voting than this short-term period demonstrated. However, for the long-run period, it will be even more difficult to separate the various factors influencing election turnout than it was for the short periods considered here.

Finally, these analyses of voting trends before and after poll tax adoption and repeal demonstrate that the tax is not the bogey man its opponents would have us believe. If it is the chief reason for low voting rates in poll tax states, its adoption would have caused more disfranchisement than took place and its repeal would have resulted in a greater and more permanent voting increase than occurred. But, in southern states where turnout is low, almost any increase is significant. An increase of five to ten percentage points should bring important changes in the political life of the region. Expressed in numbers, this increase represents a sizable number of voters—a number greater than the margin of victory in many election contests.

6. VOTING: INTERSTATE AND INTERCOUNTY COMPARISONS

IN CHAPTER 5, it was noted that a method frequently used to illustrate the effects of the poll tax upon voting is to compare voting in poll tax states with voting in non-poll tax states. The inadequacy of this method when applied to poll tax states as a group in comparison with all non-poll tax states is obvious. A refinement of this procedure is to compare voting in two states that are similar in most respects, except that poll tax payment is required in one and not in the other. Sole reliance on this manner of ascertaining the effects of the tax upon voting is open to serious question. No two states are alike in every respect apart from the fact that one has a poll tax and the other does not. If such a condition existed, the effects of the tax could be tested with scientific precision. Since many differences exist between states and since many factors influence voting in them, the results of interstate comparisons need to be taken with several grains of salt. This warning must be remembered in considering the material which follows.

Table 6 contrasts voting participation rates in all southern states, poll tax and non-poll tax, for the Democratic gubernatorial primaries in 1950 or in the year nearest to 1950. The average participation rate for southern non-poll tax states was just over four percentage points more than that for southern poll tax states. If the turnout in the North Carolina general election had been used, the differential between these two groups of states would have been about three percentage points higher. Due to Republican strength, more citizens vote in the general election in this state than in the Democratic primary.[1] In the 1948 gubernatorial election, 35 per cent of all adult citizens voted.

It cannot be concluded that the poll tax was the sole reason for the difference in voting behavior between these states. This fact is evident from the spread between the percentage of adult citizens who voted in Mississippi and the percentage who voted in Virginia. In 1950, Mississippians voted at a rate more than

Table 6. PERCENTAGES OF ALL CITIZENS 21 AND OVER VOTING IN 1950 DEMOCRATIC GUBERNATORIAL PRIMARIES: POLL TAX STATES AND NON-POLL TAX STATES OF THE SOUTH

POLL TAX STATES		NON-POLL TAX STATES	
State	*Per Cent*	*State*	*Per Cent*
Mississippi[a]	33.8	Louisiana[b]	42.0
Arkansas	29.5	Florida[b]	33.8
Texas	23.7	South Carolina[c]	30.2
Alabama	23.1	Georgia[d]	26.9
Virginia[e]	16.1	Tennessee[c]	24.4
		North Carolina[b]	19.0
Average	25.2		29.4

[a] 1951 primary.
[b] 1948 primary.
[c] No poll tax required to vote in primary.
[d] Based on all citizens eighteen and over.
[e] 1949 primary.

double the rate at which Virginians voted. Both states had cumulative poll taxes. The difference in turnout between Mississippi and Virginia was considerably greater than the difference between Mississippi, a poll tax state, and Louisiana, a non-poll tax state. The Mississippi rate exceeded that of four non-poll tax states and tied with that of Florida. As V. O. Key demonstrated, whites in Mississippi, Louisiana, and South Carolina have voted for some time at a higher rate than whites in other southern states.[2] The presence or absence of the poll tax apparently has not had a significant effect upon this trend.

[1] See Key, pp. 493-95.
[2] *Ibid.*, pp. 495-96.

No valid conclusions about the disfranchising effects of the poll tax may be drawn from Table 6. An attempt to draw conclusions would ignore the many other underlying factors which influence the turnout of voters. For instance, intensity of election contests affects voter turnout. Participation rates for only one election are shown in Table 6. Presumably the election did not arouse the same amount of interest in each state. A comparison of voting rates for a single election may not present a fair picture of the normal turnout in some states. A contrast like that contained in Table 6 does not take into consideration such important factors as the suffrage effect of the Byrd machine in Virginia. Thus, even when this method for discovering the suffrage effects of the poll tax is restricted to southern states, it is a highly questionable means of proving anything about the tax.[3]

Contrasting Kentucky, a state that never had a voter poll tax, with Tennessee, a state that required poll tax payment from 1890 until recently, has been a favorite device. Jennings Perry, an early leader in the Tennessee poll tax repeal movement and in the effort to pass a federal anti-poll tax bill, is the originator of this contrast.[4] He argues that these states are sufficiently alike to make a comparison of voting participation valid. They border one another, their populations have kept within 100,000 of each other for some seventy years and

. . . they share the same mountains, the same valleys, the same soil, the same agriculture, the same population stock, the same origins

[3] A similar comparison was made for the 1940 Democratic gubernatorial primaries. At this time, seven states (Georgia and Tennessee in addition to those listed in Table 6) required poll tax payment to vote in primary elections; four did not. The year 1940 was selected to avoid difficulties resulting from judicial nullification of the white primary in 1944. Percentages were computed on the basis of white citizens 21 and over. This comparison yielded a significant difference between these two groups of states. The average rate for southern non-poll tax states was more than twenty percentage points higher than that for southern poll tax states. All non-poll tax states had a turnout rate in excess of poll tax states except North Carolina and its turnout rate in the general election was greater than the rate of any poll tax state. However, the results of the comparison do not alter the conclusions stated.

[4] *Democracy Begins at Home: The Tennessee Fight On the Poll Tax* (Philadelphia and New York, 1944), p. 215.

in transmontane migration, the same historical figures. . . . Their settlers funneled through the Cumberland Gap together, importing the same religious denominations, the same culture, the same political credos, the same politics.[5]

Figure 13 contrasts Kentucky and Tennessee as to the percentages of all adult citizens who voted in presidential elections from 1872 to 1952. By 1952, the poll tax no longer affected voting in Tennessee. The turnout rate was similar until Tennessee adopted the poll tax. Afterwards the spread in voting participation became significant although it was not until 1900 that it became really noticeable. Since the 1920's, participation has increased in the Volunteer State and the gap between the two states has tended to close. This trend stands out particularly in 1952, the first election after the poll tax was nullified in Tennessee.

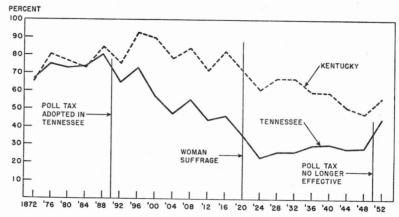

FIGURE 13. Interstate Comparison: Percentages of All Citizens 21 and Over Voting in Presidential Elections, Kentucky and Tennessee, 1872-1952.

The poll tax cannot be held accountable for all the difference in voting behavior. Although the Republican party is stronger in Tennessee than in most southern states, it has been stronger in Kentucky than in Tennessee over most of this period. For instance, Kentucky went Republican in the McKinley-Bryan race of 1896 while Tennessee did not. This campaign virtually

5 *Ibid.*, p. 213.

killed off the Republican party as a fighting organization in southern states but Kentucky Republicans were not defeated. In the 1944 presidential race, Republicans in Kentucky polled 40 per cent or more of the vote in 69 of 120 counties while Republicans in Tennessee polled the same percentage in 43 of 95 counties.[6] In 1948, the Republican candidate received 41.5 per cent of the total vote in Kentucky and 36.9 per cent in Tennessee. In 1952, however, the Republicans carried Tennessee by a slight margin while the Democrats barely won Kentucky's electoral vote. The greater strength of the Republican party should account for a considerable part of the higher turnout in the Blue Grass State. The great interest aroused by the 1952 campaign was undoubtedly more responsible for the increased turnout in Tennessee than was poll tax elimination. To maintain that the poll tax is the only factor responsible for the difference is to misinterpret observable political facts and to overemphasize decimal points and a well-constructed graph.[7]

While the Kentucky-Tennessee comparison has been the one most frequently used, some contrast of voting participation in North Carolina and Virginia has also been made.[8] Since even greater differences exist between North Carolina and Virginia than between Kentucky and Tennessee, this comparison must be taken with even greater reserve. Undoubtedly the statewide machine control which has long existed in Virginia accounts for most of the low turnout there.[9] North Carolina has not had a comparable political organization. In addition, the strength of the North Carolina Republican party increases turnout in Tarheel general elections.

[6] See Edgar E. Robinson, *They Voted For Roosevelt: The Presidential Vote 1932-1944* (Stanford, 1947), pp. 97-102 and 154-58.

[7] See Key, p. 609.

[8] See Virginius Dabney, "Shall the South's Poll Tax Go?" *New York Times Magazine*, February 12, 1939, p. 9. In 1950, Estes Kefauver told North Carolina Young Democrats that the larger vote of their state over that of Tennessee was due to the absence of the poll tax in North Carolina. Tuscaloosa *News*, February 13, 1950. Clark Foreman contrasted voting turnout in one election in West Virginia and Virginia, North Carolina and South Carolina, and Minnesota and Alabama and implied that the poll tax was the sole cause of the differences noted. *Hearings on H. R. 29*, p. 148.

[9] Key, pp. 19-20.

Voting in presidential elections in North Carolina and Virginia was compared for the same period as in Kentucky and Tennessee. North Carolina always had a higher turnout rate than Virginia whether a poll tax was in effect or not. The rate for both states declined sharply after adoption of disfranchising measures in 1900 and 1902 respectively. Since then, their participation rates in presidential elections have remained about equally divided, roughly by about twenty percentage points. Poll tax repeal in North Carolina had no apparent effect in increasing participation. There has been a slight tendency in recent years for the voting rates of these states to draw closer together despite the fact that one does not have, and the other has, a voter poll tax. Comparison of the participation rates of North Carolina and Virginia does not yield any accurate information about the effects of the poll tax upon voting.

Therefore, the results of the interstate comparison method of ascertaining the suffrage effects of the poll tax are of dubious value and open to criticism. Any inferences regarding the amount of disfranchisement caused by the tax based solely upon this method are of slight worth.

INTERCOUNTY COMPARISONS

A considerably more rewarding method of analysis is to collate the county-by-county tax payment rates within a single state. By analyzing voting both before and after adoption and repeal, an estimate of the overall disfranchising effects of the tax was made. In addition, the Louisiana and Alabama analyses indicated that a poll tax disfranchises more women than men. By comparing county-by-county tax payment rates within one state, other social groups most affected by the tax may be found.

An intercounty comparison for Arkansas and Texas follows. The investigation is limited to these states because usable data are unavailable in the other states.[10]

---

[10] An abortive attempt was made to apply the intercounty comparison method to Tennessee, using the 1940 poll tax receipts. While Tennessee did not publish

In Arkansas, the spread between counties in the proportion of adults over 21 paying the poll tax is substantial. For 1949,

Table 7. DISTRIBUTION OF ARKANSAS COUNTIES ACCORDING TO PERCENTAGE OF ALL ADULTS 21 AND OVER PAYING POLL TAX IN 1949

PERCENTAGE RANGE	NUMBER OF COUNTIES
20-29.9	4
30-39.9	9
40-49.9	36
50-59.9	21
60 and above	5
Median County of State 48.0	Total 75

the range was from 67.1 per cent in Perry County to 21.6 per cent in Crittenden County. Table 7 allocates counties to varying percentage ranges.[11]

---

the number of persons paying the tax in each county, the Department of Education published the county-by-county yield in its *Annual Statistical Report*. It was assumed that the number paying could be computed by dividing the tax rate into the amount received. However, the reports were found unusable for this purpose. The situation in South Carolina was similar. County reports of poll tax receipts were published by the State Superintendent of Education. An attempt to use them uncovered so many inaccuracies that no trustworthy intercounty comparison could be made. The intercounty method may not be used for Alabama, Mississippi or Virginia because of their cumulative requirements. For use of this method by Professor Key, see *Southern Politics*, pp. 609-17.

11 The county-by-county figures of poll tax payments since 1948 were obtained from the Director, Arkansas Department of Finance and Administration. Figures for years 1929 through 1948 are in Heard and Strong, pp. 35-36. Since the Arkansas tax is $1.00 and non-cumulative, receipts equal the number of taxpayers. The 1949 receipts were used because the tax was paid then to vote in the 1950 primaries. Receipts issued in 1950 were used for the 1950 general election. Percentages are based upon total population 21 and over since Arkansas does not exempt persons from payment because of age. The 1950 census reports were used for the population figures. Since the tax was paid in 1949, the use of the 1950 figures introduces a slight margin of error but not a significant one.

What causes these variations in poll tax payment rates? One way to seek the answer is to compare counties having the highest payment rates with counties having the lowest payment rates to see if these two groups are different in any characteristics. Table 8 shows that counties with the highest payment rates tend to be rural, with a small non-white (i.e. Negro) population, and with relatively few persons per square mile. Alternatively counties having the lowest payment rates tend to be more urbanized, to have a larger proportion of non-whites and a greater density of population than the first set of counties. Table 8 indicates that urbanism, density of population, and the proportion of Negroes in the population are associated with the poll tax payment rate in Arkansas. An attempt to analyze further the effect of these factors upon poll tax payment follows.[12]

Table 8. ARKANSAS COUNTIES WITH HIGHEST PERCENTAGES OF POLL TAX PAYMENT, 1949*

County	Per Cent Adults Paying Poll Tax	Per Cent Population Urban	Per Cent Population Non-white	Population Per Square Mile
Perry	67.1	....	4.1	10.8
Grant	63.7	....	8.2	14.3
Yell	62.0	....	3.9	15.1
Cleveland	61.2	....	24.2	14.9
Marion	58.4	....	....	13.7
Conway	57.8	30.2	23.6	32.4
Stone	57.5	....	0.1	12.6
Van Buren	56.3	....	1.2	13.6
Franklin	56.2	....	1.6	20.1
Sharp	55.6	....	0.1	15.1
Montgomery	55.5	....	0.5	8.3
Dallas	55.0	30.2	39.2	18.5
Scott	54.4	....	1.3	11.2
Searcy	54.1	....	....	15.7
Cleburne	53.9	....	....	19.3
Average	57.9	4.0	7.2	15.7

12 On the hypothesis that the economically better-off pay the poll tax at a higher rate than the poor, an attempt was made to test the relationship between economic well-being and poll tax payment. Farm tenancy was selected as an index of economic standing because agriculture plays an important role in the Arkansas economy and because of the availability of county-by-county

ARKANSAS COUNTIES WITH LOWEST PERCENTAGES OF POLL TAX
PAYMENT, 1949

County	Per Cent Adults Paying Poll Tax	Per Cent Population Urban	Per Cent Population Non-white	Population Per Square Mile
Sebastian	40.7	74.7	6.7	121.4
Columbia	40.1	24.0	39.1	37.5
Chicot	39.4	29.9	54.6	34.5
Poinsett	38.7	16.8	8.3	51.6
Monroe	38.2	34.4	48.8	31.7
Clay	37.9	9.6	. . . .	41.0
Izard	37.8	. . . .	1.0	17.3
Crawford	37.7	28.2	2.9	38.0
Lincoln	37.7	. . . .	53.3	30.2
Mississippi	36.4	25.8	26.9	89.4
Jefferson	35.0	48.8	49.8	85.5
St. Francis	28.2	20.6	57.4	57.9
Phillips	27.2	37.5	59.7	65.7
Lee	24.0	18.6	59.4	39.2
Crittenden	21.6	19.3	66.8	75.7
Average	34.7	25.9	35.6	54.4
The State	43.9	33.0	22.4	36.3
Median County of State	48.0	24.0	9.6	28.0

* Information on urbanism, non-white population, and density of population obtained from 1950 census reports.

information on farm tenancy in census reports. It was assumed that counties with the highest rates of farm tenancy would be the poorer counties and those with the lowest rates of farm tenancy, the wealthier ones. However, analysis revealed that high rates of farm tenancy are associated with a high proportion of Negroes and that the significant factor was probably the presence of Negroes and not the farm tenancy ratio. Further, many small farmers in hill counties are farm owners but are far from economically well-off. In addition, where there is a large amount of farm tenancy, there are also many large landowners of considerable wealth. Thus, farm tenancy is not a valid index of relative economic status on a county-by-county basis. A comparison of the 1949 median income of families and unrelated individuals was also made for the highest and lowest payment counties. The lowest payment counties had a slightly higher average median income than the highest payment ones, contrary to the assumption about the relationship between income status and poll tax payment. The higher incidence of urbanization in the lowest payment counties probably accounts for their higher incomes. Urbanization appears to be more important in influencing the poll tax payment rate than the income level. Since the tax amount is small, relatively minor variations in income do not affect the payment rate.

The relation between urbanism and poll tax payment is examined in Table 9. Rates of payment are listed for those counties which contained a city of more than 10,000 persons in 1950. None of these eleven counties was among the fifteen highest payment counties and only one (Garland) had a rate of payment exceeding that of the median county of the state. On the other hand, four (Sebastian, Jefferson, Mississippi, and Phillips) were among the counties with the lowest payment rates. The table indicates that urbanism has a significant effect upon the rate of poll tax payment. However, this factor cannot be tested with great accuracy in the Wonder State because of the few cities with any sizable population.

Table 9. THE POLL TAX AND URBANISM

(Rates of poll tax payment in counties containing a city of more than 10,000 persons, Arkansas, 1949.)

County	Principal City	Population of City, 1950	Per Cent Adults Paying Poll Tax
Pulaski	Little Rock	102,213	42.6
	North Little Rock	44,091	
Sebastian	Fort Smith	47,942	40.7
Jefferson	Pine Bluff	37,162	35.0
Garland	Hot Springs	29,307	49.3
Union	El Dorado	23,076	43.5
Washington	Fayetteville	17,071	41.4
Craighead	Jonesboro	16,310	42.1
Mississippi	Blytheville	16,234	36.4
Miller	Texarkana	15,875	44.6
Ouachita	Camden	11,372	47.0
Phillips	Helena	11,236	27.2
Median County of State			48.0

Density of population is related to urbanism. Table 8 showed that the highest payment counties tended to have fewer persons per square mile than the lowest payment counties. In Table 10, this relationship is examined by comparing poll tax payment rates in rural counties with less than twenty persons per square mile with poll tax payment rates in counties containing some urban population and with more than fifty persons per square mile. The median rate for the sparsely

populated counties is well above both the median rates for the
state and for the most densely populated counties. The table
substantiates the tendency noted in Table 8 and suggests that
the greater the density of population the lower will be the rate
of poll tax payment.

Table 10. THE POLL TAX AND POPULATION DENSITY
(Comparison of poll tax payment rates in rural counties with less than twenty
persons per square mile with poll tax payment rates in partially urban counties
with more than fifty persons per square mile, Arkansas, 1949.)

County	Population Per Sq. Mile	Per Cent Adults Paying Poll Tax	County	Population Per Sq. Mile	Per Cent Adults Paying Poll Tax
Cleburne	19.3	53.9	Pulaski	251.8	42.6
Izard	17.3	37.8	Sebastian	121.4	40.7
Pike	16.3	49.8	Mississippi	89.4	36.4
Searcy	15.7	54.1	Jefferson	85.5	35.0
Fulton	15.1	49.9	Crittenden	75.7	21.6
Sharp	15.1	55.6	Craighead	70.6	42.1
Yell	15.1	62.0	Phillips	65.7	27.2
Cleveland	14.9	61.2	Garland	65.3	49.3
Grant	14.3	63.7	St. Francis	57.9	28.2
Madison	14.1	48.9	Miller	52.0	44.6
Marion	13.7	58.4	Washington	51.9	41.4
Van Buren	13.6	56.3	Poinsett	51.6	38.7
Stone	12.6	57.5	Greene	50.3	45.0
Calhoun	11.4	66.2			
Scott	11.2	54.4			
Perry	10.8	67.1			
Newton	10.6	44.8			
Montgomery	8.3	55.5			
Average		55.4			37.9
Median		55.55			40.7
Median County of State		35.1			

Table 8 discloses that most high-payment counties had few
Negroes while most low-payment counties had a significant
proportion of Negroes. Since Negroes are not generally
encouraged to vote in southern states, it is logical that many of
them do not pay their poll taxes and that the presence of many
Negroes depresses the rate at which the tax is paid. Arkansas
counties with the lowest poll tax payment rates in 1949 were
mainly situated along the eastern border where the Negro

population is concentrated. The six counties with a 1950 Negro population exceeding fifty per cent were among the fifteen counties with the lowest payment rates the preceding year. However, five of these low-payment counties had less than ten per cent of Negroes in their population.

To test further the influence of the Negro upon poll tax payment, Table 11 compares one group of counties with a negligible Negro population with another group with a sizable Negro population. Since urbanism affects the rate of payment, only completely rural counties are included. The factor of urbanism is held constant while the Negro factor is examined. The table generally upholds the conclusion reached after examining the counties with the highest and lowest rates of payment. The median for the counties with few or no Negroes is approximately seven percentage points above the median for the counties with a large Negro population. However, there is only one percentage point difference between the averages

Table 11. THE POLL TAX AND THE NEGRO

(Comparison of poll tax payment rates in rural counties with one per cent or less non-white population with poll tax payment rates in rural counties with more than twenty per cent non-white population, Arkansas, 1949.)

COUNTY	PER CENT ADULTS PAYING POLL TAX	COUNTY	PER CENT ADULTS PAYING POLL TAX	PER CENT POPULATION NON-WHITE
Marion	58.4	Calhoun	66.2	34.4
Stone	57.5	Cleveland	61.2	24.4
Sharp	55.6	Lonoke	46.8	24.4
Montgomery	55.5	Woodruff	42.7	37.6
Searcy	54.1	Lincoln	37.7	53.3
Cleburne	53.9			
Carroll	53.4			
Baxter	52.5			
Fulton	49.9			
Madison	48.9			
Newton	44.8			
Izard	37.8			
Average	51.9		50.9	
Median	53.65		46.8	
Median County of State	48.0			

for the two sets of counties and two rural counties with a sizable Negro population have higher payment rates than any of the rural counties without or with few Negroes. The presence of additional factors is indicated.

An additional factor which may be examined for its effect upon poll tax payment is the party vote. Increased party competition should bring a higher vote and a higher rate of poll tax payment. This factor could not be tested in Table 8 because the table was based on receipts issued in 1949 and these receipts were not used in an election where party competition existed. In Table 12, the payment rates for two sets of counties differing in the proportion of votes cast for the different parties in the 1948 presidential election are compared. The first group is composed of counties where the vote was divided between the Democratic and Republican parties so that competition existed between them. The second group is composed of counties where the Democratic party polled in excess

Table 12. THE POLL TAX AND PARTY VOTE

(Comparison of poll tax payment rates in counties casting between forty and sixty per cent of total vote in 1948 presidential election for either Republican or Democratic party with poll tax payment rates in counties casting more than seventy per cent of total vote for Democratic party, all counties rural and with non-white population of five per cent or less, Arkansas.)

COUNTY	PER CENT TOTAL VOTE, 1948 PRES. ELEC. Rep.	Dem.	PER CENT ADULTS PAYING POLL TAX	COUNTY	PER CENT TOTAL VOTE, 1948 PRES. ELEC. Dem.	PER CENT ADULTS PAYING POLL TAX
Madison	51.2	47.5	92.0	Izard	81.9	35.0
Newton	50.3	48.5	62.7	Searcy	77.6	58.0
Carroll	41.4	55.1	61.7	Yell	77.1	54.6
				Franklin	76.1	52.3
				Montgomery	75.2	56.4
				Pike	73.8	49.0
				Cleburne	73.3	45.4
				Marion	72.6	54.4
				Scott	72.2	38.6
				Sharp	71.5	48.3
Average			72.1			49.2
Median			62.7			50.7
Median County of State			45.2			

of seventy per cent of the total vote. To cancel the effect of some of the other factors, only rural counties with a non-white population of five per cent or less were included. The States Rights party polled more than ten per cent of the total vote in only two of these counties (Scott and Sharp).

Table 12 indicates that party competition in Arkansas helps to increase the rate of poll tax payment. The rate for the three two-party counties exceeded the rate for all the one-party counties. The average of the first set of counties was over twenty percentage points higher than that for the second group. The 1949 payment rates of these same counties were also compared. For this year, the rates were lower in the two-party counties than in the one-party counties. The average of the first group was nearly five percentage points lower than that of the second group. Party competition did not enter into poll tax payment in 1949 since receipts for this year were used for the 1950 primary but not for the general election. Analysis of the 1952 payment rates also substantiates the party factor. Because of the Eisenhower candidacy, an unusually large number of Republican votes were cast in Arkansas in 1952. One group of counties casting over 55 per cent of the total vote for Eisenhower was contrasted with a group casting over 55 per cent of the total vote for Stevenson. As in Table 12, all counties were rural and had a non-white population of five per cent or less. In most cases, they were identical to the counties in Table 12.[13] All the over 55 per cent Republican counties had a higher payment rate than the over 55 per cent Democratic ones. The average rate for Republican counties was more than twenty percentage points higher than that for Democratic counties. Party competition, therefore, appears to affect the rate of poll tax payment in Arkansas. An intense intra-party strife may be as, or more, influential in encouraging poll tax payment but is more difficult to test than competition between parties.[14]

---

[13] The first group included Carroll, Madison, Newton, and Searcy; the second, Franklin, Izard, Marion, Perry, Pike, Scott, Sharp, and Yell.

[14] In computing the 1948 and 1952 county-by-county rates of payment, the 1950 population figures were used. A slight margin of error was thereby introduced but it is believed that it was insufficient to affect the results significantly.

Poll tax payment rates in 1939 and 1940 were also analyzed. The results were similar to those for the 1949 analysis. Urbanism, density of population, the Negro, and party competition also influenced payment rates a decade earlier. The effects of urbanism and population density stood out more clearly in 1949 than in 1939 while the Negro factor did not influence poll tax payment as much in 1949 as in 1939. The effect of party competition was comparable. In 1940, when poll tax receipts were used for the presidential election, two-party counties paid the tax in a higher proportion than one-party counties. In 1939, when receipts were used only for the Democratic primary, no significant difference existed between these two groups of counties.

The county-by-county comparison of poll tax payment rates in 1939 and 1949 also revealed a consistency between the high and low payment counties. Eight of the fifteen highest-payment counties in 1939 were among the same grouping in 1949 and eleven of the fifteen lowest-payment counties in 1939 were among similar counties in 1949. Only one county, Poinsett, moved from a high-payment group in 1939 to a low-payment one in 1949. Crittenden County had the lowest rate of payment in both years as well as in 1940 and 1952. It was one of the lowest in 1941 and 1948.

The Arkansas poll tax payment rate is rising. In 1939, the rate for the median county of the state was 35.1 per cent; in 1949, 48 per cent and in 1952, 50.3 per cent. This increase in the proportion of adults paying the tax indicates that the requirement is not as significant as formerly in restricting the suffrage in Arkansas. The increased rate of payment probably reflects greater interest in elections as well as the rise in dollar income and the lowered value of the dollar.

The county-by-county analysis of Arkansas poll tax payment rates points to the following conclusions: first, the denser the population the lower will be the rate of payment; second, urban residents tend to pay the tax at a lower rate than rural residents although this factor could not be adequately tested due to the scarcity of large urban communities; third, the presence of a large number of Negroes tends to lower the rate of payment although this factor was not as significant as the others nor as significant as it was ten years earlier; fourth, when receipts were used for voting in a presidential election, the tax was paid at a higher rate in two-party counties than in those where the Democratic party predominated; fifth, the payment rate has increased in recent years, indicating that the tax does not keep as many persons from voting as formerly.

The same widespread range in poll tax payment rates exists in Texas. In 1950, the spread was from 94 per cent in McMullen County to 25.3 per cent in El Paso County. They were also the highest and lowest counties in 1940 when McMullen had the surprising high of 100.8 per cent and El Paso 24.2 per cent. The number of counties grouped according to various percentage ranges is listed in Table 13.[15]

Table 13. DISTRIBUTION OF TEXAS COUNTIES ACCORDING TO PERCENTAGE OF PERSONS 21-60 PAYING POLL TAX IN 1950

PERCENTAGE RANGE	NUMBER OF COUNTIES
20-29.9	5
30-39.9	37
40-49.9	78
50-59.9	72
60-69.9	47
70-79.9	11
80 and above	4
Median 51.4	Total 254

The tests applied to the analysis of poll tax payment in Arkansas may also be used for Texas to discover why payment rates vary and to see if the results of these tests are similar. Because of the large number of counties in Texas, the county-by-county analysis has greater validity for this state than for Arkansas. The many Texas counties make it possible to test several different groups of counties which are similar except for one variable.

[15] The number of poll tax receipts was obtained from the *Texas Almanac and State Industrial Guide, 1952-53*. The percentages are based upon all persons 21 to 60 years of age. Texas exempts those persons 60 and above. Population figures were derived from the 1950 census report.

The 26 Texas counties with the highest and lowest percentages of poll tax payment in 1950 were contrasted. These counties have characteristics similar to the fifteen high and low payment Arkansas counties contrasted. The Texas high-payment counties in 1950 were predominantly rural and sparsely populated and had a small non-white population whereas the low-payment counties were more urbanized and more heavily populated and had more non-whites.

Two factors not tested in Arkansas—the proportion of foreign-born whites in the population and the number of persons per motor vehicle—were analyzed in Texas. It was assumed that the concentration of Mexican-Americans in certain Texas areas might affect the poll tax payment rate.[16] The high-payment counties had fewer foreign-born whites than the low-payment counties. The low-payment counties showed a relationship between the proportion of non-whites (primarily Negroes) and the proportion of foreign-born whites. One factor tended to complement the other, each having its effect upon lowering the poll tax payment rate. Where the percentage of non-whites was low, the percentage of foreign-born whites in most cases was relatively high so that the presence of many Mexican-Americans seemed to have the same effect upon poll tax payment rates as the presence of many Negroes.

Since the number of registered motor vehicles is available for Texas counties, this information was used to test the hypothesis that poll tax payment is higher in well-to-do counties than in those of a lower economic standing. The motor vehicle registration datum was used on the assumption that the fewer persons per motor vehicle, the higher the economic standing of the county would be. High-payment counties tended to have fewer persons per motor vehicle than those with the lowest payment rates. The average for the high-payment counties was slightly below the number of persons per motor vehicle for the state as a whole, while that for the low-payment counties exceeded the state-wide figure. If the ratio of persons per motor vehicle is related to the economic standing of a

16 The foreign-born white group in Texas consists primarily of Mexican-Americans; 70.9 per cent of the total number in 1950 were Mexican-Americans.

county, it would appear that the counties of highest poll tax payment are wealthier than those where payment rates are lowest.[17]

Many of the 26 high and low payment counties in 1950 were among the 26 high and low payment counties in 1940. Eleven of the 1950 high-payment counties were among the 26 high-payment counties in 1940 while twelve of the 1950 low-payment counties were among the similar ones a decade earlier. One 1950 high-payment county, Starr, was among the 1940 low-payment counties. No 1950 low-payment county was among the 1940 high-payment counties. There was not, however, as much continuity between the 1950 and 1940 high and low payment counties in Texas as in Arkansas. In 1940 as in 1950, the high-payment counties were mainly rural, sparsely populated, and primarily white in composition while the low-payment counties were more urbanized, more heavily populated and had more Negroes than the high-payment ones. Also the high-payment counties had fewer foreign-born whites and fewer persons per motor vehicle than the low-payment ones. Although these general characteristics were comparable, there were differences in degree between the 1940 and 1950 high and low payment counties. The 1950 high-payment counties were more urbanized than the 1940 ones, probably reflecting the increased urbanization of the state. The 1950 low-payment counties had fewer Negroes than the 1940 low-payment counties, fewer than the state-wide decrease in the Negro population would justify. This difference probably resulted from increased voting by Negroes. The spread between the number of persons per motor vehicle in the high and low payment counties was not as great in 1950 as in 1940. The increased number of automo-

[17] Information on urbanism, non-white population, density of population, and foreign-born population obtained from 1950 census report. Number of motor vehicles registered obtained from *Texas Almanac and State Industrial Guide, 1952-53*. The use of the motor vehicle ratio as a measure of relative economic standing may be open to question but no more satisfactory standard could be found. These counties were also compared on the basis of the median income of families and unrelated individuals for 1949 but significant results were not obtained. The median incomes for the high-payment counties were slightly less than those for the low-payment counties. The difference between them was too small to be significant.

biles and the rise in living standards appears to explain this variation. The proportion of foreign-born whites in high and low payment counties was about the same in both years.

In 1940, all counties with the highest percentages of poll tax payment were west of the ninety-eighth meridian which is just west of Austin, the capital. The majority of the low-payment counties were east of this line and along or near the Mexican border. Locating these counties on a map reveals that the high-payment ones were situated in the sparsely populated, predominantly rural and largely white sections of the state, whereas the counties with the lowest payment rates were in the more heavily populated, more urbanized sections where either more Negroes or more foreign-born whites lived. The same tendency was present in 1950 although the high and low payment counties were more scattered over the state. Not all high-payment counties were west of the ninety-eighth meridian; Hood, Franklin, Trinity, and San Augustine were not, and the meridian cut through Wilson and Jim Wells. Most of these counties had little urbanism, few Negroes, few foreign-born whites, small population density, and a relatively small population per motor vehicle. However, Trinity was over one-fourth non-white; San Augustine was 28.4 per cent urban and 34.7 per cent non-white; and Jim Wells was 70.1 per cent urban. Factors not studied here must have produced the high poll tax payment rates in these counties. Fifteen of the 26 low-payment counties in 1950 were east of the ninety-eighth meridian and four more were along the Mexican border. The other seven were scattered throughout the western part of the state in the same general area as the high-payment counties. Urbanism explains the low payment rates in all these counties. The proportion of urbanism ranged from 47.2 per cent to 92.6 per cent. All but one contained a city of over 10,000 persons.[18]

The previous analysis revealed that the poll tax is paid at a lower rate in counties with a large urban population than in rural counties. Tables 14 and 15 test further the urbanism factor. Table 14 lists the tax payment rates of counties

18 These seven counties were Bexar (San Antonio), Mitchell, Potter (Amarillo), Scurry (Snyder), Taylor (Abilene), Tom Green (San Angelo), Wichita (Wichita Falls).

containing a city of more than 20,000 persons as of 1950. The median tax payment rate for these counties is approximately fifteen percentage points less than the median rate for all counties. None of these 31 counties had a rate exceeding the median rate for all counties. Counties having the largest cities are listed first. This arrangement helps to illustrate further the influence of urbanization in lowering the tax payment rate. The rate tends to be less in counties containing the largest cities. None of these counties was among the 26 counties with the highest poll tax payment rates. Fifteen were among the 26 counties of lowest payment, including five of the seven counties which contained a city of over 100,000. El Paso, the county with the lowest poll tax payment rate, was in this group. A similar analysis of 1940 rates was made for counties having a city over 10,000 persons with the result being generally the same.

Table 15 compares poll tax payment rates in completely rural counties with rates in counties having an urban population of fifty per cent or more. The non-white population of all counties was five per cent or less as of 1950. Thus, the urbanism factor is tested while the Negro factor remains constant. The table bears out the conclusion that rural residents are more apt to pay their poll taxes than persons in urban communities. The median rate for rural counties is sixteen percentage points higher than the median rate for urban counties. The 1940 analysis of a similar group of counties produced comparable results.

Similar findings were obtained when other groups of counties differing in urbanization were contrasted. A group of rural counties was compared with a number of counties having an urban population in excess of fifty per cent. All counties had a non-white population of five to ten per cent. The median tax payment rate for the rural counties was just over 23 percentage points higher than that for the urban ones. Eight rural counties and fourteen urban ones were in this grouping. Poll tax payment rates in counties containing a city of more than 10,000 persons were compared with rates in counties without such a city. The non-white population of both sets of counties was between ten and fifteen per cent. The

Table 14. THE POLL TAX AND URBANISM
(Rates of poll tax payment in Texas counties containing a city of more than 20,000 persons, 1950.)

County	Principal City	Population of City	Per Cent Adults 21-60 Paying Poll Tax
Harris	Houston	596,163	33.5
	Baytown	22,983	
	Pasadena	22,483	
Dallas	Dallas	434,462	26.2
	University Park	24,275	
Bexar	San Antonio	408,442	32.3
Tarrant	Fort Worth	278,778	27.2
Travis	Austin	132,459	37.0
El Paso	El Paso	130,485	25.3
Nueces	Corpus Christi	108,287	42.7
Jefferson	Beaumont	94,014	42.6
	Port Arthur	57,530	
McLennan	Waco	84,706	36.9
Potter	Amarillo	74,246	33.7
Lubbock	Lubbock	71,747	36.3
Wichita	Wichita Falls	68,042	30.3
Galveston	Galveston	66,568	43.8
Tom Green	San Angelo	52,093	34.6
Webb	Laredo	51,910	46.5
Taylor	Abilene	45,570	31.4
Smith	Tyler	38,968	35.5
Cameron	Brownsville	36,066	33.9
	Harlingen	23,229	
Brazoria	* Brazosport	30,000	48.0
Ector	Odessa	29,495	39.8
Bell	Temple	25,467	26.5
Bowie	Texarkana	24,753	37.0
Gregg	Longview	24,502	46.4
Harrison	Marshall	22,327	29.9
Midland	Midland	21,713	42.1
Lamar	Paris	21,643	37.2
Denton	Denton	21,372	32.9
Orange	Orange	21,174	48.4
Brown	Brownwood	20,181	48.8
Grayson	Sherman	20,150	37.2
Hidalgo	McAllen	20,067	33.5

Average			36.7
Median			36.3
Median of all counties			51.4

*Not a single city. A group city name applied to the industrial and port area embracing the incorporated places of Freeport, Velasco and Lake Jackson and unincorporated places of Clute, Oyster Creek and Jones Creek. Population is estimated. See Texas Almanac and State Industrial Guide, 1952-53. p. 84.

Table 15. THE POLL TAX AND URBANISM

(Comparison of poll tax payment rates in rural counties with poll tax payment rates in counties with an urban population of more than fifty per cent, all counties with non-white population of five per cent or less, Texas, 1950.)

COUNTY[a]	PER CENT ADULTS 21— 60 PAYING POLL TAX	COUNTY[b]	PER CENT POPULATION URBAN	PER CENT ADULTS 21— 60 PAYING POLL TAX
Archer	59.6	Potter	92.6	33.7
Armstrong	75.9	Webb	92.5	46.5
Bailey	57.6	Val Verde	85.4	38.5
Bandera	65.0	Nueces	85.3	42.7
Blanco	76.9	Jim Hogg	79.8	76.2
Borden	58.4	Randall	78.8	40.6
Bosque	57.6	Kleberg	76.8	50.0
Briscoe	65.1	Comal	74.6	44.7
Burnet	49.1	El Paso	74.3	25.3
Callahan	53.7	Ochiltree	73.3	56.5
Carson	55.1	Brooks	73.0	60.9
Castro	65.1	Crockett	72.5	44.4
Cochran	61.6	Brewster	72.0	48.3
Coke	63.5	Taylor	71.9	31.4
Concho	59.6	Dallam	71.8	52.7
Crane	61.4	Brown	70.5	48.8
Culberson	66.0	Sutton	70.3	55.1
Edwards	59.5	Hutchinson	70.2	41.9
Glasscock	66.1	Ector	70.1	39.8
Hansford	59.3	Jim Wells	70.0	69.1
Hood	66.5	Nolan	68.8	43.9
Hudspeth	36.8	Winkler	68.7	47.1
Irion	84.2	Reeves	68.6	42.5
Jeff Davis	67.9	Gray	67.1	41.4
Kendall	58.3	Andrews	65.9	56.7
Kenedy	46.8	Hemphill	65.5	64.4
Kent	55.2	Howard	64.7	49.4
Kimble	72.9	Menard	64.3	65.9
Lipscomb	66.0	Zavala	64.3	37.8
Live Oak	58.4	Young	62.5	45.1
Average	63.7			47.9
Median	63.5			47.15
Median of all counties	51.4			

[a] Fifty-one counties fell within this group. The others were Loving, McMullen, Martin, Mason, Mills, Oldham, Parmer, Regan, Real, Roberts, Schleicher, Shackelford, Sherman, Somervell, Sterling, Stonewall, Terrell, Throckmorton, Wilson, Yoakum, Zapata.

[b] Forty-eight counties fell within this group. The others were Baylor, Bee, Cameron, Cooke, Deaf Smith, Eastland, Erath, Garza, Hidalgo, Kerr, LaSalle, Llano, McCulloch, Maverick, Scurry, Stephens, Upton, Uvalde.

median rate for counties without a sizable city was over seventeen percentage points more than the median rate for counties containing a city of more than 10,000. In this grouping, there were thirteen counties without a city of 10,000 and seven counties with such a city. The spread in the poll tax payment rates between the urban and rural counties was greater in 1950 than in 1940.

The factor of population density is tested in Table 16 where poll tax payment rates in rural counties with five persons or less per square mile are compared with rates in counties with some urban population and with more than twenty persons per square mile. To limit the effect of other factors, the analysis was restricted to counties with less than five per cent of both non-whites and foreign-born whites. Tax payment rates were considerably higher in the sparsely populated counties than in the more heavily populated ones. The median rate for the first group was approximately 22 percentage points higher than that for the second set. All but two of the more heavily populated counties had a lower payment rate than the sparsely populated county with the lowest rate. A definite relationship between high rates of poll tax payment and a low population ratio is indicated. An analysis for 1940 yielded similar results.

A tendency for the rate of poll tax payment to be lower where the proportion of Negroes is high has been previously noted. This relationship is examined further in Table 17 where payment rates in counties with a non-white population of less than two per cent are contrasted with payment rates in counties with a non-white population of over fifteen per cent. To hold constant urbanism and Mexican-Americanism, only rural counties with less than five per cent of foreign-born whites were included. While the table indicates that the proportion of Negroes in the population affects the poll tax payment rate, this factor is not as significant as urbanism. The median rate for counties with few Negroes was just over eleven percentage points higher than that for counties with a significant number of Negroes. In 1940, the median tax payment rate for counties with few Negroes was over 22 percentage points higher than that for counties with a sizable Negro population. This difference between 1940 and 1950 substan-

Table 16. THE POLL TAX AND POPULATION DENSITY

(Comparison of poll tax payment rates in rural counties with less than five persons per square mile with poll tax payment rates in partially urban counties with more than twenty persons per square mile, all counties less than five per cent Negro and less than five per cent foreign-born white, Texas, 1950.)

COUNTY	PER CENT ADULTS 21— 60 PAYING POLL TAX	COUNTY	POPULATION PER SQ. MILE	PER CENT POPULATION URBAN	PER CENT ADULTS 21— 60 PAYING POLL TAX
McMullen	94.0	Jim Wells	33.1	70.0	69.1
Irion	84.2	Karnes	22.6	39.8	59.9
Roberts	82.8	Hockley	22.6	40.5	49.8
Throckmorton	78.9	Eastland	25.1	53.7	49.5
Armstrong	75.9	Howard	29.3	64.7	49.4
Loving	74.4	Cooke	24.6	50.8	49.0
Stonewall	73.5	Brown	30.1	70.5	48.8
Kimble	72.9	Bee	21.6	51.4	48.2
Oldham	68.2	Parker	23.8	37.6	44.7
Real	68.1	Nolan	21.5	68.8	43.9
Glasscock	66.1	Nueces	197.5	85.3	42.7
Lipscomb	66.0	Hutchinson	35.7	70.2	41.9
Briscoe	65.1	San Patricio	52.0	44.8	41.8
Sherman	64.5	Gray	26.4	67.1	41.4
Coke	63.5	Ector	46.4	70.1	39.8
Sterling	62.0	Hale	28.8	49.8	39.7
Crane	61.4	Potter	81.4	92.6	33.7
Schleicher	61.0	Taylor	69.4	71.9	31.4
Hansford	59.3	Scurry	25.1	52.7	31.1
Borden	58.4				
Reagan	56.3				
Kent	55.2				
Average	68.7				45.0
Median	66.05				43.9
Median of all counties	51.4				

tiates the earlier conclusion that increased voting by Negroes means that more are paying the poll tax than formerly and, therefore, the presence of a large Negro population is less significant now in reducing the poll tax payment rate.

A comparison was also made between one group of counties with a non-white population of two per cent or less and another group with a non-white population of more than twenty per cent. All of them had an urban population of 25 per cent or more and a foreign-born white population of five per cent or less. Thirty counties fell in both categories. As in Table

17, counties with few Negroes had higher poll tax payment rates than counties with a heavier concentration of Negroes. The median rate for the first group was nearly twelve percentage points more than that for the second group. In 1940, the median for the first group was fourteen percentage points more than that for the second group. Thus, in counties with a sizable

Table 17. THE POLL TAX AND THE NEGRO

(Comparison of poll tax payment rates in counties two per cent or less non-white with poll tax payment rates in counties more than fifteen per cent non-white, all counties rural and with less than five per cent foreign-born whites, Texas, 1950.)

County	Per Cent Adults 21—60 Paying Poll Tax	County	Per Cent Population Non-White	Per Cent Adults 21—60 Paying Poll Tax
McMullen	94.0	Trinity	26.8	74.1
Irion	84.2	Chambers	19.7	64.9
Roberts	82.8	Sabine	26.1	63.7
Throckmorton	78.9	Burleson	32.3	60.6
Armstrong	75.9	Austin	20.6	60.0
Loving	74.4	Rockwall	27.5	55.6
Kimble	72.9	San Jacinto	52.5	54.0
Yoakum	69.7	Madison	32.8	52.4
Parmer	69.4	Leon	39.4	50.2
Oldham	68.2	Newton	35.3	48.7
Real	68.1	Tyler	19.8	48.3
Hood	66.5	Morris	33.2	45.0
Glasscock	66.1	Waller	52.9	42.5
Lipscomb	66.0			
Castro	65.1			
Bandera	65.0			
Mills	64.9			
Sherman	64.5			
Mason	63.9			
Coke	63.5			
Sterling	62.0			
Archer	59.6			
Concho	59.6			
Hansford	59.3			
Live Oak	58.4			
Kendall	58.3			
Somervell	57.5			
Carson	55.1			
Callahan	53.7			
Average	67.2			55.4
Median	65.1			54.0
Median of all counties	51.4			

urban population, as well as in counties with a completely rural population, the presence of many Negroes tends to depress the poll tax payment rate. An objection might be raised that the possibility for a considerable variation in the proportion of urbanization is too great to draw valid conclusions from the comparison. The median rate of urbanization for counties with few Negroes was approximately thirteen percentage points

Table 18. THE POLL TAX AND THE MEXICAN-AMERICAN
(Comparison of poll tax payment rates in counties with one per cent or less foreign-born whites with poll tax payment rates in counties with more than five per cent foreign-born whites, all counties rural and less than five per cent non-white, Texas, 1950.)

COUNTY	PER CENT ADULTS 21— 60 PAYING POLL TAX	COUNTY	PER CENT POPULATION FOR.-BORN WHITE	PER CENT ADULTS 21— 60 PAYING POLL TAX
Roberts	82.8	Jeff Davis	9.1	67.9
Throckmorton	78.9	Culberson	6.4	66.0
Blanco	76.9	Zapata	19.7	60.3
Armstrong	75.9	Edwards	8.8	59.5
Stonewall	73.5	Kenedy	15.3	46.8
Yoakum	69.7	Terrell	11.8	45.0
Parmer	69.4	Hudspeth	31.9	36.8
Oldham	68.2			
Hood	66.5			
Briscoe	65.1			
Castro	65.1			
Mills	64.9			
Sherman	64.5			
Coke	63.5			
Sterling	62.0			
Cochran	61.6			
Crane	61.4			
Shackelford	60.1			
Archer	59.6			
Hansford	59.3			
Borden	58.4			
Bailey	57.6			
Somervell	57.5			
Reagan	56.3			
Carson	55.1			
Callahan	53.7			
Burnet	49.1			
Average	64.3			54.6
Median	63.5			59.5
Median of all counties	51.4			

higher than the median for counties with a large number of Negroes. Because of the effect of urbanism upon poll tax payment, this higher rate of urbanization in the first group of counties should have worked to lower their tax payment rates. Since the tax payment rates were higher in the counties with few Negroes, despite this difference in urbanism, the effect of a large Negro population in depressing the poll tax payment rate is further emphasized.

A comparison of counties with the highest and lowest poll tax payment rates indicates that the high-payment counties had fewer foreign-born whites than the low payment counties. Table 18 shows the results of an effort to isolate this factor more specifically. The table tests the effect of a sizable number of Mexican-Americans since they constitute most of the foreign-born whites in Texas. Poll tax payment rates in one set of counties with one per cent or less foreign-born whites are contrasted with poll tax payment rates in another set of counties with more than five per cent foreign-born whites. The urban and Negro factors are held constant by confining the comparison to rural counties with less than five per cent non-whites. The median payment rate for counties with few Mexican-Americans is only four percentage points higher than that for counties with a significant number of Mexican-Americans. The presence of a sizable number of Mexican-Americans appears to aid in lowering the poll tax payment rate but this factor does not stand out as clearly as those previously examined. It is noteworthy that Hudspeth, the county with easily the largest proportion of foreign-born whites, had the lowest payment rate of all these counties. In 1940, the foreign-born white factor had more effect upon poll tax payment. The median rate for counties with few Mexican-Americans was nearly ten percentage points higher than that for counties with a large number of Mexican-Americans.

The relationship between the number of persons per registered motor vehicle, as a yardstick of the relative wealth of a county, and the poll tax payment rate is tested in Figure 14 by correlating these two items. To eliminate as many variables as possible, only rural counties with less than five per cent of both non-whites and foreign-born whites and with a population of less than 3,000 persons in the 21-60 age group were included. While the results of the scatter diagram are not conclusive, the tendency is for payment rates to be higher where the ratio of persons per motor vehicle is the lowest. If the motor vehicle ratio is an adequate measuring stick, the diagram helps to sustain the earlier tentative conclusion that the tax is paid at a higher rate in wealthy, than in poor, counties. The considerable scattering of the points indicates the influence of factors not considered here.[19]   The presence of additional factors and perhaps also the fact that payment of an annual $1.75 tax is not greatly affected by income levels was revealed by

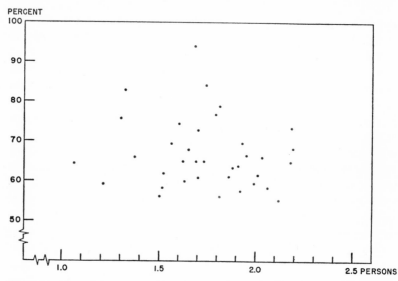

FIGURE 14. The Poll Tax and Wealth: Rates of Poll Tax Payment Compared with Number of Persons Per Registered Motor Vehicle, All Counties Rural, with Less than Five Per Cent of Both Non-whites and Foreign-born Whites and Under 3,000 Persons from 21-60, Texas, 1950.

comparing two groups of counties with different median incomes. One group had a median income for families and unrelated individuals in 1949 of less than $2,000; the other had a median income above $3,000. All counties were rural and had less than five per cent of non-whites and foreign-born whites. Twenty-two counties fell in the first category and nine

[19] See Key, p. 616, for a similar figure based on 1940 poll tax payment rates.

COMPARISONS   167

in the second. Counties with the lower median income had a median poll tax payment rate just over three percentage points higher than that for counties with the higher median income—a result opposite from what it should have been if income level significantly affects the rate of poll tax payment.

In Arkansas, party competition tended to increase the rate of poll tax payment. This factor was also tested in Texas but without significant results. The 26 highest and lowest payment counties in the 1948 presidential election year were compared with reference to the percentage of total votes cast for the Republican party. The median of the Republican vote percentages for the lowest-payment counties was nearly nine percentage points higher than that for the highest-payment counties. If party competition worked to encourage poll tax payment in Texas, the result should have been the opposite. To test this factor further, the twenty most Republican counties were contrasted with the twenty least Republican counties. Republicanism was judged by the returns in the 1948 presidential election. The median payment rate of counties with few Republicans was approximately nine percentage points higher than the median for counties with a significant Republican turnout. Poll tax payment rates in a group of counties that cast over twenty per cent of the total vote for the Republican ticket were compared with the payment rates in a group of counties that gave ten per cent or less of the total vote to the GOP. To cancel the effect of other factors, only rural counties with a non-white and foreign-born white population of less than five per cent were included. Twelve counties fell within the first grouping and nine within the second. In this instance, counties with the largest percentage of votes for the Republican candidate had a median poll tax payment rate of just over five percentage points more than counties of least Republicanism. This difference is not of great significance, especially in view of the small number of counties involved. Similar tests yielded comparable results for 1940.

Bi-partyism does not appear to be a factor associated with high rates of poll tax payment in Texas. Texas and Arkansas may differ because there are few Texas counties where a large

Republican vote is cast. In addition, the Republican party in Texas is mainly a presidential party. In local elections, little competition occurs between parties. Thus, the party clash does not stimulate voting and, as a corollary, poll tax payment. In Arkansas, Republicans are strong enough in some counties to engage in local contests with Democrats. A consequence of this fact appeared in the Arkansas analysis.[20]

The intercounty analysis of Texas poll tax payments reveals that urbanism, concentration of population, a large Negro population and a large Mexican-American population reduces the rate of payment. A relationship between low economic standing, measured by the motor vehicle ratio, and a low rate of poll tax payment exists although the results are not as conclusive as those obtained from the other factors. Analysis of poll tax payment and income levels does not show a positive relationship and modifies the conclusions with reference to the relation between poll tax payment and the motor vehicle ratio. The relationship between urbanism and a low rate of poll tax payment is more positive in Texas than in Arkansas. Due to the greater number of sizable urban areas in the Lone Star State, this factor could be tested with greater validity and the results are more significant than for Arkansas. The testing of the relationship between party and poll tax payment yielded different results in these states with a positive relationship under some circumstances in Arkansas and a negative one in Texas.

THE POLL TAX AND ECONOMIC CONDITIONS

The relationship between the poll tax and economic conditions is important enough to test further. One way is to compare tax payment rates over a series of years with some significant economic condition in a particular state. In applying this method the same problem arises that was met in the inter-county analysis, i.e., the difficulty of finding

---

[20] The 1952 presidential election was not used for this comparison because the results were not a true indication of Texas Republicanism. The majority of votes for Eisenhower were cast for him as an individual and not as leader of the Republican party.

meaningful economic data. Data that cover a series of years and indicate the economic status of a particular state are not readily available. Analysis was also limited by the inadequacy of poll tax data. For instance, if information on Arkansas poll tax payments had been available before 1929, the analysis could have covered a longer period with possibly more adequate results. The economic indices with which poll tax payment rates are compared are per capita income, cash receipts from farming, and the price of cotton.[21]

Figures 15 and 16 compare the percentage of persons paying the poll tax with per capita income from 1929 through 1953 in Arkansas and from 1930 through 1952 in Texas. In Arkansas, the tax payment rates and per capita income are compared for all these years whereas in Texas information is presented only for election years. Fluctuations in the Arkansas payment rates indicate that fewer persons paid the tax in non-election years than in election years. The change that occurred in 1939 resulted from the alteration in the time of poll tax payment.[22] The Texas fluctuations show that more Texans pay the tax during presidential election years than in other years.

These figures indicate that the payment rate tends to decline as per capita income declines and to rise as per capita income rises. This relationship is most noticeable in Arkansas. A smaller percentage of persons paid the poll tax there in 1933, at the depth of the depression, than in any other year during the period charted. As per capita income increased, a greater proportion of Arkansans paid the tax. The relationship between poll tax payment and per capita income is not as close in Texas, but an inclination for the payment rate to decline

[21] Information on which the following figures are based was obtained from the following sources: Arkansas poll tax payments from State Comptroller's Office (see also Heard and Strong, pp. 35-36); Texas poll tax receipts from *Texas Almanac and State Industrial Guide, 1949-50* and *1952-53* and letter to author from S. C. Reed, Dallas *Morning News,* dated August 24, 1955; per capita income from U.S. Dept. of Commerce, *Survey of Current Business,* XXIX (August, 1949) and XXXIV (August, 1954); cash receipts from farming and price of cotton from U.S. Dept. of Agriculture, *Yearbook of Agriculture,* years through 1935, and *Agricultural Statistics,* years 1936 through 1954.

[22] See Chapter 2.

with a drop in income and to edge upward with an improvement in the economic situation exists. If it were possible to compare poll tax payment and per capita income in a state

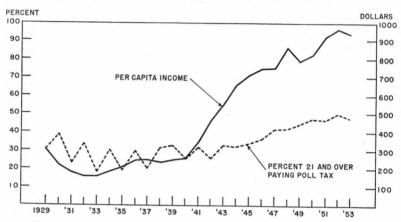

FIGURE 15. Comparison of Percentages of All Persons 21 and Over Paying Poll Tax with Changes in Per Capita Income, Arkansas, 1929-1953.

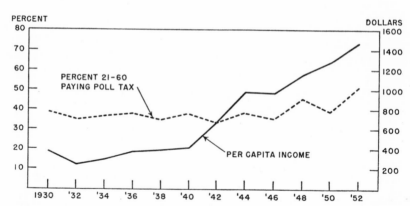

FIGURE 16. Comparison of Percentages of All Persons 21-60 Paying Poll Tax with Changes in Per Capita Income, Texas, 1930-1952.

with a cumulative tax, the relationship would undoubtedly be more striking because of the greater economic burden of a cumulative tax.

Another significant economic datum with which poll tax payment may be compared is cash receipts from farming.

Where agriculture plays a basic role in the economy, farm income serves as a valid indicator of prosperity. Figure 17 contrasts the percentage of Arkansas citizens paying the poll tax with the cash receipts from farming for 1929 through 1953. A significant correlation between them is evident. Tax payment tends to decrease when farm income declines and to increase when farm income rises.

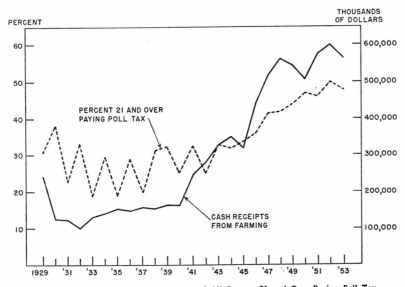

FIGURE 17. Comparison of Percentages of All Persons 21 and Over Paying Poll Tax with Cash Receipts from Farming, Arkansas, 1929-1953.

An additional way to observe the relationship between the poll tax and economic conditions is to compare tax payment with the price received for a commodity which has an important influence upon the economy. Cotton has long been such a commodity in the South. Figures 18 and 19 compare the relationship between the price of cotton and poll tax payment in Arkansas from 1930 through 1953 and in Texas from 1922 through 1952. The Texas figure contrasts odd-numbered price years with even-numbered tax years. Because of collection schedules, income received from cotton for the year preceding the year of tax collection will influence the payment rate that year more than cotton income of the same year as the tax year.

The situation is different in Arkansas where the tax may be paid up to October 1.

The charts reveal a significant relationship between fluctuations in the cotton price and the poll tax payment rate.   The

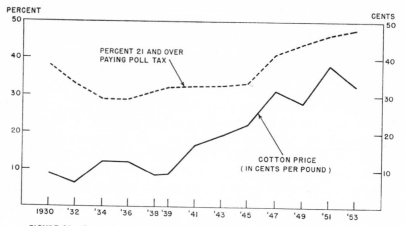

FIGURE 18. Comparison of Percentages of All Persons 21 and Over Paying Poll Tax with the Price of Cotton, Arkansas, 1930-1953.

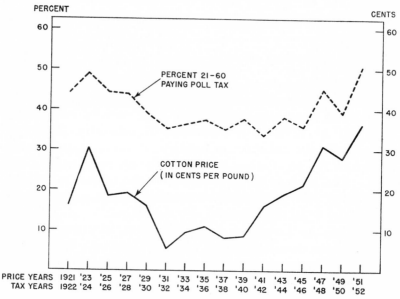

FIGURE 19. Comparison of Percentages of All Persons 21-60 Paying Poll Tax with the Price of Cotton, Texas, 1922-1952.

connection between them is particularly striking in Texas. The figure shows a progressive decline in poll tax payment along with a steady drop in the price of cotton during the twenties. In the thirties, both tended to level off. Beginning in 1939, the cotton price rose and a few years later the tax payment rate increased.[23] However, fluctuations in the cotton price have been more violent than have those in the poll tax payment rate. Also, fluctuations in the tax payment rate beginning in 1936 suggest the inauguration of a tendency for presidential years to have an effect partially independent of economic conditions.

The number of persons who pay the poll tax is, therefore, influenced by economic conditions. In times of economic depression and low income, a tax requirement will discourage more citizens from becoming qualified voters. It restricts the suffrage significantly when the economic level is low and is an important deterrent to low income individuals at any time. The tax is not now as important a means of disfranchisement as when it was first adopted. Because of the rise in per capita income and the decline in the value of the dollar, the tax is no longer the hurdle to many individuals that it was formerly.

SUMMARY AND CONCLUSIONS

The methods used in this study have not fully answered the question of who pays and who does not pay the poll tax or of what social groups it most affects. But they have indicated that poll tax payment is influenced by urbanism, density of population, the number of Negroes or other unassimilated groups in the population, and the economic conditions of the area. The analysis suggests that the urban voter, the Negro voter, and the economically depressed voter are especially injured by a tax requirement.

Why should the urban resident be more adversely affected by a poll tax than his country cousin? The same factors that dissuade individuals from voting probably also dissuade them from paying their poll taxes and, contrariwise, the factors that

[23] See a comparable chart in Key, p. 601.

induce individuals to vote also induce them to satisfy the tax requirement. In *Southern Politics,* V. O. Key demonstrated that city dwellers in the South have a lower degree of electoral interest than farm and small town residents.[24]   If influences are at work which produce greater interest in elections in rural areas than in urban centers, it is not surprising that proportionately more persons pay the tax in the country than in the city.   The lower ratio of payment in the city may not mean that the city inhabitant is more adversely affected by the poll tax than the rural resident.   It may simply reflect a lower interest in elections.   However, there is reason to believe that the tax operates to the disadvantage of the urban citizen. Administrative procedures associated with it tend to encourage payment by rural citizens more than by urban residents.   In most places, the citizen must pay his tax at the county courthouse.   Employment in industry makes it inconvenient for urban residents to make this annual or biennial pilgrimage. Time would be lost from work in many cases.   On the other hand, a trip to the county seat is often an eagerly anticipated event for southern rural residents.   The courthouse is a place for renewing old friendships and exchanging gossip as well as for paying taxes and transacting other business.   The fact that administration of poll tax collection often gives greater encouragement to pay to real estate owners than to renters may also help to explain the higher rate of payment in rural areas.   The lower poll tax payment rate in urban areas results largely from lower political participation in the cities and partially from the effect of the tax upon the urban voter.

If the presence of many Negroes lowers the rate of poll tax payment, is the tax the primary means of preventing them from voting?   This is a popular assumption.   Examination of tax administration disclosed that Negroes are usually not discriminated against when they offer to pay their poll taxes. Prospective voters are discouraged by other means.   The white primary was formerly of greater significance than the poll tax in keeping Negroes from the polls.   Literacy tests and registration requirements constitute high hurdles for them.   Less

[24] Pp. 510-13.

obvious explanations for low voting participation by Negroes may be summed up in the phrase "Politics is white folks' business." The poll tax has not been the major deterrent to Negro voting. It has affected white citizens more directly than Negroes. In 1940, Ralph Bunche concluded:

It is something more than a mere catch-phrase to say of the South and its poll tax provisions that it is the registrar—and the Democratic party officials who set the qualifications for voting in the primary—who disfranchise the Negro, while the tax collector disfranchises the [poor] white man.[25]

The collapse of the white primary altered the situation which existed when Mr. Bunche wrote. Democratic party officials cannot disfranchise Negroes as they could before 1944. The fall of the white primary gave Negroes an incentive to vote and to pay their poll taxes that they did not have previously. In the past, relatively few Negroes paid their poll taxes, not solely because they could not, but primarily because they had little incentive to pay them. Now that they have an inducement to vote, the poll tax, especially a cumulative one, will be a more direct hindrance. As other restrictive measures cease to be effective, the poll tax may take on more importance as a restriction on Negro voting. However, the Texas analysis indicated that more Negroes were paying their poll taxes in 1950 than in 1940.

It should be noted that Negroes are in the economic class that tends to be harmed most by a tax requirement for the suffrage. A connection exists between economic conditions and poll tax payment. If a smaller proportion pay the tax in times of depression than in times of prosperity, it is evident

---

25 P. 629. See also Key, pp. 597-98. A Negro graduate student sought to find out why Negroes did not vote in Texas. He sent questionnaires to counties in the areas of greatest Negro density and received usable returns from 39 counties. Using these returns, he concluded that the chief reason for Negro non-voting was the one-party system. Not one Negro mentioned the poll tax as a cause of non-voting among Negroes. William M. Ellison, Jr., "Negro Suffrage in Texas and Its Exercise" (Mss., M.A. Thesis, Colorado State College of Education, 1943), pp. 84-86. John Temple Graves, the southern journalist, has stated that the poll tax operates more against white than Negro voting and that, with or without the poll tax, the South knows a score of ways to keep the Negro from voting. *The Fighting South* (New York, 1943), pp. 159-240.

that the tax tends to bear more harshly upon individuals at the bottom of the economic scale than upon those higher up.   It has this effect whatever the race of the individual.   Because many southern Negroes are in the lowest income group, the tax will operate to discourage them from voting providing other more effective methods of disfranchisement are removed. Groups like Negroes and Texas Mexican-Americans, standing on the fringes of society, in it but not of it, have little incentive to meet a tax requirement for voting since the society gives them no encouragement to participate in its political processes. These are also the economically depressed groups, a fact which further aids in discouraging them from paying a voting tax. The poll tax is not the primary cause of their failure to participate in elections.   They do not participate because society dissuades them from doing so.   A tax requirement aids to some extent to achieve this end.

Although it is logical that a tax on voting should be a greater deterrent to those at the bottom of the economic ladder than to those on higher rungs, the lower classes, judged economically, vote at a reduced rate in sections where there is no poll tax as well as where there is one.   Studies of voting behavior have consistently disclosed that participation declines at each stage down the economic scale.[26]   Thus, the groups least able to pay a poll tax are also the ones least interested in voting. This fact undoubtedly helps to explain why tax repeal has not been followed by greater increases in turnout.   The analysis also indicated that, as a result of higher incomes and reduced value of the dollar, the poll tax is no longer the economic burden that it once was and, therefore, a close relationship between income and poll tax payment may not exist.

The one-party, or no-party, system[27] of the South is largely responsible for the political ills of the region.   Lack of political competition and lack of an effective party organization affect election turnout.   Similarly, they affect the extent to which citizens pay their poll taxes.   The analysis yielded an indication

[26] Key, *Politics, Parties, and Pressure Groups* (3rd ed., New York, 1952), pp. 571-75.
[27] See Key, *Southern Politics*, p. 385.

of a relation between party competition and poll tax payment. Although not conclusive, the results showed a tendency for party competition to encourage more persons to pay the tax. Competition within a single party undoubtedly has the same effect although this factor was not specifically tested. The effect of intra-party rivalry over a juicy political plum may be seen in Table 5 which shows the effect upon poll tax collections of an election for probate judge in an Alabama county.[28] The poll tax may be paid at a higher rate in some areas than in others because of a more effective and better organized political machine or because of a particularly intense election contest.

The methods used did not reveal all groups who are adversely affected by a poll tax requirement and all factors which influence poll tax payment. Other methods, such as the sampling procedure made familiar by the Gallup Poll, would have to be used to explore this question further. Since studies of voting behavior have generally shown that women vote less frequently than men, it is probable that such an approach would reveal that fewer women pay the poll tax than men. Examination of the form of the tax indicated that the tax tends to bear more harshly on women than men and analysis of the results of poll tax repeal in Louisiana and of reduction of the cumulative feature in Alabama disclosed that more white women had been prevented from voting by the tax than either white men or Negroes.

[28] See p. 81.

7. REPEAL BY STATES–I

IN PRECEDING CHAPTERS, the poll tax has been examined as to its origins, its forms, its administration, its relation to political corruption, and its disfranchising effects. The remainder of this study is devoted to the movement to repeal the tax. This movement, especially the attempt to enact a national anti-poll tax bill, focused public attention upon the tax. Out of it came charges and counter charges about the tax and its political effects. Since the repeal movement has played so important a role in the recent history of the southern poll tax, the following chapters will consider this movement: (1) in those states where the tax has been abolished; (2) in those states retaining it as a suffrage requirement; and (3) in the national government.

NORTH CAROLINA

Poll tax repeal attracted little attention in the southern state where the tax was first removed as a voting requirement. When the voters of North Carolina decided in 1920 to abolish the tax, they did not vote separately on this question. Five amendments were presented, three in one group and two in another. Poll tax repeal was grouped with an amendment reducing the residence requirements for voting. The other amendments pertained to taxation; the most important one authorized an income tax. Although the two amendments applicable to the suffrage were separated from the strictly tax amendments, all amendments tended to be considered together. They were debated throughout the state but discussion was confined primarily to the merits or demerits of the income tax amendment.

The removal of the poll tax attracted no unusual attention.[1]

Abolition of the poll tax and reduction of the residence requirements were approved by 235,608 to 83,366 votes. Only 26.1 per cent of those voting opposed. Of the 100 counties, only eight had a majority vote against the amendments and only nineteen had a vote over forty per cent against them. These amendments, which were directed toward easing restrictions on voting, received more support than the disfranchising amendment of 1900. Support came from all sections. Slight opposition was registered primarily in the eastern half of the state, the area of Negro concentration. Of the eight counties casting a majority vote against the amendments, three had a Negro population of more than 50 per cent, one of 44.6 per cent and two of just over 31 per cent. These counties are in the middle and eastern part of the state.[2] However, two counties had a Negro population of less than twenty per cent and were situated in the western half of the state although not along the western border.[3] It was shown in Chapter 1 that the chief objection to adoption of the disfranchising amendment of 1900 came from the western, mountainous, predominantly white section of the state. The vote on poll tax repeal and shorter residence periods shows a tendency for the main opposition to come from areas with a large proportion of Negroes. This fact indicates that some persons believed poll tax repeal and lower residence requirements would encourage Negro voting.

LOUISIANA

Poll tax repeal received more attention and publicity in other states where the tax was abolished than it did in North Carolina. Huey Long was the chief figure in the Louisiana repeal movement. Long ruled Louisiana in 1934. With his backing, repeal was achieved without great difficulty. The Kingfish did not support repeal because of any philosophical convictions concerning the right of the majority to vote in a democracy.

1 Walter J. Matherly, "The Repeal of the Poll Tax in the South," *Proceedings of the National Conference of Social Work, 1942,* pp. 130-31.

2 Durham, Halifax, Orange, Pitt, Vance, and Warren. For county-by-county figures, see *North Carolina Manual, 1923,* pp. 341-42.

3 Gaston and Stanly.

He favored repeal because he felt that it would redound to his advantage. Most of his support came from lower income groups, those who were most directly injured by a tax upon the suffrage. The poll tax drained the funds of his organization since it was necessary to pay it for many of his followers. Its removal would relieve this drain and might help to swell the ranks of Long supporters.

Another possible reason for Long's action was that he believed poll tax repeal would enable him to destroy the remaining centers of opposition to his rule. The principal surviving opposition was in parishes ruled by sheriffs who had paid the poll taxes of large numbers of voters and thus controlled their votes. Huey desired to free these voters from their obligations to their local sheriffs—"to free them so they would be able to vote for the Kingfish."

The main fight for approval of the Louisiana repeal amendment occurred in the House of Representatives. Only one dissenting vote was cast in the Senate. The vote in the House was 68 to 30. Constitutional amendments in Louisiana require approval of two-thirds of the total membership of each house. Since there were 100 members in the House, the poll tax repeal amendment carried with a margin of one vote to spare. According to an AF of L representative, the three principal economic interests in the state—sugar, oil, and lumber—wanted the tax retained. Since these interests had been instrumental in securing the election of several members of the legislature, they exercised considerable control in that body. Before the poll tax amendment came to a vote, Long lacked about three votes in the House for the necessary two-thirds. Someone suggested to the AF of L representative that the needed votes could be obtained if organized labor would come out with a handbill indicating support for repeal. Accordingly, a number of such handbills were printed and placed on the desks of the legislators. Shortly thereafter, the proposed amendment carried.

The House members who opposed repeal came from the northern and middle portions of the state and from the parish of Orleans.[4] A comparison between this vote and the centers

4 Representatives from the following parishes voted against repeal: Caddo (one nay to three yeas); Calcasieu (also a yea vote); Claiborne; East Baton Rouge;

of anti-Long strength shows that most of the parishes whose representatives voted against repeal were anti-Long parishes. Of the fifteen parishes with at least one representative against poll tax abolition, ten parishes were consistently anti-Long.[5] This fact indicates that some representatives may have opposed the proposed amendment simply because Long was backing it. It also supports the statement of the AF of L member that the economic interests were opposed, since these interests were anti-Long. The parishes whose representatives voted against repeal also tended to have large Negro populations. Nine of these fifteen parishes had a Negro population in excess of forty per cent; six of the nine had a Negro population over fifty per cent.

After the proposed amendment won legislative approval, no further difficulty arose in securing its ratification by popular referendum. The vote was overwhelmingly in support of repeal, 154,394 to 31,719. Of those voting, 83 per cent favored abolition.[6] Most of the opposition came from the northern part of the state and from parishes bordering the Mississippi River. A relationship exists between the House vote against poll tax repeal and the principal opposition in the popular referendum. The opposition came from parishes with a heavy Negro population. Of the fifteen parishes with the highest proportion of Negroes, eleven were among the sixteen with the largest percentage voting against the amendment. This fact indicates that the voters in these parishes believed the poll tax was an effective means of disfranchising Negroes, a belief which also appeared to be present fourteen years earlier in North Carolina.[7]

East Feliciana; Madison; Orleans (thirteen nays and six yeas); Ouachita (also a yea vote); Richland; St. Helena; St. Mary (also a yea vote; the one opposition vote in the Senate came from this parish); Vermilion; West Baton Rouge; West Feliciana; and Winn.

[5] For the location of the areas of anti-Long strength, see Key, *Southern Politics*, Figure 34, p. 177.

[6] For the parish-by-parish vote, see Heard and Strong, p. 76.

[7] The sixteen parishes with a vote of 27 per cent and above against the amendment were: Madison, 56.3; DeSoto, 55.2; Claiborne, 44.9; Tensas, 42.9; East Carroll, 38.6; Lincoln, 37.9; Morehouse, 37.5; Caddo, 34.2; Iberville, 33.6; Richland, 33.6; East Feliciana, 30.5; Rapides, 28.6; Bossier, 28.1; Franklin, 27.2; West Feliciana, 27.1; Concordia, 27.0.

Huey Long did not make voting easy by obtaining poll tax repeal. The tax was replaced by a requirement that, for two years prior to an election, a voter must, in addition to being registered, sign his name on the sheriff's poll book and get a sheriff's certificate that he had done so. He was supposed to present the certificate before voting. This procedure was revoked in 1940. At present, citizens may qualify to vote by complying with the usual requirements governing registration of voters.[8]

FLORIDA

The movement for poll tax abolition in Florida was led primarily by the liberal wing of the Democratic party, the so-called New Dealers. This faction was headed by Claude Pepper, at that time a United States senator.

Several attempts to lift the tax were made in the Florida legislature before repeal was finally achieved in 1937. Senator Arthur Gomez of Key West introduced repeal measures in 1931, 1933, and 1935. Several measures were proposed in the 1937 session. The one sponsored by Representative Robert L. Hodges of Orange County won approval. It did not abolish the poll tax completely but merely repealed that part of the law which made its payment a voting requirement.[9]

The vote on the repeal proposal indicates that it passed without difficulty. It was approved by 69 to 21 in the House and 32 to 4 in the Senate.[10] The measure passed the House with ease but it did not get by the more conservative Senate as easily.

Florida's legislature had a "pet bills night" at the close of each session. By this device, the legislators could get a "pet bill" considered before adjournment. They drew numbers and,

---

[8] *Acts of Louisiana, 1934*, Act 230, pp. 710-12; *ibid., 1940*, Act 374, pp. 1409-10; *ibid., 1942*, "Constitutional Amendments 1940," p. 3. See also Matherly, p. 131.

[9] Virginia D. Collins, pp. 42-43. In 1941, the tax was completely repealed by legislative action. It could be restored at any time because the constitution was not amended to forbid the legislature from doing so.

[10] *Ibid.*

in numerical order, were permitted to present one bill for immediate consideration. Only non-controversial legislation could be offered. Otherwise debate would ensue and tie up the proceedings, thereby defeating the purpose of the practice.

Senators John R. Beacham of West Palm Beach and Ernest R. Graham of Miami led in pushing the poll tax measure through in this manner. Senator Graham believed that he could not be re-elected if the poll tax remained in effect. Racing and gambling groups in his district, Dade County, bought votes by paying poll taxes. The senator felt that the racing interests, with their money and poll tax purchasing practices, would defeat him. Realizing that the opponents of repeal planned to let the bill die in committee, the two senators decided to use the pet bill procedure to get the proposal before the Senate. Senator Graham arranged to be one of the last to present a pet bill, thus avoiding any challenges from the opposition concerning the controversial nature of his measure. The two senators who were to present bills after him were not opposed to repeal and did not object when Senator Graham offered his bill. When the proposal was before the Senate, many senators who did not want it feared to oppose it because of public support for abolition. According to Representative Hodges, who introduced the bill, it would not have passed the Senate except for this maneuver.

Following the surprise passage of the poll tax measure, speculation arose as to what Governor Fred P. Cone would do. Senator Graham went to see him in the governor's mansion where he was ill in bed. To find out his attitude toward the bill, he asked the governor for one of the pens which he would use in signing it. The governor replied that he was not sure that he would sign it; that it was not a good bill. As Senator Graham was leaving, he met a close associate of the governor who lived as one of the family in the governor's mansion. The senator approached him with his problem. The governor's confidant also indicated that he did not favor the bill and suggested that since Senator Graham would receive credit for getting it through the Senate, he had no reason to worry about it any more. The senator explained that he would be defeated unless the tax were repealed. The governor's friend then promised to do what he could. Shortly thereafter Governor Cone signed the bill.[11]

The poll tax was abolished in Florida largely because it was being used to influence elections. Senator Graham supported its removal for this reason. The House sponsor, Representative Hodges, stated that opposition to the tax arose because political machines in many large cities were buying tax receipts and were using them to control elections. He introduced the measure at the request of a labor leader. Labor favored abolition because it could not raise sufficient funds to purchase tax receipts in competition with business, gambling and racing interests. In this connection, the time of repeal is important, the depression period of the thirties. Due to the depression, many white voters were reluctant or unable to pay poll taxes and were disfranchised unless their taxes were paid for them. Politicians had difficulty in raising the money needed to pay the poll taxes of prospective supporters. Therefore, the economic effects of the tax during a period of depression helped to create a demand for its elimination as a voting requirement.

Apparently Senator Pepper and his supporters advocated repeal because they felt that such action would redound to Senator Pepper's advantage in the 1938 senatorial election. The argument is that many local politicians who controlled poll tax receipts were displeased with Senator Pepper's New Deal record; that Pepper and his supporters feared defeat if the old system were continued; and that they felt they could increase their support by getting the tax abolished.[12]

In addition, the 1937 legislature has been characterized as a "liberal legislature" and as one inclined to be sympathetic to poll tax repeal. The race issue was not injected into the controversy and was not a factor in the fight.

An important objection to poll tax abolition in Florida involved the revenue feature of the tax. The relationship between the tax and the schools has been a standard defense for retention of this voting requirement. The first tax repeal

[11] An unsuccessful effort was made to restore the poll tax at the next session of the legislature.

[12] Stoney, "Suffrage in the South: The Poll Tax," p. 42.

measure voted on in the 1937 House was defeated largely because of opposition by the school lobby. This group was apparently won over by an agreement to increase state grants-in-aid to the counties for teachers' salaries. Subsequently, the Hodges bill passed. Retention of the tax until 1941 as a revenue measure was probably another concession to the school group.

GEORGIA

In Georgia, poll tax repeal was achieved in 1945 when Ellis Arnall was governor. The repeal movement began in October, 1944 when it was announced that a group of southerners would undertake a study of the effects of the poll tax upon the suffrage.[13] The initiative for this proposed study came from Roscoe C. Martin, then director of the Bureau of Public Administration at the University of Alabama. Mr. Martin interested Governor Arnall in the study and, in early December, 1944 the governor issued a call for a "factual appraisal of the poll tax."

As Governor of a southern state, and one which levies the poll tax, I am tired of seeing the South attacked by those in other sections of our country because some of our southern states require the payment of a poll tax as a prerequisite for voting. Its operation may be injurious to our governmental processes, and again it may not have that effect at all. I think it is time for us in the South to take stock and find out for ourselves what practical effects the poll tax has.

To that end a factual, careful study of the poll tax is needed and should be made. So far most of the agitation for and against the poll tax and most of the discussion about it have been based on prejudice and emotion rather than on impartial analysis of concrete facts. In simple truth, not much is known about the poll tax, beyond what casual observation teaches, for no careful study of that tax in operation has been made. It is this lack of an adequate factual basis for consideration of the poll tax that the proposed study is designed to remedy.

The governor indicated that he would defend the tax if it was found wise to do so and that he would condemn it if it was

13 New York *Times,* October 25, 1944.

found to be injurious to democratic institutions. He emphasized that the tax was a state, not a national, problem.[14]

Shortly after Governor Arnall's announcement, a Committee
of Editors and Writers of the South held an interracial conference in Atlanta. Mark Ethridge, publisher of the Louisville
Courier Journal, was primarily responsible for the conference
and served as its chairman. The officers of the Southern Conference for Human Welfare also helped to organize the meeting.

The conference gave special attention to the poll tax. In
discussing the purpose of the meeting, Mr. Ethridge noted that
the legislatures of seven of the then eight poll tax states were
soon to meet. He hoped that the conference would provide
editors and others with useful information in supporting poll
tax repeal.[15] Ralph McGill, editor of the Atlanta *Constitution*
and advisor to Governor Arnall, attempted to prevent the meeting because of its possible effect upon the governor's stand on
the poll tax. The governor's position was that he had not
made up his mind about the tax and that he would not until
the proposed poll tax study had been completed. Mr. McGill
did not want the governor to be forced into committing himself at this time.

The conference received considerable publicity. It made a
strong appeal for poll tax abolition. Governor Arnall's suggestion for a poll tax study to take a year was criticized as an
unnecessary evasion of an issue which should be settled immediately.[16]

The next development was a surprising one. Eugene Talmadge, Georgia's perennial governor, race-baiter and cracker
politician, came out in an editorial in his newspaper, *The
Statesman,* for poll tax repeal. His editorial appeared just

[14] Memphis *Commercial Appeal,* December 10, 1944. The idea for a factual
study of the poll tax was later expanded into a study of the electoral process in
the South. The results are in Key's *Southern Politics.* See "Foreword," p. vi.
See also Rowland Egger and Weldon Cooper, *Research, Education, and Regional-
ism: The Bureau of Public Administration of the University of Alabama, 1938-
1948* (University, Ala., 1949), p. 95.

[15] New York *Times,* December 22, 1944.

[16] Clark Foreman, "Georgia Kills the Poll Tax," *New Republic,* CXII (February 26, 1945), 291.

before the 1945 session of the legislature. John Temple Graves commented:

Ole Gene, meanwhile, has come out against the poll tax, to the awful embarrassment of some of his grass roots friends but with a political wisdom that is going to pay dividends. It won't be hard for him to make his followers see that the poll tax has nothing to do with Negro voting. Neither should it be hard to make them see that, with Gene among the 'outs' now, a broadening of the franchise is indicated. When you control the machine you want as few voters as possible so that the machine's proportion will be as big as possible. But when somebody else's machine controls, you need some new voters from the hills to swamp it.[17]

On January 9, 1945, Governor Arnall urged the legislature to study the question of poll tax abolition carefully but did not advocate repeal.[18] But on January 23, he suddenly asked for repeal and announced that if the legislature did not act, he would suspend the tax by executive order.[19] The governor was forced to take this step by Talmadge's surprise move.

Soon after the appearance of Talmadge's editorial, Mr. Frank McCallister, head of the Georgia Workers Education Service, lunched with Mrs. Roosevelt at the White House. He showed the Talmadge editorial to the First Lady because he feared that the Talmadge forces were taking the "ball" away from Governor Arnall and the liberals. He asked Mrs. Roosevelt to call the matter to the attention of the President and she promised to do so. Later she wrote him that the President had telephoned Governor Arnall and suggested that he take positive action. Soon afterwards the governor made his strong request for repeal to the legislature. John Temple Graves commented:

The governor has just asked for repeal of the tax, and the picture of brave and liberal leadership is dimmed by this Talmadge support. It is dimmed, too, by the fact that Governor Arnall waited too long to take the step.[20]

The legislature acted quickly on the governor's suggestion. By February 5, both houses had agreed on a repeal proposal

---

[17] Birmingham *Age-Herald,* January 18, 1945.
[18] New York *Times,* January 10, 1945.
[19] *Ibid.,* January 24, 1945.
[20] Birmingham *Age-Herald,* January 18, 1945.

and on a permanent registration system.[21] The vote in the House was 141 to 51 and, in the Senate, 41 to 3.[22] The name of Henry Wallace was frequently mentioned in the debate. Opponents of repeal asserted that the legislation stemmed from his address at the 1944 Democratic convention in Chicago in which he said that the poll tax must go.[23] They emphasized Governor Arnall's support of Roosevelt and Wallace.[24]

Since 1945, attempts have been made by supporters of Herman Talmadge to restore the principle of a poll tax in Georgia. Outright restoration of the tax was not tried. Rather it was proposed to alter the voter registration system by providing for biennial, rather than permanent, registration and requiring payment of a $1.00 fee at each registration period. The fee would have been a poll tax in disguise. However, this scheme was not adopted. Georgia's registration laws were rewritten in 1949 but the permanent registration system was continued and no fee was levied.[25]

SOUTH CAROLINA

Repeal of the South Carolina poll tax was completed in 1951. For some time before repeal, many South Carolinians recognized that their tax had little significance since it did not apply to primary elections nor to women, was non-cumulative and amounted to only $1.00 per year.

If there was a widespread belief that the tax had outlived its usefulness as a voting restriction, why was it not removed sooner? Political leaders excused their failure to act on the ground that the threat of federal action forced them to defend the tax. United States Senator Burnet R. Maybank told a Senate committee in 1948:

[21] *Georgia Laws, 1945,* p. 129.

[22] Knoxville *Journal,* February 6, 1945.

[23] Birmingham *Age-Herald,* January 25, 1945.

[24] A new state constitution was under consideration when poll tax abolition was approved. Despite agitation for poll tax repeal, the constitutional commission, chaired by Governor Arnall, did not at first eliminate the tax requirement from the suffrage article. The proposed constitution was altered following repeal by the legislature. See Saye, I, 95-101; II, 540 and 553.

[25] *Georgia Laws, 1949,* pp. 1204-27.

We have tried on several occasions to repeal it. Each time we have had a bill up before the legislature, there has been agitation from Washington that has hurt us in our effort to repeal the tax. We hope that this committee will not report the bill out. We hope that it will be left with us in South Carolina to repeal it when we are able to do so.[26]

This excuse was not valid. The threat of federal action encouraged, rather than discouraged, the repeal movement in South Carolina. Because of lack of concern about this tax, it is doubtful that any serious efforts to lift it would have been made if attention had not been first focused on it by congressional action. When he was governor, J. Strom Thurmond asked for repeal by the state to prevent national action.[27]

A constitutional amendment to repeal the poll tax was readily approved by the legislature in 1949. The Senate passed it without opposition on February 1; the House of Representatives adopted it by a vote of 89 to 7 on March 3.[28] The seven negative votes came primarily from the upcountry, the area with a predominantly white population and with lower income levels than the coastal section.[29] If the tax seriously restricted voting by whites in South Carolina, it is doubtful that opposition would have come from this section.

Until 1949, the House had prevented adoption of a poll tax repeal resolution. It rejected the proposal in 1946 and 1947. The chief opponent was Representative Calhoun Thomas from Beaufort County, the southernmost coastal county and a county with a large Negro population. He relied upon the cliché that poll tax repeal would enable many Negroes to vote in general elections. Negro voting might bring racial trouble in the low-country counties. Representative Thomas also argued that

[26] *Hearings on H. R. 29*, p. 104. Senator Olin D. Johnston testified similarly. See p. 134. Both men had been governors of the state.

[27] New York *Times*, July 19, 1948; Columbia *Record*, October 30 and November 1, 1950.

[28] *Journal of the Senate*, 1st sess., 88th General Assembly, South Carolina, pp. 106-07, and *Journal of the House of Representatives*, 1st sess., 88th General Assembly, South Carolina, p. 535.

[29] Negative votes were cast by representatives from the following counties: Anderson, Clarendon, Lancaster, Saluda, Spartanburg, and Union.

South Carolina would have a two-party system if voting were made too easy.[30]

Why was poll tax repeal approved so readily by the House in 1949 when it was defeated in preceding sessions? Apparently approval for repeal was delayed until settlement of litigation over South Carolina's white primary. The federal court decisions in 1947 and 1948 which invalidated South Carolina's attempts to evade the Allwright decision made leaders of the state realize that election reform was in order.[31] Therefore, the legislature was ready to repeal the poll tax and to adopt a general election law. The poll tax abolition resolution was approved first. A general election law was considered in 1949 but was not enacted until 1950. It made the voting qualifications for the Democratic primary identical with those for the general election and thereby permitted Negroes to participate.[32] Poll tax repeal in South Carolina rode in on the coattails of a general election reform movement which resulted from the advice of District Judge J. Waties Waring to his fellow Carolinians that "it is time to fall in step with the other states and to adopt the American way of conducting elections."[33]

Another reason for legislative approval of poll tax repeal in 1949 was the belief that South Carolina's congressmen would thereby be strengthened in their efforts to defeat the federal anti-poll tax bill. Some of the state senators who sponsored the resolution were close political friends of the state's congressmen. They decided that if action to remove the tax were begun within the state, a weapon would be provided their Washington representatives in arguing against the federal bill.

---

[30] "Why South Carolina Keeps the Poll Tax," *Christian Century*, LXIII (February 6, 1946), 166; Kenneth J. Foreman, "South Carolina Retains Poll Tax," p. 243. Calhoun Thomas was not a member of the House in 1949 when the repeal proposal passed.

[31] The cases were *Elmore* v. *Rice*, 72 F. Supp. 516 (1947), *Rice* v. *Elmore*, 165 F (2d) 387 (1948) and 333 U. S. 875 (1948), and *Brown* v. *Baskin*, 78 F. Supp. 933 (1948). For a discussion of South Carolina's white primary and these cases, see Key, *Southern Politics*, pp. 626-32.

[32] *Acts of South Carolina, 1950*, No. 858, pp. 2059-2116 and Henry Lesesne, "Summing Up in South Carolina," New York *Herald-Tribune*, October 21, 1950.

[33] *Elmore* v. *Rice*, 72 F. Supp. 516, 528 (1947).

The state legislature acted when southern senators were filibustering to save the filibuster. The attempt to amend the rules of the United States Senate was made as a preliminary to consideration of the Truman civil rights program. Thus, the time for state action was opportune.

The legislature took the lead in abolishing the poll tax. Although Governor Thurmond advocated repeal, he did not work actively for it. It is unlikely that he was instrumental in getting the resolution introduced since at least one of the Senate sponsors, W. Lewis Wallace, was his bitter opponent. Within the legislature, the conservatives led the movement. Liberals or progressives are usually assumed to be behind a reform of this kind. The proposal originated in the Senate, the more conservative branch of the legislature, and passed without opposition. The sponsors were classed among the more conservative members of the Senate.[34] The measure was not introduced at the insistence of any state-wide labor, Negro or veterans' organizations. Legislative approval of poll tax repeal in South Carolina resulted from the decision of conservative leaders that the time for repeal had arrived.

The outstanding fact about poll tax repeal following legislative approval was the lack of interest in the proposal. No one seemed concerned whether the tax was eliminated or retained, thereby proving that it had ceased to have any significance as a suffrage requirement.[35] Governor Thurmond urged approval for all of the three state-wide constitutional amendments, one of which was the poll tax amendment.[36] Many state newspapers supported abolition of the tax but generally little interest was

---

[34] The resolution was sponsored by Senators W. Lewis Wallace, O. T. Wallace, Wilbur G. Grant, and J. Ralph Gasque of York, Charleston, Chester, and Marion counties respectively.

[35] Alderman Duncan, "S. C. Expected to Eliminate Poll Tax," Columbia *Record,* October 30, 1950; Henry Lesesne, "Summing Up in South Carolina," and "Poll Tax Loses Ground," New York *Herald-Tribune,* October 21 and November 12, 1950.

[36] Columbia *Record,* November 1, 1950. Amendment No. 1 provided for elimination of the poll tax. Since it did not cover municipal elections, Amendment No. 2 proposed lifting the tax from these elections. It was approved by a smaller vote than Amendment No. 1.

shown. No organizations fought for repeal, with the possible exception of the NAACP, and even the NAACP was not very active in the movement.

The negative attitude toward poll tax repeal was clearly revealed in the results of the referendum held on November 7, 1950. Only 38,490 citizens bothered to vote; 28,030 approved and 10,460 opposed. Poll tax removal was, therefore, favored by 72.8 per cent of those who voted. Most opposition votes were recorded in the southern part of the state, the area of many Negroes. A majority voted against repeal in only two of the 46 counties, Dorchester, 50.7 per cent, and Jasper, 51.6 per cent. They are southern counties with a population over fifty per cent Negro. In only five counties was the vote between fifty and sixty per cent for repeal. In all others, it was more than sixty per cent for abolition. Two of the five counties in the fifty to sixty per cent range, Beaufort and Hampton, are in the southern section and have large Negro populations. Another, Calhoun, is centrally located but also has a heavy concentration of Negroes. The remaining two, Newberry and Greenville, are in the northwestern section and have smaller, although not insignificant, Negro populations. Analysis of the vote indicates that little interest in poll tax repeal was aroused, that little opposition was encountered, and that the opposition which developed came primarily from counties with large Negro populations. The last point shows the persistence of the belief in the tax as a device to disfranchise Negroes.[37]

The vote on poll tax repeal cannot be said to represent public opinion on this issue in South Carolina. It represented the opinion of courthouse politicians that the time for removal of the tax had arrived. The smallness of the vote is apparent when it is noted that, as of 1950, the state had a population of 760,843 whites 21 and over. Based solely on the white adult population, the per cent who voted on the poll tax amendment was only 5.1. Simultaneously, more votes were cast for James F. Byrnes, the Democratic gubernatorial candidate, than for

[37] For the county-by-county figures, see *Supplemental Report of the Secretary of State to the General Assembly of South Carolina,* Election November 7, 1950, p. 35.

the poll tax amendment. Mr. Byrnes received more than 50,000 votes without any real opposition.[38]

Elimination of South Carolina's poll tax became final on February 13, 1951 when, in accordance with the constitutional amendment process, the legislature ratified the repeal amendment.[39]

TENNESSEE

Poll tax repeal in Tennessee was completed in 1953 although the tax ceased to be of any significance as a suffrage requirement in 1951. Because of the difficulty of amending the constitution, a law was adopted on February 28, 1951, which indirectly killed the tax. The measure provided that only the tax assessed for the year 1871 had to be paid to qualify for voting. Since few, if any, male voters were alive who were liable for a poll tax eighty years ago, the act meant that Tennessee no longer had an effective poll tax. Finally, as a result of a limited constitutional convention, an amendment providing for elimination of the tax was adopted on November 3, 1953.

Efforts to repeal the poll tax in the Volunteer State began more than thirty years before they were successful but it was not until the 1938 gubernatorial campaign that the issue became an important one in state politics.[40] The high point in the movement begun in 1938 was reached in 1943 when the legislature repealed the tax only to have it restored in short order by the Tennessee Supreme Court. Silliman Evans, owner and publisher of the Nashville *Tennessean,* and Jennings Perry, its editor, began and led the 1938-1943 fight. In the course of the campaign, the Chattanooga *Times,* Knoxville *News-Sentinel,* and Memphis *Press-Scimitar* gave their support.

Although the *Tennessean* was very voluble in its campaign for poll tax abolition, the sincerity of the paper's stand has

---

38 A total of nine votes was cast for six additional persons.

39 *Acts of South Carolina, 1951,* No. 23, pp. 24-25.

40 Henry N. Williams, "The Poll Tax and Constitutional Problems Involved in its Repeal," *University of Chicago Law Review,* XI (February, 1944), 177.

been questioned. Observers believed that Silliman Evans was more interested in fighting Edward H. Crump, the Memphis boss and state political puppeteer, than in lifting the poll tax. In large measure, he turned the fight against the tax into a fight against Boss Crump.[41] Although Crump announced in favor of repeal (probably with tongue in cheek), the *Tennessean* worked to bind him and the tax together in the public mind. By so doing, the *Tennessean* may have forced the "Red Snapper" into defending the tax and fighting back. Repeal of Tennessee's poll tax might have been accomplished sooner if the *Tennessean* had not been so vigorous in attacking Mr. Crump.[42]

In its anti-poll tax fight, the *Tennessean* received aid from organizations like the League of Women Voters, Railroad Brotherhoods, Grange, Farm Bureau, Industrial Council, Parent-Teacher Association, and YWCA. These groups united into a Committee for Majority Rule. The committee was not very effective. The ties that bound the groups composing it were weak and the committee met only once. Individual members of some of these organizations worked hard but the organizations linked in a Committee for Majority Rule were of little importance in the repeal movement.[43]

When the Tennessee legislature eliminated the poll tax in 1943, it removed the tax both as a voting prerequisite and as a revenue measure.[44] Abolition by legislative act alone without a constitutional change was short-lived. Approximately six weeks after the act passed, Sheriff Burch Biggs of Polk County brought suit challenging its constitutionality. Sheriff Biggs was the political power in the piedmont counties of lower

[41]Although not stated, this point is evident in Jennings Perry's *Democracy Begins at Home,* which tells the story of this effort to repeal the Tennessee poll tax.

[42] Further support for this charge against Mr. Evans arises from the fact that the *Tennessean* did not give significant attention to an anti-poll tax measure introduced in the 1947 legislature until it was apparent that the Crump faction opposed it. Then the paper gave the bill front page publicity. Other newspapers in the state had been giving the proposal publicity all along.

[43] Perry, pp. 102 and 132.

[44] *Public Acts of Tennessee, 1943,* Chapters 37 and 38.

Tennessee, in the area of Ducktown and the Tennessee Copper Company.[45]

Sheriff Biggs brought his suit under the state's Declaratory Judgment Act. He contended that the poll tax could be removed only by a constitutional amendment. He asked for an injunction to forbid the Polk County election commission from conducting an election without requiring payment of the tax and to prevent the Tennessee secretary of state and comptroller from defraying the expenses of such an election.[46] The case was first heard in the chancery court of Polk County with Chancellor T. L. Stewart presiding.[47] The Chancellor ruled in May, 1943, and sustained the plea of Sheriff Biggs. The case then went to the State Supreme Court.

About the time *Biggs* v. *Beeler* came before the Supreme Court, a change occurred in its membership. A vacancy was filled by Frank H. Gailor of Memphis. Before appointment, the new justice was a loyal Crump supporter. Another justice, Alan Prewitt, was known as a Crump man. Both Prewitt and Alexander Chambliss were regarded as being primarily politicians rather than judges. The remaining justices, Chief Justice Grafton Green and Justice A. B. Neil, were characterized as able and conscientious men who would not allow interference with their judicial independence.[48] The court divided according to this classification of its membership. Justices Chambliss, Prewitt, and Gailor supported Chancellor Stewart's decision and held the statutory repeal measures unconstitutional while Justices Green and Neil dissented on the ground that legislative

[45] Sheriff Biggs addressed a Democratic caucus of the state legislature at the time of passage of the repeal measure. He said he and his son, Broughton, could not continue to deliver Democratic majorities if abolition succeeded. He warned that many Republicans would be elected to the legislature if the tax were repealed. When his suit had its first hearing, he is supposed to have advised the press that "there won't be a Democrat in office in East Tennessee" if the repeal law should be upheld. Perry, p. 224.

[46] Perry, p. 222; *Constitution*, Art. II, sec. 28; Art. IV, sec. 1, and Art. XI, sec. 12.

[47] Chancellor Stewart was the father of Tom Stewart, a Crump protégé and United States senator at the time.

[48] Perry, pp. 225-31.

acts which repealed previous statutes were not unconstitutional.[49]

Justice Chambliss read the majority opinion. He held that the poll tax constitutional provisions were mandatory but not self-executing. In answer to the question whether the legislature, after it had effected a constitutional mandate, could later revoke what it had done, Justice Chambliss ruled that it could not. He admitted that he could not support his position by citation of any previous case and that the general rule is that a succeeding legislature may revoke the act of a former one. He indicated that the court was dealing with an exception to this general rule.

. . . we have here a case where a constitutional mandate, if originally "dormant" and "inoperative," has had vitality breathed into it, has been "rendered effective by supplemental legislation," is now a live, active, operative thing, and to kill and destroy it requires affirmative action, which may be taken only by its creator through constitutional amendment, or convention, not by either the Legislature or the Courts.[50]

He stated that the constitutional mandate had been so "welded into intimate and permanent union" with the statute that the two had become one and indivisible; that the effect of divorcing the statute would be to nullify and defeat the operation of the constitutional mandate.

The minority justices took sharp issue with the majority opinion. After acidly commenting that the conclusion was not supported by any authority and was not sound in principle, Chief Justice Green stated:

Stripped of its eloquence and ethics, the substance of the majority opinion is that obedience to a mandate of the Constitution by one Legislature introduces into that instrument a warrant to this Court to compel obedience to the mandate by a subsequent Legislature. But the Legislature cannot amend the Constitution nor can it bind future Legislatures.[51]

Justice Neil wrote:

We are here faced with the incongruity, if not absolute absurdity, of being called upon to yield obedience, and compel obedience, to

49 *Biggs* v. *Beeler,* 173 S. W. (2d) 144 (1943).
50 *Ibid.,* 147.
51 *Ibid.,* 149.

a statute that has been repealed and a constitutional provision that is admittedly not self-executing, Such a thing is unknown to the history of English and American jurisprudence.[52]

It is apparent that the Tennessee Supreme Court decision was primarily political and not based upon accepted legal principles. Since the legislature had to effectuate the constitutional provisions, it should have been able to rescind its own acts. The dissenting opinions rested upon sounder legal arguments than that of the majority. A popular comment following the decision was, "We have won the popular decision and the legal decision. But Crump still 'has the votes'."[53]

The decision in the Biggs case temporarily deflated the Tennessee repeal movement. Initially the leaders believed that passage of a federal anti-poll tax measure or amendment of the state constitution were the only ways left to remove the tax. The latter course seemed impossible since, until 1953, the constitution had never been amended. Some repeal advocates, such as Jennings Perry and Silliman Evans, turned their efforts toward passage of a federal anti-poll tax bill.[54]

---

[52] *Ibid.*, 150.

[53] Quoted by Perry, p. 239. The decision was concerned primarily with the tax as a source of revenue. The tax as a suffrage requirement was not considered directly but the court ruled that its repeal as a suffrage measure was inseparable from its repeal as a revenue device. If repeal of the revenue feature were unconstitutional, repeal of the suffrage requirement was also. The opinion was criticized on the ground that since the legislature had lifted the tax as a suffrage requirement in 1871, it could do so again. This criticism failed to take into account that the case revolved around the revenue features. This part of the tax had not been set aside until 1943.

[54] J. D. Johnson, an Afton storekeeper, attempted to challenge the poll tax through the state courts. He filed a suit against the tax collectors to recover his tax. John W. Kilgo, a former Republican candidate for governor and opponent of the poll tax, was his attorney. Justice of the Peace J. B. Sentelle of Greeneville heard the case. In March, 1945, Magistrate Sentelle ruled for Mr. Johnson, despite the decision of the State Supreme Court in *Biggs* v. *Beeler*. The county and state officials involved appealed to the Circuit Court of Greene County and that court overruled the local magistrate on the basis of the Biggs decision. The case was appealed to the State and United States Supreme courts. The first court affirmed the lower court decision; the latter court refused to review it. Darel McConkey, "One Man's Fight for Everybody's Freedom," *Christian Science Monitor Magazine*, September 22, 1945, p. 4; New York *Times*, March 30, 1945, and December 24, 1946.

Other poll tax opponents sought ways of limiting, within the confines of the Biggs decision, the application of the Tennessee poll tax. Not long after this decision was announced, Henry N. Williams, a Vanderbilt professor, suggested some steps which could be taken.[55] The tax could be repealed as a suffrage requirement but retained as a revenue measure. Since the legislature removed the tax from the suffrage in 1871, precedent for such action existed and the courts would probably uphold it. It was also possible for the legislature to remove the tax as a requirement for primary and municipal elections and to exempt women, since the constitution mentioned only general elections and "all male citizens."

Action had been taken in 1941 to reduce the amount of the poll tax. While the fight for repeal was underway, the attorney general ruled that counties could eliminate their $1.00 tax. Repeal advocates worked for elimination of both county and state taxes. As a result, approximately one-third of the 95 counties dropped the local tax requirement.[56]

After 1943, bills aimed at alleviating the tax requirement were introduced in each session of the legislature but none won approval until 1949. In this session, the legislature went far in lightening the tax while remaining within the confines of the Biggs decision. The tax was lifted as a requirement for primary elections, and women, veterans of World Wars I and II, and blind persons were exempted from payment. In 1951, the legislature passed the measure which provided that only the tax assessed for the year 1871 need be paid to vote, thus indirectly abolishing the tax. This act related solely to the suffrage feature and did not remove the tax as a source of revenue.[57]

Complete repeal of the tax as a suffrage requirement was achieved in 1953. In the spring, a limited constitutional convention proposed an amendment to abolish the tax and on November 3, this amendment was approved by the voters.[58] Eight amendments were adopted at this time by a light vote;

[55] Williams, pp. 177-83.
[56] Perry, pp. 139 and 164; Nashville *Tennessean*, July 6, 1944.
[57] *Public Acts of Tennessee, 1951*, Chapter 63.
[58] New York *Times*, May 3, 31, and November 8, 1953.

the poll tax one received the largest affirmative vote, 130,751 for to 48,079 against. Even though the tax was no longer of any significance, a majority in 15 of the 95 counties voted against the repeal amendment. These counties were small, predominantly rural, and located primarily in east and middle Tennessee.[59]

In summary, the voter poll tax has been abolished in North Carolina, Louisiana, Florida, Georgia, South Carolina, and Tennessee. Practical politicians, rather than starry-eyed reformers, were primarily responsible for the success of state repeal. Although in some instances reform groups played important roles, abolition was achieved mainly because hard-headed political leaders decided that tax removal would benefit them or that the time for such action had arrived. In Louisiana, Huey Long led in eliminating the requirement because he believed this action would be to his advantage. In Florida, the movement was led by practical politicians who reasoned that tax repeal would increase the vote of groups supporting them and thus aid them in retaining their offices. These leaders represented the liberal wing in Florida politics. In Georgia, the lead was also taken by liberal forces headed by Ellis Arnall but they were given a shove by Eugene Talmadge. But in South Carolina, the initiative came from conservatives. Repeal was a by-product of attempts to evade the Allwright decision. When these attempts were nullified by federal court action, conservative political leaders decided to effect an overall suffrage reform. Removal of the poll tax, which had long ceased to have any importance as a suffrage restriction in this state, was one of the steps taken. In Tennessee, Silliman Evans

59 They were Benton, Cannon, De Kalb, Grainger, Hancock, Houston, Jackson, Macon, Overton, Perry, Robertson, Smith, Union, Van Buren, and Warren. Only two of these counties had any part of their populations classified as urban in the 1950 census. Robertson and Warren were 24.1 per cent and 34 per cent urban respectively. Robertson was also the only county with any significant number of Negroes. In 1950, 17.9 per cent of its population was non-white. Returns in the referendum obtained from Office, Secretary of State, *Constitutional Referendum Election,* November 3, 1953, mimeo.

and Jennings Perry of the Nashville *Tennessean* instituted a
vigorous fight for tax repeal in the late 1930's. This fight
largely resolved into a campaign against Boss Crump, but
created widespread public support for ending the tax requirement. Various citizen and labor groups helped. Such a
powerful climate of opinion favorable to poll tax elimination
developed that modifications in the tax requirement were
inevitable even though the state court would not permit statutory repeal. To a greater extent than in the other states,
initiative for repeal came largely from forces outside the
normal political channels. The grass-roots sentiment for repeal
forced political leaders to act and finally resulted in complete
removal of the poll tax from the suffrage.

8. REPEAL BY STATES—II

ATTEMPTS TO REPEAL THE POLL TAX have also been made in those states which still retain the tax requirement. The movement has been strongest in Virginia and Texas, relatively strong in Arkansas and Alabama, and weakest in Mississippi.

VIRGINIA

The voters of both Virginia and Texas rejected in November, 1949 constitutional amendments which would have removed the poll tax as a voting requirement. The question presented to them was in neither case as simple and straightforward as the proposal presented to the voters of South Carolina in 1950. Virginia voters were given a package of amendments which would have abolished the poll tax as a voting requirement, substituted annual for permanent registration, authorized literacy tests and a non-suffrage poll tax at a higher annual rate than the tax then in effect. In Texas, the poll tax repeal amendment was presented along with nine other proposals, some of them exceedingly unpopular. In addition, the Texas repeal amendment carried a proposal for annual registration and authorized the legislature to prescribe a registration fee.

The Virginia poll tax repeal movement goes back at least to 1940 when a group of liberal Virginia Democrats met and formulated a long-range campaign designed to obtain poll tax abolition and defeat of the Byrd machine. While working for increased social services, some members of this group con-

cluded that the Byrd forces and the economic groups which
benefit by and support the Byrd politics had opposed increased
expenditures for almost everything, especially for education,
health, and public welfare. They concluded that a major
reason why the organization was not more responsive to
popular needs was the restricted electorate. They also believed
that the poll tax was the keystone in maintaining this restricted
electorate. The group assumed that poll tax abolition would
result in broadening the suffrage which in turn would make
possible the defeat of the Byrd machine. The leaders were
Moss A. Plunkett of Roanoke, Francis Pickens Miller of Fair-
fax, and David George and Martin A. Hutchinson of
Richmond.

In June, 1941, some of these same liberal Democrats established the Virginia Electoral Reform League to push the fight
for poll tax abolition. The Virginia League was an outgrowth
of the Southern Electoral Reform League which was formed
February 1, 1941 by individuals interested in lifting the
southern poll tax. Moss Plunkett assumed the leadership of
the Virginia League.[1] Following its formation, the Virginia
League began an educational campaign to arouse public support for tax repeal. It also exerted pressure upon the state
legislature for a poll tax repeal constitutional amendment.

About this time, due to the efforts of Governor James H.
Price, the Virginia Advisory Legislative Council undertook a
study of the election laws.[2] In March, 1941, the council
appointed a subcommittee to study the suffrage provisions of
the state's constitution. The members were Professor Robert
K. Gooch of the Department of Political Science at the
University of Virginia, chairman; Colonel James P. Woods, a

[1] Statement of Moss A. Plunkett, *Hearings on S. 1280*, p. 72, and New York
Times, February 2, 1941. The Virginia and Southern leagues are now inactive.
Although local leagues in each poll tax state were originally planned, Georgia
was the only other state which had an active one. Those in other states
were little more than skeleton organizations since the Southern Conference for
Human Welfare had already established state units which were actively fighting
the poll tax.

[2] *Report of the Subcommittee for a Study of Constitutional Provisions Concerning Voting in Virginia*, mimeo., p. 1. Hereafter cited as *Report of the
Subcommittee*.

Roanoke attorney; and Ted Dalton, a Radford attorney and
the Republican member. They were highly regarded. Byrd
organization men were not in the majority. Senator Leonard
G. Muse of Roanoke, a member of the council, made the selec-
tions. He had the reputation of being a liberal member of the
legislature. Moss Plunkett has speculated that Senator Muse
was given the opportunity to select the subcommittee by
mistake.[3]

The subcommittee held two public hearings, one in Richmond on July 5, 1941 and the other in Roanoke on August 23,
1941. The Virginia Electoral Reform League presented a
strong case for poll tax repeal before both hearings. In its
report, the majority recommended elimination of the tax and
establishment of a registration system based on a fair, just, and
impartial literacy test.[4] Colonel Woods filed a minority report
in which he recommended lowering the tax but not abolishing
it.[5] The majority indicated its awareness of the difficulty in
carrying out its recommendations. It noted that a highly
restricted suffrage had entered into the people's habits of
thought and that "a consequent inertia exists which takes the
form of unquestioning acceptance and of unreasoned hostility
to change." It also commented that "certain elements . . .
regard the status quo as being to their continued advantage."[6]

Virginians did not learn the contents of the Gooch report
until some time after its submission. Before the General
Assembly met in January, 1942, the reports of the other two
subcommittees were published but not that of the Gooch subcommittee. The failure to publish the Gooch report was
particularly striking because the public hearings of this
subcommittee had attracted larger audiences and aroused more
interest than those of the other subcommittees. On February
12, the Richmond *Times-Dispatch* asked:

What did these eminent gentlemen find, and what did they recom-
mend? Thunderous silence has enveloped the whole matter since
early last fall. . . . We are forced reluctantly to the conclusion that

3 *Hearings on S. 1280*, p. 72.
4 *Report of the Subcommittee*, p. 2.
5 Statement of Moss A. Plunkett, *Hearings on S. 1280*, p. 73.
6 *Report of the Subcommittee*, p. 2.

the report contained a minimum of whitewash and a maximum of forthright criticism of the status quo, and that its contents did not find favor with the political powers that be....[7]

Also on February 12, the House of Delegates and Senate committees on privileges and elections held a joint hearing on a proposed poll tax repeal constitutional amendment. Among those testifying was Moss Plunkett of the Virginia Electoral Reform League. He created a sensation by reading the Gooch subcommittee report. League members had obtained a copy and decided to read it to the committees since they feared that these legislators had neither seen nor heard of the report.[8] The Richmond *Times-Dispatch* commented: "Exhumation of the Gooch subcommittee report . . . must have been a first-magnitude bombshell for those who have kept this documentary dynamite under wraps for several months...."[9] Despite the recommendations of the subcommittee and the support for them, the legislature did not at this time initiate action to repeal the tax.

The next significant development came in 1945 during the administration of Governor Colgate W. Darden, Jr. Upon the governor's recommendation, a commission was created to study the suffrage laws. It was composed of nine members with Stuart B. Campbell, a member of the House of Delegates, as chairman. Two were from the Senate, three from the House and four from outside the legislature. The Senate and House appointed their members and the governor appointed the non-legislative members. Both Democrats and Republicans were represented.[10] The commission held a series of meetings beginning in June, 1945 and reported to the governor and legislature on December 15, 1945. The suffrage amendments

---

[7] As quoted in "Foreword" to mimeographed version of *Report of the Subcommittee*, distributed by the Virginia Electoral Reform League.

[8] Statement of Moss A. Plunkett, *Hearings on S. 1280*, p. 73.

[9] February 14, 1942.

[10] Besides Mr. Campbell, the other members were: Robert C. Vaden, vice-chairman, and William D. Medley, from the Senate; Vernon C. Smith and W. R. Shaffer, from the House of Delegates; Judge John Paul, Charles J. Smith, W. L. Prieur, Jr., and J. Frank Wysor, appointed by the governor. Judge Paul and W. R. Shaffer were the Republican members.

presented to the voters in November, 1949 were based upon the recommendations of this commission.

The commission held three public hearings. Representatives of the Virginia Electoral Reform League testified. They were instructed, as previous witnesses had been instructed, not to discuss the poll tax. Despite these instructions, the League spokesmen got the commission to permit them to discuss the tax requirement.[11] Subsequently, one of the commission's recommendations supported poll tax repeal.[12]

As a substitute for the poll tax, the suffrage commission suggested an annual registration system for all voters registered since January 1, 1904.[13] It indicated that the poll tax fulfills an important function under Virginia's permanent registration system. Since registration lists are purged only occasionally, if at all, the certified lists of poll taxpayers are the only rosters of qualified voters. Abolition of the tax would require another

[11] David George represented the League and gave the standard arguments against the tax. In informal discussion with members of the commission afterwards, he remarked that, while on principle he opposed the tax, he felt that it would work to the benefit of the liberal forces eventually if it were retained. He stated that the liberals were going to start paying the tax for their people as the machine had been doing. He painted a picture of an ever-increasing union membership with the opportunity which that gave for systematic poll tax payment. He dramatized the possibility of large unions sending in large sums to qualify voters. He noted that liberal Democrats could systematize the paying of poll taxes as the organization had, the only difference being that there were more anti-organization people than organization people. Mr. George believes that his informal remarks accomplished more than his formal testimony.

[12] The commission was not unanimously agreed on this recommendation. Two of the nine members opposed, but they approved the plan proposed as a substitute should the tax be abolished. *Report of the Commission to the Governor and the General Assembly of Virginia*, Senate Document No. 8 (1946), p. 26. Hereafter cited as *Report of the Commission*. A subcommittee of the Democratic State Central Committee submitted recommendations for revision of election laws on December 1, 1945. This subcommittee was concerned about block payment of poll taxes and its recommendations relative to the tax were directed toward preventing this practice. Poll tax abolition was not suggested. Democratic State Central Committee of Virginia, *Recommendations for Revision of Election Laws*, Report of Subcommittee Appointed under Resolution of September 22, 1945, pp. 12-17.

[13] Voters registered before this date are on the "permanent roll." *Constitution*, sec. 19.

method of obtaining lists of qualified voters, and annual registration was recommended. The commission suggested that an
individual could register yearly in one of three ways: by
personal application to local boards of election; by payment,
prior to the penalty date, of all taxes, except real estate taxes,
assessed against him for the preceding year; or by voting in the
preceding year. It recommended that this registration should
be accomplished 120 days before both primary and general
elections.[14]

To compensate for the loss of poll tax revenue, the commission proposed that the General Assembly be authorized to levy
a school tax of not more than $3.00 on all residents over 21 and
that payment of this tax should be made a condition precedent
to the issuance of any license or permit for any privilege. It
also proposed that counties and cities be authorized to levy an
additional tax not to exceed $1.00 to be applied to county or
city purposes. Thus, a poll tax was to be continued and the
annual amount possibly increased but it was no longer to be
connected with the suffrage. An additional major recommendation was that the voter should be required to meet "such
tests as to literacy and such further requirements as the General
Assembly may prescribe."[15]

The recommendations of the suffrage commission did not
provide for greater ease of voting in the Old Dominion
although poll tax repeal was approved. By its suggestions for
annual voter registration to be accomplished four months
before an election and for literacy tests and "such further
requirements," its report was directed toward increasing, rather
than alleviating, restrictions on voting.

Most of these recommendations were incorporated into pro-
posed constitutional amendments which were introduced in the
House of Delegates during the 1946 session by G. Alvin
Massenburg and the three members of the commission from

[14] *Report of the Commission,* pp. 21 and 12. If this suggestion had been
adopted, the deadline for registration for primary elections would have been
about a month earlier than the poll tax deadline. For general elections, the
registration deadline would have been about two months later than the poll
tax one.

[15] *Ibid.,* pp. 14-15 and 11.

the House, Stuart B. Campbell, Vernon C. Smith, and W. R. Shaffer. They became known as the Campbell amendments. The House approved them by a 57 to 37 vote without making any major changes. C. G. Quesenbery of Waynesboro, John B. Spiers of Radford, and Robert Whitehead of Nelson led the opposition.[16] The vote in the Senate was 34 to 3. Major M. Hillard of Portsmouth, Lloyd M. Robinette of Lee, and William N. Neff of Abingdon cast the three negative votes. The Senate adopted one major change which the House approved, i.e., a provision that no tax or fee should ever be levied as a voting prerequisite.

During the 1948 session, the House approved the proposals 77 to 20. In the Senate, Senator Robinette cast the sole dissenting vote.[17] E. Blackburn Moore of Berryville, the floor leader, led the debate in the House for the amendments while Robert C. Vaden, vice-chairman of the suffrage commission, introduced them in the Senate. Delegate Whitehead led the House opposition.[18]

On the final day of the 1948 session, the General Assembly provided for submitting the Campbell amendments to the voters in November, 1949. No constitutional reason existed why the popular vote could not have been held in November, 1948. The excuse for the delay was to prevent the vote on these amendments from coinciding with the presidential election. Virginia separates national, state, and local elections. It was argued that this matter, primarily a state one, should be considered at a state election and not at a presidential election. Perhaps a more correct explanation for the postponement is that the Byrd organization did not want to contend with any change in the suffrage laws during the 1949 gubernatorial

16 Delegate Spiers was chairman of the Virginia Advisory Legislative Council when Governor Price requested it to study the election laws.

17 Amendments to the Virginia constitution must receive the approval of two successive sessions of the General Assembly and be ratified by a popular referendum. An election of a new House of Delegates must intervene between the two sessions of the General Assembly. *Constitution,* sec. 196.

18 Based upon an article entitled "Tuesday's Referendum Will Climax Study of Suffrage Changes Inaugurated in 1945," Richmond *Times-Dispatch,* November 6, 1949, sec. II.

election.[19]   These amendments, which involved changes to twelve sections of the constitution and the addition of two subsections, were presented to the voters in one package, an all or nothing affair.

The fight over the Campbell amendments both within the legislature and during the referendum campaign presented an anomalous situation.   Many persons who had been pressing hardest for poll tax repeal led the fight in opposition, while leaders of the Byrd organization, who had previously resisted abolition of the poll tax, urged approval.   Advocates of poll tax removal opposed repeal when it was presented with provisions for annual voter registration and literacy tests to be prescribed subsequently by the legislature.   In general, they argued that the amendments, although providing for poll tax abolition, would not make voting easier but would increase voting restrictions and give the Byrd machine tighter control over elections.   They urged Virginians to wait until they could get poll tax repeal with no strings attached.[20]

Although major opponents of the Byrd organization fought the Campbell amendments and top organization leaders supported them, the lines of conflict were not drawn on clear-cut pro- or anti-machine lines.   Some Byrd opponents and advocates of poll tax abolition backed the suffrage package despite its faults.   The Richmond *Times-Dispatch* stood out in this group. Editor Virginius Dabney had long supported poll tax elimination.   He felt that Virginians should take it when offered.[21]

[19] Robert H. Woods, Republican candidate for the United States Senate in 1948, stated: "But a Democrat machine, interested in controlling the gubernatorial primary next August, did not want the voting list enlarged. . . . To carry out its purpose, the Byrd-Robertson-Tuck machine had its legislative puppets defer the vote on the constitutional amendment until November, 1949." Richmond *Times-Dispatch*, October 3, 1948.

[20] One Richmond resident wrote a "Voter's Soliloquy," based upon the more famous one of Hamlet.   The dilemma presented to many Virginians by the Campbell amendments was summed up in the following lines:

   . . . To end the tax,

To end? Perchance but to begin.

   Ay, there's the rub,

For in that end of tax, what laws may come.

Adele Clark, Richmond *Times-Dispatch*, October 8, 1949.

[21] Editorials, Richmond *Times-Dispatch*, October 6 and November 6, 1949.

Neither were the amendments supported by all units of the Byrd organization. Even some of the top leaders showed little enthusiasm for the proposed changes. Many of the lower echelons were quietly opposed[22] and, as is indicated by the vote, did not support the amendments as requested by their leaders. Many county officials and local politicians, particularly those in counties with large Negro populations, opposed poll tax repeal. They wished to retain the tax because they believed that it helped to discourage a large Negro vote. Local politicians have generally tended to favor the tax requirement because they know that it is useful in keeping the electorate small and in retaining their control over the voters. In 1949, they preferred to continue with a proved method rather than to experiment with the plan offered by the suffrage commission.

Opponents of the Campbell amendments took the initiative after the amendments were placed before the voters. The supporters did not wage an aggressive campaign. Many of them did not make any public statements until shortly before the vote. Opponents, however, began their campaign early and continued right up to election day. The opposition was compounded of organizations representing labor, Negroes, veterans, and the churches. Both the CIO and AF of L were active, one through its Political Action Committee and the other through its Labor League for Political Education. Leading Negro organizations fought hard to defeat the amendments. They were the Virginia branch of the NAACP, led by Dr. J. M. Tinsley of Richmond; the Virginia Voters League, led by Dr. Luther Jackson of Petersburg; and the Virginia Civil Rights Organization, led by Dr. H. T. Penn of Roanoke. The Virginia Department of Amvets opposed the Campbell amendments as did the Virginia Council of Churches. Negro ministers associated in the Baptist Ministers' Conference voted to devote three minutes at morning services to explain to their flocks why they should vote against the amendments.

See similar viewpoint in editorial from the Norfolk *Virginian-Pilot,* reprinted in Richmond *Times-Dispatch,* October 13, 1949.

22 See Richmond *Times-Dispatch,* November 9, 1949.

Opposition to the suffrage package was bipartisan. Leading Republicans spoke against it as did the liberal anti-Byrd wing of the Democratic party. The 1949 Republican gubernatorial candidate, Walter Johnson, asked dissenting Democrats to vote for him and against the Campbell amendments, thereby defeating the Byrd machine on two counts. He promised, if elected, to push for poll tax repeal without substituting something worse. The most significant opposition came from liberal Democrats. Francis Pickens Miller and his supporters during the 1949 Democratic gubernatorial primary provided the principal leadership.[23] Senator Lloyd M. Robinette and Delegate Robert Whitehead, the chief opponents of the Campbell amendments in the legislature, also worked hard to defeat them. These opponents directed their arguments primarily against the discretionary power given to the General Assembly by the amendments, against authorization for an annual registration system with registration books closed four months before each election, and against the confused wording of the question submitted to the voters.[24]

In October, 1949, representatives of the Republican party, of anti-Byrd Democrats, and of labor groups organized the Virginia Right to Vote League to defeat the Campbell amendments. The opposition forces united their efforts through this organization.[25] An Association Against the

[23] Of the four candidates in this primary, one supported the amendments, John S. Battle, the victor and the Byrd machine candidate. In addition to Miller, Horace H. Edwards and Remmie L. Arnold opposed. Miller was the most outspoken. Cabell Phillips, "New Rumblings in the Old Dominion," *New York Times Magazine*, June 19, 1949, pp. 34-35. Co-workers with Miller were Beecher E. Stallard, Richmond attorney and one-time delegate to the General Assembly; Martin A. Hutchinson and David George, Richmond attorneys and anti-Byrd Democrats.

[24] The question was so stated that it said the sections of the constitution which were to be changed "provide for the elimination of the poll tax. . . ." Actually, the voters were being asked whether they wished to adopt new sections which would eliminate the tax and institute other changes. This misleading statement not only caused confusion but also produced charges that it had been so worded deliberately to confuse. The controversy over the wording undoubtedly aided in creating opposition to and suspicion of the proposed changes. See Richmond *Times-Dispatch*, October 5, 1949 and editorial, October 6, 1949.

[25] Beecher E. Stallard called the organization meeting and Virgil H. Goode,

Suffrage Amendments was also formed.[26]   Other organizations which worked against these proposals were the College of William and Mary Voters League, the Richmond Citizens' Association and the Virginia Commonwealth League.[27]

No counterpart of the Virginia Right to Vote League was created by the groups working for adoption of the Campbell amendments.   Stuart B. Campbell, the chairman of the suffrage commission, and Attorney General J. Lindsay Almond, Jr., led in their defense.   The Democratic organization stated frequently that the proposals were not a party affair but Attorney General Almond used the occasions of party rallies to urge his listeners to support them.   He was running for re-election on the same ticket with John S. Battle, the gubernatorial nominee, and L. Preston Collins, nominee for re-election as lieutenant governor.   The two latter candidates gave a somewhat cautious and reluctant support to the amendments.   During the primary campaign, Mr. Battle stated that he did not like everything in the suffrage package although he supported it.[28]

Other political leaders active in urging ratification included William D. Medley of Arlington, former state senator and member of the suffrage commission; Robert C. Vaden, state senator and vice-chairman of the suffrage commission; and Armistead L. Boothe of Alexandria, member of the House of Delegates.   Several leaders of the Byrd organization, including State Democratic Chairman G. Alvin Massenburg, Governor William M. Tuck, Congressman Howard W. Smith and "the boss" himself, Senator Harry F. Byrd, did not publicly state their approval until shortly before the vote.   Governor Tuck issued a statement on October 22.   His statement indicates that the organization realized efforts had to be made to answer the

---

Commonwealth's attorney of Franklin County, was named permanent chairman. Richmond *Times-Dispatch*, October 9, 1949.

[26] *Ibid.*, October 18, 1949, letter signed by Dr. Howard H. Davis, the chairman.

[27] David G. George was the director of the Virginia Commonwealth League at this time with James P. Hart, Jr., chairman, and Dr. Howard H. Davis, treasurer. It was reactivated several years before this fight after having been dormant for a long period. Its long-term objective was the overthrow of the Byrd machine. *Ibid.*, November 7, 1949.

[28] *Ibid.*, editorial, October 17, 1949.

very vocal opposition since, while governor, he had not previously announced his position on any major state issue before the voters.[29] Senator Byrd gave his approval soon afterwards and stated that the amendments represented the "patriotic judgment" of the suffrage commission and the General Assembly.[30]

These leaders principally argued that Virginia should get its suffrage machinery in order before Congress passed a poll tax repeal measure. They predicted approval of a federal bill early in 1950. They did not want the state to go into the congressional election of 1950 with a state law requiring poll tax payment and a federal law prohibiting such payment. They emphasized the resulting confusion.[31]

Why did the Byrd machine back poll tax abolition at this time? The chief factor seems to have been fear of national action. Early in the summer of 1949, Congressman Burr P. Harrison advised his fellow Virginians that the tax must be abolished "to avoid the danger of ultimate federalization of elections." He believed that rejection of the Campbell amendments would greatly strengthen the advocates of a federal anti-poll tax measure while their adoption would aid those opposing a federal statute.[32]

A second factor was public pressure for repeal. Organizations like the Virginia Electoral Reform League had educated many persons in the state on the poll tax and had created demand for its removal. A political machine has to respond to articulate public demands if it wishes to retain control. Thus, the machine had to yield on the poll tax question but it carefully guaranteed its continued control over Virginia elections.

A final factor was the reaction to machine control over elections which resulted from election scandals in 1945. Two machine candidates for the Democratic nomination for lieutenant governor were involved. The Byrd organization

29 *Ibid.*, October 23, 1949.

30 *Ibid.*, October 25, 1949. Byrd's newspaper, the Winchester *Evening Star*, had endorsed the proposals earlier. It stated, however, that it did not regard them as "perfect." *Ibid.*, editorial, October 17, 1949.

31 *Ibid.*, October 7, 1949.

32 See his letter in Richmond *News-Leader*, June 21, 1949.

does not usually allow public contests for nominations but it did in this instance. The candidates were Charles R. Fenwick and L. Preston Collins. After allowing the contest to develop, the machine leaders changed their minds and issued instructions to support Fenwick. In Wise County, in the southwestern corner of the state, the local organization gave all out support to the designated candidate. Consequently, Fenwick received 3,307 votes and Collins, 122. Since the statewide count was close, Collins challenged the accuracy of the Wise County results. In the suit which followed, many corrupt election practices were revealed. Collins won the case and, with the Wise County vote thrown out, the nomination.[33] The extent of machine control over elections revealed by this case caused considerable public reaction against the Byrd organization. Observers of Virginia politics believe that because of the threat of national action, because of public support for poll tax repeal, and because of the Wise County scandals, the Byrd machine leadership decided in 1945 that the time had come to support some type of election reforms.[34]

The voters defeated the Campbell amendments overwhelmingly. Only 56,687 voted for them while 206,542 opposed. Thus, 78.5 per cent of those voting rejected these constitutional changes. The size of the opposition vote indicates that many supporters of the Byrd machine did not follow the organization on this issue. The vote disclosed more opposition than most observers thought existed. Two days before election day, one observer wrote "The vote is expected to be close."[35]

Not a single county or city went for these proposals. The vote in some localities was as much as ten to one against them. The county that came nearest to approving them was Rappahannock where the vote was 307 to 314. The vote was not close in any city. Richmond's vote of 3,011 to 21,753 was an especially large one against these changes.[36]

[33] Key, *Southern Politics*, p. 24.

[34] In its report the suffrage commission emphasized the necessity of some of the recommended changes as a method to purify elections and to eliminate fraud.

[35] James Latimer, Richmond *Times-Dispatch*, November 6, 1949.

[36] For the county and city vote, see Heard and Strong, p. 206, or Richmond *Times-Dispatch*, November 29, 1949.

Although the organization-sponsored suffrage amendments were snowed under, the organization candidate for governor, John S. Battle, won as a matter of course, receiving 184,772 votes to a total of 77,560 votes for his two opponents. Significantly, more votes were cast on the constitutional question than for the gubernatorial office. A total of 263,229 persons voted on the Campbell amendments while 262,332 persons voted for the office of governor. Normally fewer persons vote on constitutional questions than on personalities. Due to the predominance of one party in Virginia, the general election rarely excites great interest. The Campbell amendments aroused an abnormal interest in 1949. They were the issue in that election. The fact that nearly 100,000 more voters turned out in 1949 than in 1945 reveals the sizable increase in participation produced by them.[37]

Since defeat of the Campbell amendments, no further significant action has been taken to lift Virginia's poll tax. During the campaign against the Campbell proposals, the group led by Francis Pickens Miller advocated, as the best way to handle this problem, a constitutional convention limited to poll tax repeal. After defeat of the amendments, this group immediately urged anew their convention proposal.[38] However, a convention has not been called. The Byrd machine shies away from a constitutional convention because of fear that it might get out of control.[39]

Proposed constitutional amendments providing for abolition of the voter poll tax have been introduced in every legislative session since defeat of the Campbell amendments. None of these proposals has had the backing of the Byrd organization and none has won legislative approval. In 1950, a poll tax repeal resolution passed the House of Delegates by 73 to 20 votes but was killed by a five to four Senate committee vote.[40] A similar measure passed the House and was defeated in com-

[37] The total vote in 1945 was 168,764. Heard and Strong, p. 196.
[38] Richmond *Times-Dispatch*, November 10, 1949.
[39] Editorials, *ibid.*, November 9 and 11, 1949.
[40] New York *Times*, March 13, 1950. One committee member, Harry F. Byrd, Jr., said that the committee had too little time to consider the resolution.

mittee in the Senate in 1952.[41]   An unsuccessful attempt was
made to discharge the Senate committee from further
consideration of the resolution.   This method of bringing
measures to a vote is a drastic one in Virginia and is rarely
used.   In 1954, the proposal was bottled up in committee in
both houses and an effort to apply the discharge method in the
House was defeated 49 to 47.[42]   In 1956, the Privileges and
Elections committees of both houses refused to report out a poll
tax repeal resolution.   All twelve members of the Senate committee voted in secret session against the proposal while nine of
thirteen committee members in the House voted against it.
The major argument against repeal in 1956 involved the school
segregation controversy.   Virginia's lawmakers, particularly
those from southern Virginia, were in no mood to do anything
which might increase the number of Negro voters.[43]

There continues to be considerable public support in the
Old Dominion for poll tax repeal.[44]   Because of this support,
the tax will eventually be removed from the suffrage.   Since
1949, the Byrd organization has not backed repeal because
passage of a federal anti-poll tax bill has not been imminent.
If it should again appear that Congress may adopt such a
measure, the Byrd machine might be willing to set in motion
the machinery to repeal the tax and to adopt other suffrage
safeguards.   However, due to the re-agitation of the race issue
as a result of the school segregation controversy and due to lack
of congressional interest in an anti-poll tax measure, there is
little possibility of poll tax repeal in Virginia in the immediate
future.

TEXAS

Texans, too, voted on the question of poll tax abolition in
November, 1949.   Again, other matters complicated the issue.

41 Richmond *Times-Dispatch*, February 22 and March 4, 1952. The vote in
the House was 60 to 38.

42 *Ibid.*, February 20 and 26, 1954.

43 *Ibid.*, February 9, 1956 and Richmond *News-Leader*, February 8, 1956.

44 Leading repeal advocates in recent years have been the Junior Chamber
of Commerce, Virginia League of Women Voters, Virginia Federation of

As in Virginia, the proposed amendment was defeated, but the Texas situation was not as involved as the Virginia one. Texans voted separately on the tax repeal proposal. They were not presented an "all-or-nothing" package as in Virginia. However, they had ten amendments before them, some of which aroused considerable opposition. The poll tax proposal was undoubtedly affected adversely by association with other suggested constitutional changes which did not have general approval.

Support for poll tax repeal in Texas goes back at least to 1919. Proposed constitutional amendments for this purpose have been introduced in the legislature frequently since then,[45] but serious efforts to abolish the tax have been made only within recent years. Throwing the national spotlight upon the southern poll tax has helped to focus attention upon it in Texas and to push forward the movement for its elimination.

The campaign for poll tax removal has not been as tumultuous in the Lone Star State as in some poll tax states, perhaps because the tax has not restricted voting as much there as in Alabama, Mississippi, and Virginia. In addition, the Texas tax has served a positive, as well as a negative, use. It has substituted for a voter registration system. The lists of poll taxpayers constitute the official lists of qualified voters. Its repeal would necessitate establishing a voter registration system and many persons have been willing to let well enough alone.

In recent years, the issue of poll tax abolition first received considerable attention during the 1938 gubernatorial race. Surprisingly, W. Lee O'Daniel introduced the subject into that campaign. In an address at Waco, he strongly condemned the tax requirement and promised to ask the legislature to abolish it. He advocated poll tax abolition throughout six weeks of campaigning. In accepting the nomination at the Democratic convention in Beaumont, he appealed for poll tax removal, but

---

Women's Clubs, Catholic Women, Jewish War Veterans, Council of Jewish Women, Virginia Teachers' Association, and Negro organizations.

[45] Snow, pp. 67 and 70-77. Since Texas courts have ruled that the poll tax is levied by the constitution, amendment of the constitution is necessary to secure its abolition. *Solon* v. *State*, 114 S. W. 349 (1908). See also *Attorney General's Opinions*, No. 1972, January 30, 1919.

the convention shouted down a proposed platform plank supporting poll tax repeal.[46] After becoming governor, "Pappy" O'Daniel did not continue to fight for abolition of the tax. He apparently made a truce with the Texas Democratic organization soon after the election and, consequently took no further steps concerning repeal.[47] By directing attention to this issue, his efforts helped to prepare the way for later action.[48]

After the 1938 gubernatorial campaign, poll tax repeal received only spasmodic attention until the spring of 1948 when State Senator Rogers Kelley of Hidalgo County announced that he would introduce a repeal resolution in the next legislature. He noted that many citizens could not vote in his section because they could not pay the tax.[49] Before the legislature assembled, he sought the support of the state Democratic organization and in September, 1948, a poll tax repeal proposal was written into the platform at the convention in Fort Worth. In November, Senator Kelley announced that his proposal had the endorsement of the State Democratic Executive Committee, American Legion, Veterans of Foreign Wars, Texas Junior Chamber of Commerce, Jewish War Veterans, Texas League of Women Voters, American G. I. Forum, and Women's Society of Christian Service.[50]

Senator Kelley introduced his poll tax repeal resolution soon after the legislature convened in January, 1949. After consid-

---

46 Seth S. McKay, *W. Lee O'Daniel and Texas Politics, 1938-1942* (Lubbock, Tex., 1944), pp. 100-02.

47 Wayne Gard, "Disfranchised Dixie," *Christian Century,* LVI (September 20, 1939), 1136.

48 O'Daniel was reported to be unable to vote in the primary election when he was nominated because he had not paid his poll tax. New York *Times,* September 15, 1938, and Gard, p. 1136. On December 29, 1938, most Texas newspapers reported that W. Lee O'Daniel had appeared in the office of the Tax Assessor-Collector of Tarrant County to pay the poll tax for his wife and himself. He stated that he still opposed the tax but would pay it because he was soon to be governor. McKay, p. 102.

49 Dallas *Morning News,* April 28, 1948. Hidalgo County is near the Mexican border and has a heavy Mexican-American population. The fact that fewer persons pay the tax where there are many Mexican-Americans has been shown in Chapter 6.

50 *Ibid.,* November 7, 1948.

erable delay, it passed both houses in June.[51]   It substituted a
voter registration system for the poll tax requirement and
provided that the voter must register before February 1 preceding each election.   Thus, the registration deadline was the
same as the poll tax payment deadline.   The legislature was
authorized to establish the specific system of registration and
to prescribe a registration fee.[52]

No such contest as the Virginia one developed following
submission of the proposal to the people. Since poll tax repeal
was not complicated by association with many suffrage changes
as in Virginia, most of those groups and individuals who had
supported repeal approved the amendment and worked for it.
However, some of them opposed the proposed registration
system.   They did not want a registration fee substituted for
the poll tax and may have voted against the repeal amendment
for this reason.[53]   The contest also differed from the one in
Virginia in that Texans appear to have less interest in the poll
tax question than Virginians.

Support for the poll tax repeal amendment came from the
State Democratic Executive Committee; from labor, veterans',
church, and women's organizations; from some branches of the

[51] *Ibid.*, June 15, 1949. The sponsor in the House of Representatives, S. J.
Isaacks of El Paso, was also from a county with a large Mexican-American
population. Austin *American,* April 27, 1949.

[52] *General Laws of Texas, 1949,* S. J. R. No. 1. In anticipation of poll tax
repeal, the legislature passed an act establishing a registration system. The act
was to be effective only if the poll tax repeal amendment was ratified. It provided for annual registration during the period from October 1 to February 1,
a period corresponding with the time of poll tax payment. It empowered
counties to levy a registration fee of no more than fifty cents, divided equally
between the state and county. Dallas *Morning News,* July 7, 1949.

[53] Some legislators attempted to set the registration fee at $1.00 but were
defeated by supporters of poll tax repeal. Senator Kelley refused to sign the
conference report which approved the fifty cents registration fee. *Ibid.* By substituting a registration fee for a poll tax, Texas was, in effect, reducing the
annual charge for voting from $1.75 to fifty cents. Since the fee was permissive,
all counties might not have required its payment. Also since it would have
been possible to lift the fee by legislative action alone, it would have been
easier to remove than the poll tax. Substitution of a registration fee for poll
tax payment represented a modification of Texas suffrage restrictions if not
an outright lowering of the bars.

Chamber of Commerce and from some bar associations. Senator Kelley continued to support it although he opposed the authorization of a registration fee. Early in October, he called a meeting in Austin to map a drive for repeal. He admitted that considerable "disorganized opposition" existed but stated that both Democratic and Republican leaders wanted the tax lifted. Among Republicans favoring the proposal were the late R. B. Creager, Republican boss of the state; Henry Zweifel, state chairman from Fort Worth; and Jack Porter, senatorial candidate from Houston.[54] A number of Democratic leaders backed it because they believed that a registration system would enable them to keep Republicans out of the Democratic primary.[55]

Texas congressmen actively supported poll tax elimination. House Speaker Sam Rayburn, Representative Wright Patman, and Senator Lyndon Johnson made a statewide radio appeal for approval of the amendment shortly before the people voted.[56] Senator Tom Connally was reported as favoring the amendment.[57] These representatives backed it primarily because they feared that an anti-poll tax bill would be passed by Congress. They wanted the state to repeal the tax before the national government acted. They warned their fellow citizens that voting requirements would be different in national and state elections if a federal act were passed and the tax retained at the state level. A principal reason why Texans were willing to consider lifting the voter poll tax in 1949 appears to have been the possibility of the passage of a federal anti-poll tax bill.

The opposition to poll tax repeal was largely unorganized and passive. The Dallas *Morning News* opposed repeal.[58] Some branches of the Chamber of Commerce and some bar associa-

54 Richard M. Morehead, Dallas *Morning News*, October 4, 1949.

55 *Ibid.*, October 19, 1949. The conditional registration law provided for a closed primary. Some rank and file Republicans disliked the provision for registration of party affiliation. They felt that it would hurt them, especially in local races where there were usually no Republican candidates. Morehead, October 4, 1949.

56 Dallas *Morning News*, November 4, 1949.

57 Morehead, October 4, 1949.

58 Editorials, Dallas *Morning News*, October 13, 20, and November 8, 1949.

tions opposed while others supported the amendment. A majority of the letters on this subject which appeared in the *Morning News* were from poll tax supporters. It might be concluded that while leaders of both the Democratic and Republican state party organizations favored removing the tax requirement, the majority of the rank and file were not greatly interested one way or the other and were content to retain the tax instead of substituting an untried registration system.

The principal arguments against poll tax repeal were the oft repeated ones that (1) abolition would deprive the schools of a million and a half dollars annually and (2) "If a person isn't interested enough to pay $1.75 for a poll tax, he shouldn't have the privilege of voting." The school argument probably influenced many voters. A million or more dollars sounds like a large sum. Because of school financial needs, many citizens may have been unwilling to vote for repeal if the schools would lose revenue. No serious effort was made to show that the poll tax produced a very small proportion of the total school revenue.[59] Neither was it made clear that the tax was not being removed as a revenue measure but only as a voting requirement.[60] Another less important argument against poll tax abolition was that under the substitute registration system there would be no exemptions from the registration fee.[61] Some opposition votes may have come from groups exempt from poll tax payment who would have had to pay a registration fee if the tax had been lifted.

The vote on the ten amendments submitted to Texas voters in November, 1949 was very light, reflecting the general lack of interest in the proposals. The amendments were the major items on the ballot. No important office was being filled to bring out a large vote. A total of 305,834 persons voted on the poll tax repeal amendment; 133,550 voted for and 172,284 against. Of those voting, 56.3 per cent opposed poll tax aboli-

---

[59] See Chapter 2.

[60] The Dallas *Morning News* recognized this fact but argued that without an incentive to pay, the poll tax could not be collected. Editorial, October 20, 1949.

[61] *Ibid.*

tion.[62] Slightly more persons voted on the poll tax proposal than on any of the other amendments. Voting statistics indicate the small turnout. The estimated number of qualified voters in 1948 was 1,989,710 and the number who voted in 1948 was 1,238,557.[63] Only two of the ten proposed amendments were approved. Neither was controversial.[64] The amendments providing for annual legislative sessions and payment of an annual salary of $3,600 to the legislators, for women to serve on juries, for poll tax repeal, and for trial of lunacy cases without a jury aroused the greatest opposition. The most controversial proposal was the legislative one. It seems valid to conclude that poll tax repeal was harmed by being presented to the voters with several other constitutional changes, especially since some of them were unpopular. A general suspicion against all the amendments appears to have developed. Voters tended to vote against the whole lot.[65]

Was support for poll tax repeal concentrated in any particular part of Texas? In only 36 counties was a majority vote cast for repeal.[66] These counties were grouped primarily in three sections of the state: (1) along the Mexican border, (2) along the Gulf Coast, and (3) in West Texas. Three Panhandle counties voted for repeal but most counties in this part of the state supported retention.[67]

<hr>

[62] The results tallied closely with those predicted a month before the election by the Texas Poll. Joe Belden, director of the poll, reported that a statewide survey showed 55 per cent of the qualified voters wished to retain the tax, 40 per cent wished to repeal it, while 5.0 per cent had no opinion. This division of opinion was similar to that obtained in two earlier surveys, one in December, 1947 and another in May, 1949. *Ibid.*, October 3, 1949.

[63] *Texas Almanac and State Industrial Guide, 1949-1950*, p. 457 and Heard and Strong, p. 186.

[64] One authorized District Courts to sit at places other than the county seat; the other authorized the establishment of rural fire prevention districts.

[65] The fact that the two amendments which passed were approved by slim margins supports this conclusion.

[66] No vote was recorded in eight of the 254 counties. The county-by-county figures are contained in "Official Vote on Constitutional Amendments (Ten), November 8, 1949," published by Texas, Secretary of State, mimeo., undated.

[67] The following counties voted for repeal: (1) Mexican border: Duval, 99.1, Zapata, 97.4, Starr, 95.7, Webb, 90.3, Jim Wells, 80.5, Jim Hogg, 78.3, Brooks, 72.9, El Paso, 72.6, Hidalgo, 70.7, Cameron, 70.1, Nueces, 67.1, Hudspeth, 64.6,

The strongest support for poll tax abolition came from the Mexican border region.[68] In four counties there, over ninety per cent of the total vote was for repeal; the top twelve of the 36 counties for repeal were located in this section. Why were so many voters favorable to repeal in this area? Mexican-Americans are concentrated here. It was shown in Chapter 6 that the poll tax bears heavily upon them. Since the Mexican-American vote is a controllable one and since many of these people are unable or unwilling to pay the tax, considerable vote buying through poll tax payment has occurred in this region.[69] Thus, some persons may have backed poll tax repeal to ease the voting requirements while others may have favored it to decrease the cost of winning elections. Local machines may have decided that the tax was no longer needed to retain their control and that it was costing more than its worth.[70]

A significantly close relationship exists between the areas of highest oil production and the sections favorable to repeal. The important oil producing areas are along the Gulf Coast and in West Texas.[71] The CIO has been active here in organizing the oil workers, and has also long supported poll tax abolition. The favorable vote in these sections probably resulted from CIO support.[72]

Kleberg, 61.8, Willacy, 58.7, Zavala, 55.7, Maverick, 55.4, Culberson, 54.3, Kinney, 51.0; (2) Gulf Coast: Harris, 61.9, Jefferson, 59.0, Galveston, 58.5, Brazoria, 58.2, Orange, 56.3, Wharton, 50.4; (3) West Texas: Andrews, 63.7, Loving, 61.5, Ector, 58.3, Winkler, 55.2, Howard, 54.6, Midland, 53.2, Ward, 50.5; (4) Panhandle: Hutchinson, 63.6, Dallam, 55.9, Moore, 50.5; (5) unclassified: Travis, 60.4, and Bexar, 51.2.

[68] The legislative sponsors of repeal came from this region.

[69] See Chapter 4.

[70] For a discussion of the control exercised over voting in this area, see Key, *Southern Politics*, pp. 271-75. The highest percentage cast for poll tax repeal was in Duval County (99.1) which is shown by Professor Key to have a highly manageable vote. Opposition to the poll tax is not of recent origin in the Mexican border counties. Five (Cameron, Duval, Hidalgo, Starr, and Webb) voted against adoption of the tax in 1902. See Chapter 1.

[71] The Gulf Coast and Mexican counties overlap. Some poll tax repeal support in the latter counties may have come from CIO oil workers as it did in the Gulf counties.

[72] The percentages may not be significant for some West Texas counties.

Another factor which helped to produce the favorable vote of the Gulf Coast is urbanism. It has been demonstrated that the poll tax has a greater adverse effect upon urban citizens than upon rural ones. More Texans supported repeal in urban centers than in rural areas. In 1940, seventeen counties were more than fifty per cent urbanized and had a city of more than 20,000 inhabitants. Nine of these counties cast a majority vote for poll tax removal. The median percentage for repeal of all seventeen counties was 51.2 per cent while that for all counties of the state was 33.55 per cent. A comparison of the percentage voting for repeal in certain completely rural counties with the percentages voting for repeal in certain counties over fifty per cent urban further substantiates the conclusion that more support for repeal came from urban than from rural sections. To control some other factors, only counties with a Negro and foreign-born white population of not more than five per cent were used. Fifty-eight rural and thirteen urban counties met these specifications. The median percentage for repeal of the rural counties was 31.15 per cent while that of the urban counties was 39.5 per cent, a difference of over eight percentage points. Urban voters were probably more willing to approve poll tax repeal because the tax bears more severely upon them than upon rural citizens or it may have been because they are generally more willing to change than their more conservative country cousins.

The Negro was not a factor in the Texas poll tax repeal campaign. Neither the presence nor absence of Negroes affected the way in which a county voted on the repeal measure. The Negro population is concentrated in East Texas, and this section supported retention of the tax, but so did other areas where few Negroes reside. No significant results were obtained from comparing the voting rates in counties with a Negro population of two per cent or less with the rates in counties with a Negro population of more than fifteen per cent, all counties being rural with a foreign-born white population of

---

The number who voted in them was so small that the margin of favorable votes was not as great as the percentages may indicate. In Loving County, the vote was sixteen for and ten against; in Andrews, 109 for and 62 against.

less than five per cent. The effect of poll tax repeal upon the number of Negro voters received little attention during the ratification campaign. Apparently Texans no longer regard the poll tax as an important device to disfranchise the Negro. The situation is different in southern states with many Negroes.

Since 1949, no further major campaign to remove the Texas poll tax has been made. Resolutions providing for its repeal have been regularly introduced in the legislature but have not been approved. The last resolution, introduced in the 1955 session, died in committee. Most of these resolutions also authorized the establishment of a registration system and the charging of a registration fee. The registration fee provision probably is one of the main reasons why the legislature has failed to pass one of these resolutions.

ARKANSAS

In Arkansas, the first significant poll tax repeal effort occurred in 1937 and 1938. The 1937 legislature approved a proposed constitutional amendment to abolish the tax as a suffrage requirement only.[73] The AF of L was primarily responsible for the introduction of the measure. Agrarian groups, religious organizations, and women's clubs also supported it.[74]

Two basic arguments were advanced against poll tax removal at this time. The first related to the relationship between the tax and the schools. Although the tax was to be retained as a source of school revenue, opponents argued that the incentive to pay it would be lacking unless it was a suffrage requirement and that, therefore, repeal would result in reduced school revenue.[75] Brooks Hays, then a Democratic national committeeman and later congressman from the Fifth District of Arkansas, tried unsuccessfully to win the support of the public school people by arguing that in the long run they would get more

[73] *Acts of Arkansas, 1937,* p. 1410.

[74] Crawford, p. 50.

[75] See Arkansas State Policy Committee, *The Poll Tax and Suffrage,* Published Paper No. 2 (April, 1938), pp. 6-7.

money from the type of officials elected by a broader electorate than they received from the poll tax.

The second argument related to the fact that Arkansas, like Texas, uses the poll tax as a substitute for a system of voter registration. The lists of poll taxpayers serve in lieu of rosters of registered voters. Repeal opponents reasoned that elimination of the tax would upset the election procedure and that a registration system would be more expensive and involved than the poll tax system. Reluctance to deviate from the established method of listing voters was expressed in many quarters. Some persons argued that a loose registration system might be established and that the possibility of corrupt election practices would thereby be increased. Repeal advocates replied that political corruption was inevitable under the poll tax system. They charged that the tax requirement was undemocratic since it deprived large numbers of otherwise eligible voters of the ballot.[76]

President Roosevelt became involved in the Arkansas repeal movement when he wrote to Brooks Hays in September, 1938. He summarized the development of the suffrage in the United States and indicated that poll tax requirements were contrary to that development since they narrowed, rather than broadened, the suffrage. He stated that he was glad "to know that there is such a general move in those states which still have them to repeal them altogether." In concluding, the President carefully stated that he was not advising the voters of Arkansas how to vote.[77] The letter received considerable publicity both in Arkansas and outside. Brooks Hays believes that it did more harm than good.[78] Resentment arose against this expression of opinion by an outsider. Some persons may have voted against repeal for this reason.

The poll tax repeal amendment was decisively defeated in November, 1938. The vote was 42,436 for and 83,725 against

---

[76] Crawford, pp. 51-53. Brooks Hays supported repeal because, as a result of personal experiences, he had concluded that the tax encouraged corrupt election practices.

[77] *Ibid.*, p. 54.

[78] The letter made Hays the butt of several jokes since it was published soon after the famous "Dear Alben" letter and was addressed "Dear Brooks."

repeal. Thus, 66.4 per cent of those who voted opposed abolition. The turnout was light as is usual in general elections in
the South. The poll tax issue did not arouse enough interest
in Arkansas to bring additional voters to the polls. Only 11.8
per cent of the adults voted on the amendment; 7.8 per cent
of them killed it. Fewer persons voted on this question than
voted for the offices of governor and United States senator
despite the fact that these contests were decided in the primary.

Opposition to repeal was general throughout the state. Only
four of the 75 counties voted for the amendment. These
counties were not grouped together although three were located
in the northeastern part of the state.[79] All counties where
forty to fifty per cent of the voters supported repeal were in
the northern half of the state. These counties had a predominantly white population. St. Francis was the only one with a
Negro population in excess of fifty per cent where a sizable
percentage of voters backed repeal.

The vote indicates that many persons opposed repeal because
they feared increased voting by Negroes as a result of poll tax
elimination. The bogey of Negro domination was inserted into
the campaign as in similar fights in other states. Repeal advocates tried to counteract this argument by stating that no great
increase in Negro voting had occurred in those states which
had abolished the tax. They pointed out that it only confused
the issue to associate it with the race question. However, reason
did not triumph over race.

Other major causes for defeat of the amendment were:
(1) the strong fight against it by politicians; (2) the opposition
of public school people because they feared a loss of revenue;
and (3) inadequate leadership by repeal supporters.[80]

Sidney S. McMath started a new movement to abolish the
Arkansas poll tax in 1948 when, as a gubernatorial candidate,

[79] They were Izard, 70.4; Mississippi, 65.6; Arkansas, 57.0; and Randolph,
55.4. Woodruff opposed repeal by one vote; the results were 434 to 435. For
the county-by-county vote, see Heard and Strong, p. 34.

[80] Mr. Roy Prewitt, a Little Rock lawyer, led the campaign to win popular
approval for the amendment. His leadership was ineffective. Brooks Hays was
busy with other problems and unable to devote his full energies to this
campaign.

he endorsed repeal. He became interested in the tax when he and a group of World War II veterans staged a revolt in 1946 against the political machine of Mayor Leo P. McLaughlin of Hot Springs.[81]

After his election as governor, McMath announced on November 4, 1948 that he would ask the legislature to abolish the tax and to substitute a registration system. The voters had just approved, by a two to one majority, a constitutional amendment authorizing the legislature to establish a registration system.[82] The governor-elect stated that he was requesting repeal because he felt that the state should assume responsibility for abolition and thereby prevent interference by the national government.[83]

In his inaugural address on January 11, 1949, Governor McMath formally asked for a constitutional amendment to repeal the poll tax.[84] A measure to effectuate his request was introduced by administration representatives but was not passed. The legislature adjourned after blocking it and an anti-lynching bill.[85] Opposition came principally from representatives of eastern Arkansas, the plantation belt.

Poll tax repeal died in the 1949 legislature without any real fight. An experienced observer of Arkansas politics believes that it would have passed if Governor McMath had fought for it. The governor did not push the measure since he had heavy going with other parts of his program which he considered more important. If the voters had been given the opportunity to remove the tax requirement in 1949, they probably would have done so. The vote on the amendment authorizing a registration system indicated that support for poll tax repeal had grown considerably since 1938. Many voters thought that they were voting for repeal when they voted for this amendment.[86]

81 See Chapter 4.
82 *Constitution,* Amendment XXXIX.
83 John L. Fletcher, *Arkansas Gazette,* November 5, 1948.
84 *Arkansas Gazette,* January 12, 1949.
85 *Time,* LIII (March 21, 1949), 24.
86 Statement of Governor McMath, Memphis *Commercial Appeal,* November 6, 1949.

Until 1956 no concerted effort was made to revive the poll tax issue. In the spring, Sidney McMath, then in private law practice, began a new drive to remove the tax. Several labor unions and electric co-operatives backed him. Through the efforts of McMath and his associates, a poll tax repeal amendment was proposed by the initiative method and placed on the November general election ballot.

Poll tax repeal failed again in 1956, but not by as wide a margin as in 1938. The vote was 161,403 for to 210,237 against the amendment. Only 56.6 per cent of those who voted opposed repeal. The number voting was considerably greater than the turnout in 1938, undoubtedly because of the presidential election.[87]

The principal support for the 1956 poll tax repeal amendment came from organized labor and the League of Women Voters. They worked independently to win approval for the proposal. Governor Orval E. Faubus announced that he would support repeal but predicted that the amendment would not pass.

Opposition came from various sources. Many persons opposed repeal because of the tie between the poll tax and the schools. They did not want the schools to lose $500,000 in revenue. The Arkansas Education Association did not, however, take any action on the amendment.[88] Education groups concentrated on defeating a proposal to limit to thirty mills the school tax which local districts could levy.

Other persons opposed repeal because the legislature had not adopted a registration system since securing constitutional authorization in 1949. They did not want to give up the poll

[87] In addition to voting on presidential electors and a governor, the voters passed on twelve proposals, approving seven. Only two amendments received a total vote greater than that received by the poll tax proposal. Both of these resolutions related to horse racing. One, to legalize horse racing and pari-mutuel wagering in Hot Springs, passed and the other, to prohibit all horse and dog racing, lost. Although three proposals relating to the school segregation controversy were approved, fewer persons voted on them than voted on the poll tax question. Election returns were obtained from Secretary of State, Arkansas.

[88] Arkansas, League of Women Voters, *The Arkansas Voter*, II (October, 1956).

tax as a registration procedure before a substitute method had been established. They felt that they could not trust the legislature to draw up a satisfactory registration law on the spur of the moment to fill the gap left by poll tax abolition. Both the *Arkansas Gazette* and the *Arkansas Democrat* opposed repeal on this basis.[89]

There was also opposition because of the "thirty days clause." This clause provided that no person would be required to register earlier than thirty days before any election. Many voters did not understand it because it was interpreted in many different ways.

Further opposition came from both segregationists and Negroes. Segregationists believe that the poll tax helps to disfranchise Negroes. Negroes who were qualified to vote opposed because they feared that they might not be able to vote under another form of registration.

In 1956 support for poll tax repeal was more definitely concentrated in the northern and western part of the state than it was in 1938. The sixteen counties which cast a vote in excess of fifty per cent for repeal were in the northwest corner or in the central, western part of the state.[90] Most of the counties where the vote against repeal was greatest bordered the Mississippi River in the east or were in the southern part of the state. These are the counties where the Negro population is concentrated. Arkansas and Mississippi, two of the four counties which voted for repeal in 1938, cast a vote of less than forty per cent for repeal in 1956. Each county has a sizable Negro population and is located along the eastern border.

The area of major support for poll tax repeal tended to be mainly rural although two of the eleven counties with a city in excess of 10,000 were among the sixteen counties which voted for repeal.[91] Six more of these eleven counties registered a vote of between forty and fifty per cent for repeal.

89 Letter to author from editor, *Arkansas Gazette Sunday Magazine,* dated January 8, 1957.

90 They were Baxter, Benton, Boone, Carroll, Fulton, Garland, Izard, Madison, Montgomery, Pope, Saline, Scott, Searcy, Stone, Van Buren, and Washington.

91 Garland (Hot Springs) and Washington (Fayetteville).

Analysis of the vote indicates that the poll tax is still regarded as a means to disfranchise the Negro in Arkansas. Areas with large Negro populations are not yet willing to remove it from the suffrage. A slight tendency for urban areas to support repeal existed but rural areas in the northwest also favored abolition.

It should be possible to repeal Arkansas' poll tax in the near future. Both organized labor and the League of Women Voters will continue to work for repeal. Their chances of success will be improved if they work together rather than independently. If the legislature adopts a voter registration law before another repeal proposal is submitted to the voters, repeal may be supported by many who opposed it in 1956 because an alternate registration system was lacking. It should be possible to win over some who opposed because of the loss of school revenue by adequate statistics showing the insignificance of the tax as a revenue device. The primary block before poll tax repeal in Arkansas is the segregation controversy. Those persons who wish to keep Negroes politically quiescent and who regard the poll tax as a device to disfranchise them will continue to oppose repeal.

ALABAMA

Interest in altering or abolishing Alabama's cumulative poll tax has recurred at various times since 1934. Beginning with Bibb Graves, each governor, except James E. Folsom, favored a change in the cumulative feature. "Big Jim" supported complete abolition during both of his terms. Although Governors Graves, Dixon, Sparks, and Persons said that they were for a reduction of the cumulative period, none of them really worked to achieve it. No action resulted until 1953 when the cumulative period was reduced from 24 to two years by adoption of a constitutional amendment. Although this action occurred during the administration of Governor Persons, he did not play a leading role in its achievement. In March, 1951 he testified before two interim committees of the legislature that the tax had outlived its usefulness and should be abolished. If complete abolition could not be secured, then he favored restricting the cumulative requirement to two years.[92] However, the real support for this action came from outside the governor's office.

The two most important factors in preventing any alteration in Alabama's poll tax before 1953 were those of race and labor. The race issue always comes up in any discussion of the Alabama poll tax. Rural leaders have opposed both repeal and modification because they believed either action would make voting easier for urban workers and for Negroes.[93] Referring to the defeat of a repeal proposal in the 1939 legislature, a state senator said: "By playing labor and the Negro against each other, we had no trouble in killing it."[94]

Gessner T. McCorvey, former chairman of the State Democratic Executive Committee, consistently opposed any alteration in the poll tax. His position was similar to that of many leading Alabama politicians. In 1945, he advised a legislative interim committee that he considered the cumulative provision as "all important."

You let one of these citizens, whether they be white or black, fail to pay his poll tax for two or three years and get to the point where he owes $4.50, $6.00, or $7.50 in back poll tax, then you have about eliminated this person as a voter.[95]

Following judicial nullification of the "Boswell Amendment"[96] in 1949, McCorvey reiterated his support of the cumulative poll tax by stating that it was "the last bulwark left to prevent mass voting by elements in our state who are totally unfit for self-government."[97]

[92] Tuscaloosa *News*, March 2, 1951.

[93] William V. Holloway and Charles W. Smith, Jr., *Government and Politics in Alabama* (University, Ala., 1941), p. 120.

[94] Bunche, p. 750.

[95] Hugh W. Sparrow, Birmingham *News*, February 9, 1945.

[96] This amendment was adopted in 1946 to tighten the suffrage requirements after the white primary had been declared unconstitutional. It gave local boards of registrars broad discretionary power to determine whether prospective voters could "read and write, understand and explain any article of the constitution of the United States," whether they were of "good character," and whether they understood "the duties and obligations of good citizenship under a republican form of government." See Key, *Southern Politics*, pp. 559, 571-72, 632.

[97] Tuscaloosa *News*, January 30, 1949.

The principal supporters of poll tax repeal in the Cotton State are similar to the advocates of poll tax removal in other states. They represent various civic, social, religious, and labor interests. A Women's Joint Legislative Council has been active in the repeal fight. Through it, representatives of such organizations as Alabama Congress of Parents and Teachers, Alabama Federation of Women's Clubs, League of Women Voters, Alabama Women Lawyers' Association, Methodist Missionary Women, Federation of Farm Women, American Association of University Women, and Business and Professional Women's Clubs were joined together. The now defunct Alabama Policy Committee directed public attention to this question during the early and middle forties and helped in the creation of support for repeal. The AF of L, local affiliates of the CIO, and the Farmer's Union have been important backers of poll tax abolition.

Major credit for altering the cumulative period from 24 years to two years goes to the women. Because of the veteran exemption, they concluded that the tax requirement fell most heavily upon them. With something of the vigor and sense of righteousness of suffragettes, they organized to repeal the poll tax. An unsuccessful effort had been made to lower the cumulative requirement in the 1951 legislature. After this failure, women's groups over the state took up the issue of poll tax abolition. According to a leading member of the legislature, poll tax repeal or modification had been a joke and had never been given serious consideration before the 1953 legislative session.[98]

In the spring of 1953, poll tax foes joined forces preparatory to the convening of the legislature. Representatives of various women's organizations, of the CIO, and of the Young Democrats teamed up in April to work for poll tax repeal.[99] Among the women's organizations, the League of Women Voters was particularly outstanding in this effort. Leaders of the League worked hard to get a repeal proposal adopted by the legislature

[98] Statement of George Hawkins, member of the Alabama House of Representatives from Etowah County, before the Tuscaloosa County Council for Passage of the Poll Tax Amendment, December 3, 1953.

[99] Tuscaloosa *News*, April 5, 1953.

and, subsequently, directed their efforts to securing passage of
the amendment to reduce the cumulative provision. The
Business and Professional Women also played a leading role.
The individual who probably did most to spark the movement
was Hallie Farmer, the state chairman of the B and PW's
Legislative Committee and head of the Division of Social
Sciences at Alabama College in Montevallo. Other women's
groups who were active were the American Association of
University Women, Alabama Federation of Women's Clubs,
Alabama Women Lawyers' Association, and the Pilot Club.
The Young Republicans also gave their support. In addition
to the CIO, labor was represented by the AF of L, United Mine
Workers and Railroad Brotherhoods. The NAACP approved
but, wisely, was not very active in working for either repeal or
modification.

Poll tax opponents aimed for outright repeal in 1953. Unable
to get the legislature to agree, they compromised for reduction
of the cumulative period. They would not have got this
approval if they had not aroused so much support that the
legislature was forced to act. The Senate adopted the proposal
to lower the cumulative period by a vote of 24 to 7 on May 19
and the House approved it 73 to 18 on June 16.[100] It was ratified by a referendum vote on December 15, 1953.

Following legislative approval, a State Committee for Poll
Tax Reform was organized. State Representative George Hawkins of Etowah County and State Senator Elvin McCary of
Calhoun County headed it as co-chairmen. This committee
pooled the efforts of the various groups supporting the proposal. Upon the suggestion of Dr. Farmer, councils for the
passage of the poll tax amendment were organized in several
counties. The councils consolidated the efforts of these various
organizations at the local level.

Before the campaign for ratification of the amendment was
over, most of the leading politicians gave it their approval.
They included Governor Gordon Persons; Senators Lister Hill
and John Sparkman; the state chairmen of the Democratic and
Republican parties, Ben Ray and Claude O. Vardaman; Tom

100 Birmingham *Post-Herald,* May 20 and June 17, 1953.

Abernathy, Democrat turned Republican who became the Republican gubernatorial nominee in 1954; and various potential Democratic gubernatorial nominees for 1954, such as Lieutenant Governor James B. Allen, Judge Elbert Boozer, State Senator James H. Faulkner, former Governor James E. Folsom, former State Senator Bruce Henderson, and Public Service Commission President C. C. (Jack) Owen. The support of Black Belter Bruce Henderson was particularly significant as an indication of the trend. Previously he had fought any relaxation in voting requirements. However, as a gubernatorial candidate, he apparently yielded to the strong sentiment for poll tax change.[101]

Practically all the organized effort was for passage of the amendment. The principal organized opposition existed in Jefferson County and the Jefferson County Democratic Executive Committee led it. George Sulzby, Birmingham businessman, directed the efforts of this committee. Serving with him were John D. Chichester, real estate broker and former legislator, and Victor Smith, Birmingham lawyer.[102] He was also assisted by former Governor Frank Dixon who, when a gubernatorial candidate, said that he favored reduction of the cumulative period, and by Gus Thompson, chairman of the Jefferson County Board of Registrars.[103] Within Jefferson County, the Bessemer City Democratic Executive Committee adopted a resolution opposing the amendment.[104] In the Black Belt, the Bullock County Democratic Executive Committee did the same.[105] In Mobile, former State Democratic Chairman Gessner T. McCorvey spoke against lowering the cumulative period. Black Belter J. Miller Bonner, State Senator from Wilcox County, was another leading opponent.

The Jefferson County Democratic Executive Committee mailed out thousands of postcards urging voters to reject the poll tax change. These cards, headed "Urgent," called attention to a report that the Communist party supported the

[101] Rex Thomas, Tuscaloosa *News*, December 13, 1953.
[102] Fred Taylor, Birmingham *News*, December 13, 1953.
[103] *Ibid.*, December 8 and 9, 1953.
[104] Birmingham *News*, December 16, 1953.
[105] Tuscaloosa *News*, December 4, 1953.

amendment and attempted to give the impression that it was Communist inspired and, therefore, should be defeated.[106] Shortly before the vote, the committee inserted the race issue into the campaign. It ran a series of large advertisements in the Birmingham *News* and Birmingham *Post-Herald*. Emphasis was placed upon NAACP support for the poll tax amendment. The advertisements implied that adoption of the amendment would lead to the end of racial segregation in Alabama. One was headed "NAACP Urges Adoption of Poll Tax Amendment (No. 1) and Seeks Death of Racial Segregation in Alabama and the South." Another appealed to skilled labor to vote against the amendment because of NAACP support and because the NAACP was fighting to narrow the wage differential between skilled and unskilled jobs.[107] It is doubtful that the scare tactics of the Jefferson County Committee succeeded in persuading many voters to oppose the amendment. Too many of the state's civic, political, and business leaders as well as its newspapers were on the other side.[108] The extreme charges of the committee probably harmed, rather than aided, its side. Appeals to racial prejudices did not have the power in December, 1953 which they assumed following the Supreme Court school segregation decision of May, 1954.

The turnout on December 15, 1953 was light. The voters had ten amendments before them of which only two were state-wide in scope. The poll tax amendment was the only one to arouse general interest and more persons voted on it than on any other amendment. The total vote was 124,483 while less than 100,000 votes were cast on each of the nine other proposals. The poll tax amendment was ratified by 70,951 to 53,532; 57 per cent of those voting approved reducing the cumulative period. As expected, support came generally from North Alabama and from the urban areas while the opposition was concentrated in the rural Black Belt region. Although the

106 "Vulcan," Birmingham *News*, December 8, 1953.

107 See advertisements in Birmingham *News*, December 9, 10, 13, and 14, 1953 and in Birmingham *Post-Herald*, December 10, 11, and 14, 1953.

108 According to a Birmingham *News* editorial (December 13, 1953), every Alabama newspaper which expressed itself editorially on the amendment favored it except one.

amendment was approved by a comfortable margin, it was defeated in 37 of the 67 counties. The sizable affirmative vote in the large cities was primarily responsible for its ratification. In all six counties which contained a city of over 25,000 persons in 1950, the percentage vote for the amendment exceeded sixty per cent. Of the fifteen counties with a city of over 10,000 persons in 1950, the vote was against the amendment's adoption in only two counties. Both of them are Black Belt counties— one, Dallas County, in the heart of the Black Belt and the other, Russell County, with the infamous Phenix City as its county seat.

Since the Black Belt is the area of heaviest Negro concentration, it is no surprise that counties with the largest non-white population turned down the poll tax change. Of 23 counties with a non-white population in excess of forty per cent as of 1950, only three counties gave an affirmative vote for the amendment. They were Lee, Macon, and Montgomery counties. The urbanism factor apparently influenced the result in Lee and Montgomery counties.[109]　Macon County is the home of Tuskegee Institute. The presence of this famed school with its educated Negro community helps to account for the vote in this county.[110]

No one can say when Alabama's poll tax will be abolished. If in 1953 the legislature had submitted a repeal amendment to the voters, there is reason to believe that it would have been ratified. However, agitation of the race question as a consequence of the Supreme Court's school segregation decision has produced a situation unfavorable to poll tax repeal for the immediate future. A large body of opinion favorable to abolition continues to exist, especially among organized women's

[109] Opelika and Auburn are located in Lee County. Alabama Polytechnic Institute is situated at Auburn and may have had a liberalizing influence.

[110] The thirty counties casting a majority vote for the amendment, with percentages, were: Mobile, 84.4; Baldwin, 81.2; Lauderdale, 79.6; Madison, 79.3; Etowah, 75.0; Calhoun, 74.2; Colbert, 73.1; Winston, 71.7; Morgan, 71.6; Montgomery, 67.9; Marion, 65.8; Marshall, 64.9; Jackson, 64.5; Lee, 63.7; Walker, 63.7; Macon, 63.3; Cleburne, 63.0; Jefferson, 63.0; Talladega, 61.6; Cullman, 60.9; Limestone, 60.3; Tuscaloosa, 60.3; Escambia, 58.6; St. Clair, 57.9; Houston, 57.8; Geneva, 56.3; Washington, 52.8; Shelby, 52.5; Tallapoosa, 52.0; and Randolph, 51.9.

groups. In the regular session of the legislature in 1955, a resolution providing for abolition was introduced in the House of Representatives with the support of 37 members and was approved by the Ways and Means Committee by a nine to four vote.[111] Governor Folsom has continued to advocate repeal. However, the repeal resolution did not win legislative approval. Due to the widely-held association between the poll tax and the Negro, there is little possibility of removal of Alabama's poll tax until racial tensions have been alleviated. Since the tax has been greatly watered down, its eventual repeal is only a matter of time.

MISSISSIPPI

The repeal movement has made less headway in Mississippi than in any other state. During congressional debates on federal anti-poll tax bills, representatives of the Magnolia State fell back on the argument "Let the states do it." They indicated that they were working for removal of the tax in their state. Former Senator Theodore Bilbo advised his colleagues:

I have no more patience with the imposition of a poll tax than possibly the sponsors of this bill have. For 4 or 5 years I have been fighting and urging the people of my State to repeal the poll tax as a prerequisite to participation in the party primaries of the State, which could be done by an act of the legislature. . . .[112]

Despite his statement, little evidence exists of the late Senator Bilbo's "fight" for a modification of the Mississippi poll tax.

No significant movement directed toward altering the tax prerequisite exists at present. The threat of national action seemed to have an effect in this state opposite to the one it had in other states. In 1949, an observer of Mississippi politics believed that as long as the news from Washington kept poll tax repeal on the front page, Mississippi's dander would be so high that no local action would be taken. The poll tax issue is no longer front page news in Washington but the segregation controversy will operate to prevent poll tax repeal in

---

111 House Bill No. 28 and Tuscaloosa *News,* May 5, 1955.

112 88 *Congressional Record* 8833. See also p. 8841 and statement of Representative Whittington, pp. 8072-78.

Mississippi for some time. From time to time, even as recently as 1954, proposed constitutional amendments to repeal the tax have been introduced in the legislature but none has received serious consideration. Less possibility for poll tax repeal exists in this Deep South state than in any other southern poll tax state.

This survey of the repeal movement in the poll tax states disclosed that the greatest amount of support for abolition exists in Virginia, Texas, and Arkansas. Until recently, demand for tax removal had not been as strong in Alabama but the women have produced a change. Little support for any modification in the tax requirement is present in Mississippi.

In Virginia, the prospects for poll tax abolition are not bright for the immediate future. Repeal as a part of several suffrage changes was defeated in 1949 and, since then, the Byrd machine has been unwilling to allow the voters to pass on straight repeal uncomplicated by other alterations. Eventually the machine will have to do something about the demand for lifting the tax. New threats of a national bill would help to force action in the Old Dominion. However, the issue of poll tax repeal is now complicated by the school segregation controversy. Re-agitation of the race issue means that the poll tax will not be abolished in Virginia for some time.

A poll tax repeal amendment was also defeated in Texas in 1949. Future action in the Lone Star State is difficult to predict. The Texas non-cumulative tax which serves in lieu of a registration system has not aroused the indignation which the tax requirement has aroused in some other states. Apparently the tax is largely retained because of public indifference. If an active movement for its elimination should begin, the tax might be removed without great difficulty. The race issue does not stand in the way as it does elsewhere. A renewed push to adopt a national anti-poll tax bill would greatly assist repeal in Texas.

Arkansas may be the first of these five states to repeal the poll tax. Since a favorable vote of nearly 45 per cent was obtained in 1956 and since organized labor and the League of Women Voters are actively working for repeal, the chances for early passage of an amendment to abolish it are good. Repeal will be assisted if the legislature enacts a voter registration law preceding submission of another repeal amendment. The race issue is the primary deterrent to repeal and it is a greater deterrent than in Texas but less significant than in Virginia, Alabama, or Mississippi. The difficulty of securing poll tax repeal has been increased by the worsening of the segregation controversy in the Wonder State.

While recent years have produced a strong poll tax repeal movement in Alabama and while the movement nearly met with success in 1953, little possibility of poll tax removal exists at present because of the school segregation controversy and its resulting racial tensions. Some resolution of current racial problems will have to occur before the poll tax can be entirely eliminated.

Poll tax repeal will be obtained in these states only when the politicians have become convinced that such action should or must be taken. Further efforts to enact a national anti-poll tax bill will be of great help in bringing them to this conclusion. Examination of the state repeal movement indicates that repeal has been forwarded by the threat of national action. Another method of convincing the powers-that-be to support poll tax removal is for groups favoring repeal to work much harder for it. In most of these states, a greater grass-roots sentiment for abolition needs to be created than exists at present.

Labor, Negro, veterans', women's, and religious organizations have been the chief pressure groups supporting poll tax elimination. Labor and Negro organizations have been particularly active, although not to the same degree in all states. In Alabama, the women led the movement. An increase of labor's political power in the South will benefit the repeal effort.

Entrenched political interests, who believe that the tax helps them retain their control, are the principal opponents. In states with a sizable Negro population, the race issue always enters any attempt to drop or alter the tax requirement. Tax supporters use the race problem as a smoke-screen to win popular approval for poll tax retention. The outburst of racial tensions since the Supreme Court's school segregation decision has made the racial argument particularly effective. The relationship between the tax and the schools is also used to prevent lifting the tax. In some instances, public school groups take the short-term view that repeal will deprive them of a few dollars. Voters are influenced by this argument. A final argument against repeal is the familiar one that a citizen who is not interested enough to pay a small fee to vote should not be allowed to vote. This contention reflects the aristocratic leanings of many southerners. Many of them frankly believe in a limited suffrage. They also believe that the poll tax helps in keeping out of the electorate the ill-fitted and irresponsible. Therefore, many southerners continue to give it their support.

9. REPEAL BY NATION

SINCE RECENT DEVELOPMENTS involving the poll tax have largely resulted from agitation of the poll tax issue before Congress, the effort to abolish the tax by action of the national government cannot be ignored. The methods proposed, the initiators of these methods, the major groups supporting and opposing repeal by national action, the major arguments for and against such action, and the possibility for achieving repeal via this route, are important parts of the total poll tax picture.

The focusing of national attention upon the poll tax, beginning in 1939, is one phase of the trend in the United States to turn to Washington for leadership. Just as United States citizens are looking to the central government more and more for direction in such fields as agriculture, social security, labor relations, and conservation of natural resources, they are also asking the national government to safeguard their civil rights. They are no longer content that these rights be guaranteed solely by establishing constitutional limits upon governmental action. They are demanding that the government act positively to protect them. This new approach to civil rights is summed up in the report of President Truman's Committee on Civil Rights which emphasized that "the National Government of the United States must take the lead in safeguarding the civil rights of all Americans."[1] As a result of the recommendations of this committee, the Truman Civil Rights Program was placed before the American people. The most controversial and well-known parts of this program were the proposals to establish a Fair Employment Practices Commission, to outlaw

[1] *Report of the President's Committee*, p. 99.

poll tax payment for national elections, to make lynching a national crime, and to eliminate segregation in interstate transportation.

After publication of the report of the President's Committee on Civil Rights, the question of poll tax abolition through national action became a part of the general controversy stirred up by the report and by President Truman's civil rights message to Congress in February, 1948. Congressional attention to the poll tax, however, and to the problem of lynching, ante-dated their inclusion in the general civil rights package. Attention by Congress to these subjects prepared the way for the Truman Civil Rights Program and indicated an acceptance by many persons of the idea that these are problems which relate to the fundamental rights of all Americans and which, therefore, may demand action by the central government.

The campaign for poll tax repeal by the national government began as a part of the general movement for social reform which came in with the New Deal. When the New Deal program was before Congress, the belief developed that many southern congressmen had a conservative outlook because they represented a restricted electorate. The poll tax was largely to blame for the narrow base of the southern suffrage. If the tax could be removed, the suffrage would be broadened and the result would be the selection of a different type of congressman. Southern conservatives and demagogues could be replaced by liberal, progressive representatives. It will be recalled that this same assumption played a part in the state repeal movements, especially in those of Florida, Tennessee, and Virginia.

Thus, poll tax abolition was regarded as a condition precedent to shifting political control from the so-called conservatives, from representatives like John E. Rankin and Theodore G. Bilbo of Mississippi, Edward E. Cox of Georgia, Martin Dies and Hatton W. Sumners of Texas, and Howard W. Smith and Harry F. Byrd of Virginia, and to pro-New Deal congressmen. Because of this assumption, congressional attention was directed to the poll tax at the latter part of the New Deal period. The first anti-poll tax bill was introduced in 1939. Some poll tax opponents turned to Congress because they believed state action was remote. Knowing that state constitutional amendments were necessary in most cases and that the amendment process was usually a tedious and difficult one, they looked to the national government for help. In the beginning, they may have really expected to lift the tax in this way. As year after year passed without success, it seems apparent that few advocates of repeal by Congress really expected the tax to be lifted in this manner. Instead, they used Congress as a platform from which to propagandize their fight against the poll tax. They also recognized that the threat of national action was a powerful weapon to use in achieving repeal by the states.

Three methods of lifting the poll tax through national action have been attempted. The most important one is that of enacting an anti-poll tax bill to remove the tax as a voting requirement for national elections. The national repeal movement has centered on this method. A second method is that of abolishing the tax by constitutional amendment. Much of the battle over the issue of poll tax repeal via national legislation has revolved around the constitutional question. Some non-southern congressmen, although they do not support the tax as a voting qualification, believe that Congress does not have the constitutional authority to lift it by legislative action. They favor a constitutional amendment. Support for this method also comes from some southern congressmen who may regard it as a convenient way to table the troublesome poll tax issue. The final, and least publicized, method is that of challenging the constitutionality of state poll tax laws in federal courts. Although impressive arguments have been built up, no significant results have been obtained through this approach.

REPEAL BY CONGRESS

Since 1939, every session of Congress has had before it at least one bill which would eliminate the poll tax as a voting requirement in national elections. The proposal has been aptly termed the "perennial anti-poll tax bill." The House of Representatives has passed an anti-poll tax bill on five different occasions but, thanks to the filibuster, the Senate has not once approved the measure.

Lee E. Geyer, a Democrat from California, introduced the first anti-poll tax bill in the House of Representatives in August, 1939.[2] The proposal originated with the Southern Conference for Human Welfare, an organization composed of representatives from southern welfare, labor, religious, civic, and student groups and having, depending upon your point of view, a progressive, liberal, or leftist outlook.[3] A resolution was adopted at the first conference in Birmingham, Alabama, November, 1938 which supported both state and national action to end the poll tax as a voting prerequisite in primary and general elections. At the first meeting of the Executive Board, held at Chapel Hill in February, 1939, a Civil Rights Committee was established.[4] This committee decided to concentrate on poll tax abolition. It drafted the bill which Congressman Geyer introduced. An attempt was made to get a

[2] 84 *Congressional Record* 11229.

[3] The Southern Conference was organized in Birmingham, Alabama, in 1938. It grew largely out of the Alabama Policy Committee, a group which concerned itself with social, economic, and political problems of Alabama as they affected the citizens of Alabama, the rest of the South, and the Nation. The idea crystallized at a 1937 meeting of the committee that a southwide organization was needed to work toward achieving needed reforms. In July, 1938, a formal proposal for a southern conference was submitted to a group of southerners in Birmingham and the following September, an organizational meeting was called in the same city. The first conference was held in Birmingham from November 20 to 23, 1938, with some 1,200 representatives from all sections of the South present. The delegates represented churches, schools, civic clubs, student groups, YMCA and YWCA, labor organizations, industrialists, Negro groups, influential newspapers, Jewish organizations, Catholics, Protestants, Democrats, and Republicans. The organization of the Southern Conference was also influenced by reaction to the 1938 *Report on Economic Conditions of the South.* Bunche, pp. 675-76; *Report of the Proceedings of the Southern Conference for Human Welfare* (Birmingham, Ala., 1938), p. 16; and "Origin and History of the Southern Conference for Human Welfare" (n.d., 2 pp., mimeo.). The last two publications may be found in the files of the Southern Conference, which are deposited at Atlanta University, Atlanta, Ga.

[4] The committee was composed of Maury Maverick, chairman; James Morrison, vice-chairman; Joseph Gelders, secretary; and Virginia Durr. Because of Maverick's political difficulties in Texas and Morrison's in Louisiana, the work largely fell upon Gelders and Mrs. Durr. Virginia Durr's introduction of Joseph Gelders, Second Conference, SCHW, April 16, 1940. SCHW File, Atlanta University.

southern congressman to sponsor the bill but since none was willing, the committee got Lee Geyer to do so.[5] Thus, although many southerners complain that the anti-poll tax bill is another instance of Yankee meddling into their affairs, southerners originated the proposal.

About a year before introduction of the Geyer bill, President Roosevelt directed attention to the poll tax. He declared at a press conference in September, 1938, that the tax was an outmoded instrument for restricting the suffrage. He gave Virginia as an example of its effect upon voting, stating that, because of the tax, only about one-third of the white population voted there.[6] These comments were made at the same time that the President wrote to Brooks Hays, indicating his support of poll tax abolition in Arkansas. This action of the President may have encouraged leaders of the Southern Conference for Human Welfare to undertake to eliminate the poll tax through act of Congress.

Congress has considered two principal types of anti-poll tax bills. The Geyer bill represents one type and the Pepper bill another. The latter was introduced in the Senate in 1941 by Claude Pepper of Florida. The Geyer bill was drawn as an amendment to the Hatch Act of 1939 which was enacted to prevent "pernicious political activities."[7] The Geyer measure declared that the poll tax requirement caused "pernicious political activities" since the tax was frequently paid for voters by others as an inducement to vote for certain candidates. To insure honesty of elections, Congress should abolish this requirement in national elections.[8]

---

[5] Bunche, pp. 677, 682, and 759; "Origin and History of the Southern Conference for Human Welfare." See also 84 *Congressional Record* A4123-25, extension of remarks of Lee E. Geyer. The committee's secretary, Joseph Gelders, asked Geyer to introduce the bill. Letter to author from Clark Foreman, dated April 6, 1951.

[6] New York *Times*, September 10, 1938. The late Senator Carter Glass quickly challenged the President's statement. He disagreed that the poll tax caused non-voting in Virginia and offered for proof the fact that many more persons paid the tax than voted. *Ibid.*, September 12, 1938.

[7] The Hatch Act became law just three days before Congressman Geyer introduced his proposal. See Public 252, 53 *Stat.* 1147.

[8] H. R. 7534, 76th Cong.

The Pepper bill did not approach poll tax repeal by the indirect route of declaring it a cause of corrupt election practices. It stated that the tax requirement was not a qualification of voters within the meaning of Section 2, Article I of the Constitution and made it unlawful to require poll tax payment in connection with any election for national offices.[9] The Pepper bill applied to both primary and general elections, while the Geyer proposal covered only general elections. After its introduction, the approach of the Pepper bill was followed in subsequent measures considered by Congress.

Since Representative Geyer did not introduce the Southern Conference measure until the last day of the 1939 session,[10] no action was taken until the following session and little progress was made then. Hearings were held in the spring of 1940 by a subcommittee of the House Judiciary Committee but the full committee did not report the measure.[11] Geyer reintroduced the bill in January, 1941.[12] Realizing that the House Judiciary Committee, headed by Hatton Sumners of Texas, would continue to sit on the measure, he acted to bring it before the House by the discharge petition procedure.[13] The necessary number of signatures was not obtained until September, 1942. Geyer had died nearly a year before, and Joseph A. Gavagan of New York assumed the leadership of the poll tax proposal. On October 13, 1942, the House passed the Geyer bill by 254 to 84 votes.[14]

[9] S. 1280, 77th Cong.

[10] Geyer stated that he introduced it then so that there might be a full discussion of its objective and form prior to the convening of the next session. 84 *Congressional Record* A4125. He was apparently waiting to see if the Civil Rights Committee could get a southern congressman to introduce it. Statement of Joseph Gelders, SCHW Conference, Chattanooga, April 16, 1940. SCHW File, Atlanta University.

[11] Contrary to established procedure, the 1940 hearings were not published. To make available some of the information presented, the Civil Rights Committee of the Southern Conference published a digest of the hearings. All who testified were favorable to the proposal but even so the House Judiciary Committee did not act.

[12] H. R. 1024, 77th Cong.

[13] 87 *Congressional Record* 1460.

[14] 88 *Congressional Record* 8174.

By this time, the Senate had under consideration the Pepper proposal. A subcommittee of the Senate Judiciary Committee held lengthy hearings, beginning in July, 1941, and extending intermittently until October, 1942, closing the same day that the Geyer bill passed the House. After receiving the Geyer bill, the Senate Judiciary Committee decided to substitute the Pepper measure for it. Shortly thereafter, the committee reported the amended bill favorably.[15]

Once before the Senate, the anti-poll tax bill ran into a filibuster staged by southern senators led by Senator Tom Connally of Texas and dominated by Senator Bilbo of Mississippi. An unsuccessful attempt was made to apply cloture. Many senators voted against cloture, even though they favored the bill, because they feared cloture might some time be used against them.[16]

This summary of what happened to the anti-poll tax bill in the 77th Congress tells the story of what happened in following congresses. In the 78th Congress, several bills, patterned after the Pepper proposal, were introduced. The one sponsored by Representative Vito Marcantonio, the former American Labor congressman, was singled out for action.[17] The House approved it on May 25, 1943 by 265 to 110 votes.[18] Like its predecessor, it was killed by a Senate filibuster. This time Senator Connally bore the brunt of the fight instead of the unpopular Bilbo.

In the 79th Congress, the Marcantonio bill again received the major attention.[19] It passed the House on June 12, 1945 by 251 to 105 votes.[20] When the Senate took it up at the end of July, 1946, Majority Floor Leader Alben Barkley invoked the cloture rule immediately without allowing a filibuster to develop. The Senate again refused to apply cloture and another Congress ended without enacting an anti-poll tax measure.[21]

---

15 Senate Report No. 1662, 77th Cong., 2d sess.

16 88 *Congressional Record* 9065.

17 H. R. 7.

18 89 *Congressional Record* 4889.

19 H. R. 7.

20 91 *Congressional Record* 6003.

21 The Senate vote on cloture was 39 to 33. A two-thirds vote is necessary. 92 *Congressional Record* 10512.

The 80th Congress sidetracked the "communist-tainted" Marcantonio bill in favor of a similar measure sponsored by a safe and solid Republican, George H. Bender of Ohio.[22] In this Congress, all anti-poll tax proposals were referred to the new Committee on House Administration instead of to the Judiciary Committee as in previous sessions. As a result, the measure came before the House for the first time by a favorable committee report rather than by the discharge petition route. On July 21, 1947, the House approved by 290 to 112 votes its fourth anti-poll tax bill.[23] The Senate did not consider the proposal until the special session called by President Truman following the presidential nominating conventions of 1948. The measure met the same fate as that of previous ones.

In the 81st Congress, the poll tax issue and other parts of President Truman's Civil Rights Program were in effect defeated early in the first session when the attempt to amend the Senate cloture rule failed due to the united efforts of southern spokesmen. However, Congress went through the motions of trying to pass an anti-poll tax measure for the fifth time. On July 26, 1949, the House approved by 273 to 116 votes the bill sponsored by Mrs. Mary T. Norton of New Jersey, the chairman of the Committee on House Administration.[24] This proposal did not even reach the filibuster stage in the Senate. Throughout the 1950 session, it remained bottled up in the Senate Committee on Rules and Administration. The outbreak of fighting in Korea occurred about the time the Senate normally would have taken up the poll tax question. As a result of this crisis, few senators were interested in engaging in a futile debate over the poll tax.

Although anti-poll tax bills have continued to be introduced

[22] H. R. 29.

[23] 93 *Congressional Record* 9551-52.

[24] 95 *Congressional Record* 10248. Since the Rules Committee did not approve a resolution to bring the Norton bill before the House, Mrs. Norton invoked the rule which permitted the bypassing of this committee. The rule provided that the Rules Committee could be discharged from further consideration of any measure pending before it if the measure had been pending more than 21 calendar days. The procedure was adopted for the 81st Congress in an attempt to limit the power of the Rules Committee. It was not continued for the 82nd Congress. *Ibid.*, pp. 10095-97, and 10110.

in Congress, no significant action toward passage of any of them has been taken in recent years. Even the House of Representatives has not bothered to pass the proposal again. The bills have been sent to committee and allowed to die. The school segregation controversy reawakened interest in the protection of civil rights by the national government. Some of the resulting civil rights proposals included an anti-poll tax provision[25] but this provision was not included in the bill approved by the House on July 23, 1956.[26]

Passage of an anti-poll tax bill by Congress appears extremely remote. The proposal has been before Congress so long that the spark and interest in it has gone. However, it will be agitated on Capitol Hill until the tax has been abolished as a voting requirement in every state.[27]

SUPPORTERS AND OPPONENTS OF REPEAL BY CONGRESS

The principal groups who support poll tax abolition were identified when the state repeal movement was examined. Most of these same groups also favor passage of an anti-poll tax bill by Congress.

Three organizations were closely connected with the fight to lift the poll tax through congressional action. The role of the Southern Conference for Human Welfare has been indicated. The Southern Conference concentrated its activities on repeal through federal action. Another southern organization, the Southern Electoral Reform League, worked primarily to secure repeal by state action although it endorsed and worked for passage of a federal measure as well. These organizations complemented each other; one devoted its major energies to the passage of a federal bill and the other to repeal by state

25 For example H. R. 51 and H. R. 5503, 84th Cong.

26 102 *Congressional Record* (daily edition) 12766.

27 During World War II, Congress partially lifted the poll tax requirement. The Soldier's Vote Act of 1942 provided that no one in military service during wartime should be required to pay a poll tax to vote for federal officers. Public 712, 56 *Stat.* 753. Since this measure has not been repealed, it would apply if the United States again became engaged in a formal war. Scattered attempts have been made to attach an anti-poll tax provision as a rider to some other proposal. None of these attempts mustered any significant support.

action. Each lent support to the other and their membership overlapped.

The third organization was the National Committee to Abolish the Poll Tax, which, as its name indicates, was founded for the sole purpose of securing passage of a federal anti-poll tax bill. Many of the same persons active in the Southern Conference and in the Southern Electoral Reform League were also members of the National Committee. Mrs. Virginia Foster Durr developed the Civil Rights Committee of the Southern Conference into the National Committee.[28] Some of those who were associated with one or more of these three organizations were Clark Foreman, Frank P. Graham, Jennings Perry, Will Alexander, Moss A. Plunkett, David G. George, Virginia Foster Durr, Mary McLeod Bethune, Eleanor Roosevelt, Claude Pepper, George H. Bender, Vito Marcantonio, William Green, and Phillip Murray. Clark Foreman led in the work of the Southern Conference; Moss A. Plunkett and David G. George in the Southern Electoral Reform League; and Jennings Perry and Will Alexander in the National Committee.

These organizations are defunct. They were most active in the early and middle 1940's.[29] Due to lack of financial resources, internal squabblings, and waning enthusiasm, all three organizations lapsed into inactivity. They were injured, especially the Southern Conference, by the communist label pinned on them by opponents.

A variety of labor, Negro, civic, religious, and veteran organizations supported and worked for passage of a federal anti-poll tax bill. The national organizations of the CIO and AF of L as well as a number of affiliated unions were among the leaders.

[28] Letter to author from Clark Foreman, dated April 6, 1951.

[29] The Southern Conference, established in 1938, was the oldest. The Southern Electoral Reform League was organized early in 1941 and the National Committee was established about the same time. The Southern Conference was formally disbanded in November, 1948, on its tenth anniversary. *Ibid.* The Southern Electoral Reform League exists only on paper. Letter to author from Moss A. Plunkett, dated July 16, 1949. The National Committee ceased to function in 1948. On January 1, 1947, the Southern Conference withdrew its financial support of the committee. Letter to James Dombrowski from Jennings Perry, dated January 3, 1947. SCHW File, Atlanta University.

The representatives of southern branches of the CIO and AF of L were especially vocal before congressional committees.[30] Negroes were represented at congressional hearings by the NAACP, Colored Voters' League, Fraternal Council of Negro Churches, National Council of Negro Youth, National Negro Congress, National Negro Council, and National Urban League. Women's organizations like the League of Women Voters, American Association of University Women, League of Women Shoppers, Women's International League for Peace and Freedom, Women's Society of Christian Service of the Methodist Church, YWCA, and National Council of Jewish Women supported the measure. Some religious groups who favored the bill were the Church League for Industrial Democracy and the National Intercollegiate Christian Council. Other supporting organizations were the American Civil Liberties Union, Americans for Democratic Action, American Jewish Congress, Council Against Intolerance in America, National Conference of Social Work, National Federation for Constitutional Liberties, National Lawyers' Guild, People's Lobby, Southern Tenant Farmers Union, and the Communist and Socialist parties. The support of the Communist party and other left-wing organizations obviously did more harm than good to the movement. Opponents, like Representative John Rankin of Mississippi, waved the Red flag with vigor.

It is doubtful that any strong grass-roots sentiment favoring poll-tax repeal by Congress exists. No nation-wide polls have been taken on the question of whether a federal anti-poll tax bill should be enacted. Samples of public opinion indicate that the people of the United States believe that the tax should be abolished but the polls have not ascertained how they think abolition should be achieved. Since 1949, the polls have shown that poll tax repeal is favored by a majority in the South.[31]

---

30 Efforts were made to have southerners testify for a federal bill at the time of congressional hearings. This was more true of the hearings held in 1940 and 1941-1942 than of those held in 1947, 1948, and 1949.

31 The following results were obtained by the American Institute of Public Opinion to the question, "Do you think southern poll taxes should be abolished?"

Vocal opposition to a federal anti-poll tax bill came from state officials and congressional representatives of both poll tax and non-poll tax southern states. No National Committee to Retain the Poll Tax was formed; neither were there any organized pressure groups which opposed the federal bill. In the early days of the effort to pass the bill, the pressure came almost entirely from its supporters. At the first hearings, few spoke against it. At later hearings, opposition ranks considerably expanded until almost as many opposed as supported the proposal. Governors and attorney generals of the poll tax states and southern congressmen were the opposition spokesmen. The latter not only fought this challenge to states' rights on the floor of Congress but also led the opposition before congressional committees.

One way to find out where support for and opposition to passage of an anti-poll tax bill comes from is to analyze congressional roll call votes on the issue. The analysis yields the expected results. Most congressmen from the South voted against passage while most of those from other sections voted for passage. Table 19 sets forth the results of an examination of the five votes in the House of Representatives on final pas-

		Abolish	*Retain*	*No Opinion*
NATIONAL TOTAL—April, 1941		63%	25%	12%
	July, 1948	65	24	11
	April, 1949	67	22	11
	March, 1953	71	21	8
SOUTH ONLY—	April, 1941	43	45	12
	July, 1948	48	43	9
	April, 1949	53	38	9
	March, 1953	59	29	12

The 1941 question was phrased in a slightly different fashion for voters living in poll tax states. The shift in southern opinion indicates that ventilation of the issue before Congress helped create an opinion in the South favorable to removal of the tax. Since both poll and non-poll tax states were included in the computation, the increase in southern support for repeal also reflects the fact that the ranks of the non-poll tax states have grown. See *The Public Opinion Quarterly*, V (Fall, 1941), 470; XII (Fall, 1948), 567; XIII (Fall, 1949), 557; and Public Opinion News Service, American Institute of Public Opinion, "6 out of 10 Voters in South Favor Abolishing Poll Taxes," For release March 4, 1953.

sage of an anti-poll tax bill. On each occasion, over seventy per cent of the opposition votes came from southern representatives and less than four per cent of the favorable votes came from them. Since the result confirms a well-known fact, the chief significance of the analysis is its revelation of southern supporters and non-southern opponents of the federal anti-poll tax bill.

Table 19. ANALYSIS OF VOTE IN HOUSE OF REPRESENTATIVES ON FINAL PASSAGE OF ANTI-POLL TAX BILLS

	GEYER BILL 1942	MARCANTONIO BILL 1943	MARCANTONIO BILL 1945	BENDER BILL 1947	NORTON BILL 1949
Vote	254-84	265-110	251-105	290-112	273-116
Southerners for	9	5	5	6	7
Southerners against	73	83	79	90	85
Number of Southerners	102	105	105	105	105
Percentage of Southerners for	8.8	4.8	4.8	5.7	6.7
Percentage of Southerners against	71.6	79.0	75.2	85.7	81.0
Percentage of those for, Southern	3.5	1.9	2.0	2.1	2.6
Percentage of those against, Southern	86.9	75.5	75.2	80.4	73.3

Each time the House passed an anti-poll tax bill from five to nine southern congressmen voted for it. As Table 20 shows, most of the southern support came from Tennessee and Texas. At that time Tennessee was still a poll tax state. Little help came from southern non-poll tax states. Only one congressman from North Carolina voted for the Norton bill. The Tennessee supporters were Republicans from East Tennessee and Democrats from Middle Tennessee. No representative from West Tennessee, the stronghold of Boss Crump, voted for any of the bills. In Texas, the "yea" votes came from representatives of the eighth, fifteenth, and sixteenth districts. Harris County, the home of Houston, constitutes the eighth district.

Table 20. SOUTHERN REPRESENTATIVES VOTING FOR PASSAGE OF
AN ANTI-POLL TAX BILL

STATE AND DISTRICT		GEYER BILL 1942	MARCAN-TONIO BILL 1943	MARCAN-TONIO BILL 1945	BENDER BILL 1947	NORTON BILL 1949
Tenn.	1	Reece, R.	Reece, R.		Phillips, R.	Phillips, R.
	2	Jennings, R.	Jennings, R.		Jennings, R.	
	3	Kefauver, D.	Kefauver, D.		Kefauver, D.	
	4	Gore, D.		Gore, D.	Gore, D.	Gore, D.
	5	Priest, D.				
	6	Courtney, D.	Priest, D.	Priest, D.	Priest, D.	Priest, D.
	7					Sutton, D.
Texas	8	Thomas, D.		Thomas, D.	Thomas, D.	Thomas, D.
	15					Bentsen, D.
	16	Thoma-son, D.	Thoma-son, D.	Thoma-son, D.		
Ala.	9	Patrick, D.		Patrick, D.		
N. C.	8					Deane, D.

The fifteenth and sixteenth districts are composed of counties located along the Mexican border. The analysis of the Texas poll tax repeal movement indicated that the greatest support for repeal came from these same areas. The sole Alabama congressman to support the anti-poll tax proposal, Luther

Patrick, represented the ninth district, the home of Birmingham. His support may be accounted for because he came from an urban area and had strong CIO backing.[32]

An analysis was also made of the non-southern representatives who voted against passage of an anti-poll tax bill. An increasing number of non-southerners opposed the proposal. Only eleven non-southerners voted against the Geyer bill in 1942 while 31 opposed the Norton bill in 1949. Although the South produced the chief opposition, the opposition of representatives from other sections is not without significance. On most of the five measures, more Republicans than non-southern Democrats voted against them. This fact takes on greater significance when it is noted that only the 80th Congress (1947-48) was controlled by Republicans. The negative votes of these Republicans were probably based on the belief that Congress does not have constitutional power to lift the tax requirement. Their opposition may have also reflected their increasing concern for states' rights and the extreme conservatism of some. Some Republican right-wingers probably approved of a restricted suffrage and sympathized with their southern colleagues. The non-southern Democratic opponents were primarily from the border states of Kentucky, Maryland, Missouri, and Oklahoma. They reflected a "consciousness of kind" with their southern brethren.[33]

---

32 Patrick was defeated in the 1946 Democratic primary by Laurie Battle who did not have CIO support. Battle did not vote for any anti-poll tax bill.

33 In 1942, the four non-southern Republicans against the Geyer bill were: Paddock, Ill.; Fellows, Maine; Reed, N. Y.; and Rich, Penn. The seven non-southern opposition Democrats were: Bell, Mo.; Coffee, Neb.; Cartwright, Disney, and Wickersham, Okla.; and Faddis and Moser, Penn. In 1943, the seventeen non-southern Republicans against the Marcantonio bill were: Mason and Sumner, Ill.; Jensen, Iowa; Winter, Kan.; Hale, Maine; Bradley and Hoffman, Mich.; Knutson and O'Hara, Minn.; Curtis, Neb.; Douglas, O'Brien, Reed, Taber, and Wadsworth, N. Y.; Rizley, Okla.; Simpson, Penn. The ten non-southern opposition Democrats were: Bates, Chapman, Creal, Gregory, May, and Vincent, Ky.; Baldwin, Md.; Bell and Slaughter, Mo.; Stewart, Okla. In 1945, the nineteen non-southern Republicans against the Marcantonio bill were: Johnson, Mason, and Sumner, Ill.; Jensen, Iowa; Hale, Maine; Hoffman, Mich.; O'Hara, Minn.; Arnold, Cole, and Schwabe, Mo.; Curtis, Neb.; Fuller, Reed, Taber, and Wadsworth, N. Y.; Clevenger, Ohio; Rizley and Schwabe, Okla.; Rich, Penn. The seven non-southern opposition Democrats were: Greg-

A similar analysis cannot be made for the Senate since an anti-poll tax bill never came to a vote there. However, attempts were made to apply cloture on some anti-poll tax bills. Table 21 contains the results of an examination of three Senate cloture votes.[34] These votes do not show as strikingly

Table 21. ANALYSIS OF VOTE IN SENATE ON CLOTURE APPLICABLE TO ANTI-POLL TAX BILLS

	GEYER BILL 1942	MARCANTONIO BILL 1943	MARCANTONIO BILL 1945
Vote	37-41	36-44	39-33
Southerners for	1	1	1
Southerners against	19	17	19
Percentage of Southerners for	4.5	4.5	4.5
Percentage of Southerners against	86.4	77.3	86.4
Percentage of those for, southern	2.7	2.8	2.6
Percentage of those against, southern	46.3	38.6	57.6

ory and May, Ky.; Baldwin and Roe, Md.; Bell and Slaughter, Mo.; Wickersham, Okla. In 1947, the fourteen non-southern Republicans against the Bender bill were: Johnson, Ill.; Jensen, Iowa; Fellows and Hale, Maine; Hoffman, Mich.; Short, Mo.; Kilburn, Reed, Taber, and Wadsworth, N. Y.; Rizley and Schwabe, Okla.; Rich, Penn.; Byrnes, Wis. The seven non-southern opposition Democrats were: Bates, Chapman, and Gregory, Ky.; Bell, Mo.; Albert, Morris, and Peden, Okla. In 1949, the 24 non-southern Republicans against the Norton bill were: Werdel, Calif.; Mason, Ill.; Jensen, Iowa; Smith, Kan.; Fellows and Hale, Maine; Nicholson, Mass.; Bennett, Crawford, Hoffman, and Woodruff, Mich.; O'Hara, Minn.; Short, Mo.; D'Ewart, Mont.; Curtis, Neb.; Cotton, N. H.; Reed and Taber, N. Y.; Gillette, Rich, and Simpson, Penn.; Lovre, S. D.; Byrnes and Smith, Wis. The seven non-southern opposition Democrats were: Gregory, Ky.; Magee, Mo.; Davies, N. Y.; Albert, Morris, Wickersham, and Wilson, Okla.

[34] In 1948, the question of applying cloture on the Bender bill was not brought to a vote. The bill was laid aside by adjourning the Senate. When Republican leaders moved to adjourn, Administration Democrats, led by Senator Barkley, forced a roll call vote so they could state in the 1948 election

as the House votes the sectional nature of support for and opposition to the anti-poll tax measure. The general dislike of imposing cloture in the Senate accounts for the difference. Some non-southern senators, who would have voted for an anti-poll tax bill, voted against cloture. Even so, the South furnished a higher proportion of opposition votes than any other section while only one southern senator, Claude Pepper of Florida, voted for cloture. The non-southerners who voted against cloture did not come from any particular section and were nearly equally divided between both parties.

ARGUMENTS FOR AND AGAINST REPEAL BY CONGRESS

Agitation of the poll tax issue before Congress produced a great, and perhaps significant, debate on the question of Congress' power to lift this suffrage requirement. Both advocates and opponents of repeal by Congress discussed the constitutional question at length. Since the question of constitutionality was debated and examined in detail both in Congress and in scholarly journals, an exhaustive discussion of this aspect of the poll tax is not attempted.[35] However, to

---

campaign that they opposed giving up on the issue. The vote was 69 to 16; 45 Republicans, 19 southern Democrats, and five non-southern Democrats voted for adjournment while 15 non-southern Democrats and one southern Democrat (Pepper) voted against. 94 *Congressional Record* 9738. In 1950, the Norton bill died in committee.

35 A voluminous discussion of this question may be found in the *Congressional Record* and in the hearings on poll tax bills. Additional sources are: J. E. Christensen, "The Constitutionality of National Anti-poll Tax Bills," *Minnesota Law Review,* XXXIII (February, 1949), 217-54; R. A. Hogenson, "Anti-Poll Tax Legislation and the Federal Constitution," *George Washington Law Review,* XI (December, 1943), 73-79; J. E. Kallenbach, "Constitutional Aspects of Federal Anti-poll Tax Legislation," *Michigan Law Review,* XLV (April, 1947), 717-32; M. R. Lazere, "Payment of Poll Tax as a Prerequisite of Voting in a Federal Election," *Cornell Law Quarterly,* XXVIII (November, 1942), 104-10; D. O. McGovney, *The American Suffrage Medley: The Need for a National Uniform Suffrage* (Chicago, 1949), pp. 158-80; J. J. Morrison, "The Pepper Bill is Constitutional," *Lawyers Guild Review,* II (September, 1942), 1-12; J. J. Morrison and B. Algase, "H. R. 7 to Outlaw the Poll Tax in Federal Elections is Constitutional," *Lawyers Guild Review,* III (September, 1943), 9-15; "Anti-poll Tax Legislation—Constitutionality," *New York Univer-*

present a complete account of the effort to abolish the tax by act of Congress, the leading constitutional arguments for and against such action are summarized at this point.

A key constitutional argument turns on the meaning of the term "qualifications" as used in Section 2, Article I of the Constitution. Supporters and opponents of a federal anti-poll tax bill have conducted a verbal tug-of-war over whether the poll tax requirement is or is not a qualification for voting. Advocates of repeal by Congress say that the tax requirement is not a qualification because it is not reasonably related to the capacity of the citizen to participate in the choice of public officials. Ability to pay the tax does not necessarily indicate ability to vote intelligently. The tax is also not a qualification because it was adopted to restrict the suffrage; it is, therefore, a restriction upon voting rather than a qualification for voting. The advocates argue further that a valid qualification should apply to all voters and that the many exemptions from poll tax payment reveal that it is not a true qualification. A final and less effective contention is that this requirement is not a qualification because it is a tax-enforcing measure. This argument emphasizes the revenue aspect of the poll tax and holds that the voting requirement is simply a means of compelling citizens to pay it. If the tax requirement is a restriction on voting rather than a qualification for voting, then Congress may abolish it for federal elections without violating the constitutional prohibition against different qualifications for voters in elections for national officers and state legislatures.[36] In this manner, proponents of a federal bill argue that the poll tax is an arbitrary and meaningless qualification which, in reality, is not a qualification. It is a pretended qualification which prohibits large numbers of citizens from voting.[37] The argu-

---

sity Law Quarterly Review, XXI (January, 1946), 113-21; "Brief in Support of Pepper Bill," *Lawyers Guild Review*, I (March, 1942), 11-18. This bibliography is selective rather than complete.

[36] See Janice E. Christensen, "The Constitutionality of Proposed National Legislation to Abolish the Poll Tax as a Requirement for Voting in National Elections" (Mss., M. A. Thesis, University of Minnesota, 1946), pp. 38-43.

[37] See Senate Report No. 1662, 77th Cong., 2d sess., p. 2.

ment assumes that the states are limited in prescribing qualifications by the inherent meaning of the word "qualifications" and that the powers of the states over voting qualifications do not prevent the national government from questioning a requirement prescribed as a qualification by the states.[38]

To sustain their contention that the poll tax is a qualification for voting within the meaning of the Constitution, opponents of an anti-poll tax bill rely heavily upon the fact that, when the Constitution was adopted, the original states had property or tax qualifications. Thus, a tax payment requirement was a qualification according to the use of the term when it was included in the Constitution. The framers accepted these qualifications and nowhere did they give Congress power to alter them.[39] Accordingly, Congress cannot now abolish the tax in federal elections by giving the term "qualifications" a definition different from its historic meaning. The adversaries of repeal by Congress quote liberally from the founding fathers to prove that the framers intended for the states, not the national government, to control elections. They also argue that when the qualifications of race and sex were abolished, constitutional amendments were necessary. If the poll tax is to be removed by national action, a constitutional amendment will again be necessary.

Anti-poll tax bill opponents state further that if the argument relative to the meaning of "qualifications" is accepted, then the constitutional directions as to qualifications are meaningless since every qualification must by its nature be restrictive.[40] Age, citizenship, and residence qualifications are all restrictive. If a qualification ceases to be such when it is restrictive, then what meaning is left to the constitutional provisions that the qualifications to vote for congressmen shall be the same as those to vote for members of the lower house of the state legislature?

38 Christensen, "The Constitutionality of Proposed National Legislation," p. 34.

39 Senate Report No. 1662, Pt. 2, 77th Cong., 2d sess., p. 3.

40 See letter of Representative Burr P. Harrison, Richmond *News Leader*, June 21, 1949.

Opponents emphasize that enactment of a federal anti-poll tax bill would create a different set of qualifications for national and state electors. Persons voting in national elections would not all have the same qualifications as those for electors of the lower house of the state legislature, contrary to Section 2, Article I and the Seventeenth Amendment. Opponents contend that if Congress can strike down a state qualification, it can itself impose qualifications. They dwell upon the growth of national power within recent years and state that the anti-poll tax proposal is the opening wedge which will lead to the nationalization of elections. The argument is summed up as follows:

Concealed in the anti-poll tax bill is a legal weapon that could destroy our system of government and the local supervision of elections. If the bill passes, something of America will pass with it.[41]

The adversaries of a federal bill rely heavily upon the cases of *Breedlove* v. *Suttles* and *Pirtle* v. *Brown* to sustain their contention that the poll tax voting requirement is a valid qualification. In both cases, federal courts refused to strike down the tax requirement. The constitutionality of Georgia's poll tax was challenged in the Breedlove case. In 1937, the United States Supreme Court affirmed the decision of the Georgia court which dismissed the contention as to unconstitutionality. In refusing to invalidate Georgia's tax requirement, the Supreme Court unanimously ruled that:

Privilege of voting is not derived from the United States, but is conferred by the State and, save as restrained by the Fifteenth and Nineteenth Amendments and other provisions of the Federal Constitution, the State may condition suffrage as it deems appropriate.[42]

The appellant demanded in the Breedlove case that the state official qualify him to vote in state, as well as in national, elections. The Pirtle case concerned congressional elections only. It presented the question of whether a state (Tennessee)

---

[41] As quoted in Minority Views on H. R. 3199, House Report No. 912, 81st Cong., 1st sess., p. 4.

[42] 302 U. S. 277, 283.

could prevent a citizen from voting in them because he had not paid his poll tax. He was otherwise qualified to vote. In March, 1941, in an unanimous three-judge opinion, the Sixth Circuit Court of Appeals held that the right to vote in a national election is conditioned on such terms as the state imposes. It upheld Tennessee's poll tax as a requirement for participating in general elections for members of Congress and used the Breedlove case for precedent.[43]

In arguing that Congress has authority to enact an anti-poll tax measure, advocates frequently cite *United States* v. *Classic*.[44] The question presented was whether the right of qualified voters to vote and to have their ballots counted in a Louisiana congressional primary was a right secured by the Constitution. Justice Harlan F. Stone, speaking for the Court, held that the right of the people to choose their elective officers is a right established and guaranteed by the Constitution. Anti-poll tax bill supporters rely upon this opinion to uphold their contention that Congress may, in protecting this guaranteed right, abolish the poll tax for national elections. Because of it, they believed that the Supreme Court would overrule the Breedlove case when it decided the Pirtle case.[45] However, the Court refused to grant a writ of *certiorari* for the Pirtle case and thereby sustained the lower court decision.[46] Since *certiorari* was denied after the decision in the Classic case, opponents of the anti-poll tax proposal point out that, no matter how those favoring repeal by Congress interpret the Classic decision and no matter how they criticize the Breedlove decision, the Supreme Court followed the latter decision by refusing *certiorari* in the Pirtle case. They also note that the Breedlove and Pirtle cases involved the poll tax directly while the Classic case had nothing to do with the tax. They contend that the Classic case did not decide the right of Congress to interfere with the qualifications of voters and that this question was decided by the Breedlove and Pirtle decisions which upheld the poll tax requirement. Supporters reply that the Breedlove and

43 118 F. (2d) 218.
44 313 U. S. 299 (1941).
45 See statement of Senator Claude Pepper, *Hearings on S. 1280,* p. 10.
46 314 U. S. 621.

Pirtle decisions merely upheld the Georgia and Tennessee poll tax requirements and that the question of whether Congress may abolish this requirement in national elections has never been presented to the Court. Since the Classic decision went far to uphold a positive control over elections by Congress, doubts as to constitutionality should be resolved in favor of the measure and the final decision should be left to the Supreme Court.

To this point, the constitutional argument over whether or not the poll tax is a qualification for voting within the meaning of Section 2, Article I of the Constitution has been examined. The supporters of a federal bill do not base their case for its constitutionality solely upon their interpretation of this constitutional provision. They also rely upon Section 4, Article I which authorizes state legislatures to prescribe the times, places, and manner of holding elections for congressmen but provides that Congress may make or alter these regulations at any time, except as to the places of choosing senators. Since the tax requirement affects the manner of holding congressional elections and since Congress may alter regulations pertaining to the manner of holding these elections, Congress may abolish the tax under this clause.

Opponents reply that the poll tax is a voting qualification which has nothing to do with the manner of holding elections. "Manner of holding" refers to the mode of voting, i.e., to whether voting shall be secret and to the method of counting the votes. It concerns the method by which the voter's will is expressed and determined and is clearly distinguished from eligibility to vote.[47] Since the tax relates to eligibility for voting, it falls under Section 2, and not Section 4, of Article I.

Another major argument of the federal bill's supporters is that the poll tax is a tax on a national function and, therefore, may be abolished by Congress. In this connection, they emphasize the revenue feature of the tax. They maintain that the right to participate in congressional elections is granted by the Constitution and cite *Ex parte Yarbrough*[48] and *United*

[47] See McGovney, p. 162.
[48] 110 U. S. 651 (1884).

States v. *Classic* as precedents. In the Classic case, Justice Stone wrote:

While, in a loose sense, the right to vote for representatives in Congress is sometimes spoken of as a right derived from the states, . . . this statement is true only in the sense that the states are authorized by the Constitution, to legislate on the subject as provided by Sec. 2 of Art. I, to the extent that Congress has not restricted state action by the exercise of its powers to regulate elections under Sec. 4 and its more general power under Article I, Sec. 8, clause 18 of the Constitution "to make all laws which shall be necessary and proper for carrying into execution the foregoing powers."[49]

If the right to vote in congressional elections is a right granted by the Constitution, then a tax upon it is a tax upon a national function. The Supreme Court has held since *McCulloch* v. *Maryland*[50] that the states may not tax a national function. If the right to vote can be taxed by a state, then the state has the power to destroy this national function. As a matter of self-preservation, Congress must prevent any state from destroying this cornerstone of the government.[51]

Opponents answer that the national courts decided in the Breedlove and Pirtle cases that the poll tax is within the legitimate taxing powers of the states. The courts decided further that the tax requirement does not tax the right to vote. It is not limited to voters but is also laid upon aliens. In addition, because of exemptions, it is not exacted of all voters. Therefore, it is not essentially a tax upon the right to vote. The requirement that it be paid as a prerequisite to voting is a means of enforcing collection. Opponents state that the courts in these cases did not consider the right to vote for a congressman a national function at all; they considered the right to vote a state matter which could be taxed if the states so desired. Due to the decisions in the Yarbrough and Classic cases, the opposition is on weak ground in emphasizing that the right to vote is purely a state matter.[52]

49 313 U. S. 299, 315.

50 4 Wheat. 316 (1819).

51 See Senate Report No. 1662, 77th Cong., 2d sess., p. 4. This argument was the basis for the Pirtle case.

52 See Christensen, "The Constitutionality of Proposed National Legislation," pp. 62-68.

A fourth argument of the anti-poll tax bill supporters is that the tax abridges the privileges or immunities of citizens of the United States because it abridges the right to vote. States are forbidden to abridge the privileges or immunities of United States citizens by the Fourteenth Amendment. In refutation, opponents of the federal bill cite again *Breedlove* v. *Suttles* and *Pirtle* v. *Brown* in which the courts held that a poll tax voting requirement does not deny any privilege or immunity protected by the Fourteenth Amendment.[53]   They also refer to *Minor* v. *Happersett* in which the Supreme Court ruled that a woman does not have the right of suffrage as a privilege or immunity of citizenship.[54]

Advocates of an anti-poll tax bill also contend that the tax subverts the republican form of government. Therefore, an additional constitutional basis for the measure exists in Section 4, Article IV of the Constitution guaranteeing a republican form of government to every state. Since Congress, and not the courts, may decide what a republican form of government is,[55] Congress may abolish the poll tax if it concludes that the requirement subverts this form of government. In reporting favorably an anti-poll tax proposal in 1942, the majority of the Senate Judiciary Committee asked:

Can we have a republican form of government in any State if, within that State, a large portion and perhaps a majority of the citizens residing therein are denied the right to participate in governmental affairs because they are poor. . . ? The most sacred right in our republican form of government is the right to vote. . . . It must be exercised freely by free men. If it is not, then we do not have a republican form of government.[56]

Opponents reply that the framers of the Constitution did not regard poll tax and property qualifications as opposed to a republican form of government since they did not abolish them when they wrote Section 4, Article IV.[57]   They contend that

---

[53] 302 U. S. 277, 283 and 118 F. (2d) 218, 220.

[54] 21 Wall. 162, 170-71 (1875). See Christensen, "The Constitutionality of Proposed National Legislation," pp. 70-81.

[55] *Luther* v. *Borden*, 7 Howard 1 (1849).

[56] Senate Report No. 1662, 77th Cong., 2d sess., p. 6.

[57] *Ibid.*, Pt. 2, p. 4.

anti-poll tax bill supporters do not believe their argument on this point. If they really believed that the tax requirement acts to deny the republican form of government in the states, their proposal would extend to state as well as to national elections.[58]

The arguments summarized above are the major ones which have entered into the extensive and largely futile debate over constitutionality of a federal anti-poll tax bill. Some supporters also rely upon the Fifteenth Amendment as constitutional authorization. Since this amendment empowers Congress to enforce it by appropriate legislation and since the tax disfranchises Negroes, Congress can use the Fifteenth Amendment as justification for the proposed legislation.[59] Some efforts have been made to base the anti-poll tax bill on the equal protection clause of the Fourteenth Amendment. It is argued that because the tax discriminates against the poor, it violates the equal protection clause. Both arguments are weak as justifications of repeal by Congress and have not played significant roles in the constitutional debate.[60]

A strong argument against the anti-poll tax proposal pertains to the power of Congress over the election of presidential electors. The anti-poll tax bill would abolish tax payment for all national elections. Opponents emphasize that the constitutional provisions relative to voting for members of Congress and for presidential electors are different. Sections 2 and 4 of Article I do not apply to voting for presidential electors. The Constitution is silent as to who may vote for these electors and does not authorize Congress to regulate the manner of holding such elections. It provides that "each State shall appoint, in such manner as the legislature thereof may direct, a number of electors, . . ." and that Congress may determine the time of choosing the electors.[61] The anti-poll tax bill's opponents argue that state legislatures have exclusive powers over the

---

58 Senate Report No. 530, 78th Cong., 1st sess., p. 13 and Christensen, "The Constitutionality of Proposed National Legislation," pp. 82-90.

59 See remarks of Senator Wayne Morse, 94 *Congressional Record* 9718.

60 See Christensen, "The Constitutionality of Proposed National Legislation," pp. 95-99.

61 Art. II, sec. 1, para. 2 and 3.

manner or mode of appointing presidential electors and that, as applied to such elections, the bill is clearly beyond the power of Congress.[62]

In summary, the principal constitutional arguments advanced to support poll tax repeal by Congress are: (1) Section 4, Article I authorizes Congress to abolish the poll tax for national elections since the tax is not a valid voting qualification within the meaning of Section 2, Article I but relates to the manner of holding elections; (2) the broad regulatory powers given Congress under Section 4 are reinforced by the "necessary and proper" clause; (3) Congress may abolish the poll tax since it is a tax on a national function; (4) Congress may abolish the tax because it abridges a privilege of national citizenship in violation of the privileges or immunities clause of the Fourteenth Amendment; and (5) Congress may abolish the tax because it subverts the republican form of government and thus violates Section 4, Article IV. While opponents of the federal bill have an answer to each argument, their basic contention is that the poll tax requirement is a valid qualification for voting and that the national government cannot abolish a qualification which a state has established since the states have broad powers over voting qualifications.

Other pro and con arguments have been advanced besides those relative to constitutionality. Supporters of the federal bill have relied heavily upon a moral approach to the problem. They make broad claims for the tax as a major cause of the low voter turnout in poll tax states. They argue that this low participation challenges the principles which underlie our democratic beliefs. The fact that many Negroes and whites are prevented from voting in these states saps the belief in universal suffrage. Individuals come to believe that the disfranchised are incapable of self rule and, therefore, should not have the right to vote. Thus, suffrage limitations, like the poll tax, irreparably damage our democratic beliefs and cause a

[62] See Christensen, "The Constitutionality of Proposed National Legislation," pp. 100-08, and McGovney, pp. 174-80.

"moral erosion."[63]   In a democratic nation, a price tag should not be placed on the most fundamental of all political rights—the right to choose the elected officials.

Proponents also emphasize that the poll tax is a national issue rather than a purely local matter.   Since it is a national issue, the national government should deal with it.   It is a national problem because it is contrary to the major tenets of the American system and because it affects the relations of the United States with other countries.   The President's Committee on Civil Rights stated that

. . . interference with the right of a qualified citizen to vote locally cannot today remain a local problem.   An American diplomat cannot forcefully argue for free elections in foreign lands without meeting the challenge that in many sections of America qualified voters do not have free access to the polls.[64]

When the poll tax question was before Congress during World War II, the bill's advocates argued that if we were waging an all-out global war to preserve democracy, we should do something in democracy's favor at home.   Young southerners were not asked to pay a poll tax before being inducted into the armed forces.   If they could fight for their country, they should be qualified to participate in the government.   During debate on the poll tax in the spring of 1943, a young sailor expressed a common opinion when he shouted from the House visitors' gallery:

If a man doesn't have to pay to fight, why should he have to pay a tax to vote?   You're fighting the Civil War all over again.[65]

Supporters of repeal by Congress also argue that the poll tax is a national issue because of the influence exercised in the national government by representatives from poll tax states. They point to the number of committee chairmanships held by southerners when Congress is controlled by the Democratic party.   They argue that, having been chosen by a restricted electorate, these representatives have not been sympathetic to

---

63 See *Report of the President's Committee*, p. 140.

64 *Ibid.*, p. 101.

65 As quoted in George H. Bender, "The Poll Tax: A Democratic Deformity," *Free World*, VII (May, 1944), 415.

many of the social welfare measures with which Congress has been concerned since the New Deal. Poll tax removal will help to enlarge the electorate. A broadening of the suffrage will result in a different type of representative being selected, a representative who will think in terms of the interests of the whole rather than in terms of the interests of the upper strata alone.

In reply to these general arguments, opponents of repeal by Congress state that the poll tax is neither the only nor the major cause of disfranchisement, citing figures to show that many persons pay it but do not vote. Indifference is the major factor accounting for the small vote and poll tax repeal will not solve the problem of low turnout in southern elections. Some opponents object to the figures used by repeal advocates. They rightly contend that the primary is the important election in the South and that a discussion of non-voting based on general elections does not present a true picture. They incorrectly maintain that the number of voters who participate in southern primary elections compares favorably with the number who participate in primary elections in non-poll tax states.[66]

Opponents argued during World War II that a wartime period was not the time to consider a matter which would cause disunity and endanger the war effort.[67] The end of the war deprived them of this argument but they could still point to many major questions facing the country and say that these issues should be dealt with before bringing up a sectional measure like the poll tax. Some less responsible opponents, like Representative Rankin of Mississippi, were not averse to introducing the red-herring of communism. They attempted to discredit the proposal by referring to it as CIO and Communist inspired legislation.[68]

However, an increasingly larger number of southern opponents of repeal by Congress make no attempt to defend the tax nor to answer the charges levied against it by those

---

[66] See remarks of Representative William M. Whittington, 93 *Congressional Record* 9547. See also Key, *Southern Politics*, pp. 491-508, for a comparison of voting turnout in southern and non-southern states.

[67] Senate Report No. 530, 78th Cong., 1st sess., p. 7.

[68] See remarks of Representative Rankin, 93 *Congressional Record* 9523.

seeking approval for a federal bill. They admit that the poll tax is an outmoded device. Some congressmen from states which have abolished the tax advise their colleagues that they supported and worked for repeal in their states; others state that they favor repeal in their states. These opponents of the federal bill agree that the tax should be abolished but want it removed by state, rather than national, action. Perhaps this is a result which the backers of the anti-poll tax bill hoped to achieve.

REPEAL BY CONSTITUTIONAL AMENDMENT

Since the constitutional argument has dominated the effort to enact a federal anti-poll tax bill, it is not surprising that attempts have been made to abolish the tax by a constitutional amendment. Although several proposed amendments have been introduced in Congress, no significant progress has been made to lift the tax in this way. Only one proposal, that introduced by Senator Joseph C. O'Mahoney of Wyoming in the 79th Congress, got as far as to be reported out of committee.[69] None has been voted on in either house.

Support for such an amendment has increased slightly within recent years. Several southern representatives now support it. Some advocates of repeal by Congress concluded, after many failures to enact an anti-poll tax bill, that this approach should be followed.[70] When a poll tax amendment was first suggested, some congressmen supported it because, while they favored abolition of the tax, they believed that Congress could not remove it. Senator O'Mahoney of Wyoming is representa-

[69] Senate Report No. 614, 79th Cong., 1st sess.

[70] During debate on the Bender bill in 1948, Senator Pepper, after reaffirming his belief in the constitutionality of the measure, gave support to a constitutional amendment because of the opposition on constitutional grounds. He said: ". . . if we could have an agreement here that instead of pressing for the statutory repeal of the poll tax, we could with only short debate submit to the States a constitutional amendment for the abolition of the poll tax, without any litigation in the courts being necessary, the matter could be settled by the people. That would seem to me, taking everything into consideration at the present time, to be the best practical approach to the elimination of the poll tax." 94 *Congressional Record,* 9464.

tive of such congressmen. Others were undoubtedly "talking for the record" when they indicated approval for a constitutional amendment. They were southern representatives who could safely support it since they knew an amendment had little chance of approval and ratification.

Southern representatives appear to support a constitutional amendment more sincerely now than they did in the early days of the poll tax fight. Beginning with the 81st Congress, Senator Spessard L. Holland of Florida has regularly introduced for himself and several senators from southern and border states a joint resolution proposing abolition of the poll tax by constitutional amendment.[71] In the House, Brooks Hays of Arkansas has sponsored a poll tax repeal amendment.[72] Shortly before the House began consideration of the Norton bill in June, 1949, Hays tried unsuccessfully to get his measure out of the Judiciary Committee by a discharge petition. He informed the House:

I am convinced that a majority of the people have concluded that the seven States retaining the poll tax should in the interest of uniformity on this point be required to do away with the tax. We who feel that, while an undesirable tax, it is a legitimate exercise of State authority, have made no headway in convincing those in other States of the soundness of this position. It is, therefore, time to settle the issue, but it must be settled in an honorable and proper way by amending the Constitution.[73]

Therefore, recent support for a constitutional amendment to abolish the poll tax has come primarily from the South. A basic difference exists between the amendments now sponsored

[71] S. J. Res. 34, 81st Cong.; S. J. Res. 12, 82nd Cong.; S. J. Res. 25, 83rd Cong.; and S. J. Res. 29, 84th Cong. Holland has been joined by such senators as McClellan and Fulbright of Arkansas; Smathers of Florida; George of Georgia; Ellender and Long of Louisiana; Tydings and O'Conor of Maryland; Hoey, Broughton, Smith, Ervin, and Scott of North Carolina; Thurmond of South Carolina; Connally of Texas; and Robertson and Byrd of Virginia. For his statement when introducing the proposal in January, 1955, see 101 *Congressional Record* 730-31.

[72] See H. J. Res. 214, 81st Cong.

[73] 95 *Congressional Record* 7937. In 1949, Hays proposed a compromise program on the civil rights controversy. Poll tax repeal by constitutional amendment was one part of the program. See *ibid.*, p. 770.

by southern congressmen and the earlier ones sponsored by a Republican congressman from Tennessee, John Jennings, Jr.; by the Democratic senator from Wyoming, Joseph C. O'Mahoney; and by 35 Republican senators.[74] The first proposals sought to abolish the tax requirement for both national and state elections. The later ones, sponsored by either the southern senators or by Representative Hays, would remove the tax only from national elections. They go no further than the anti-poll tax bills. Most of these proposals also forbid any tax or property qualification.

Anti-poll tax bill supporters object to repeal by constitutional amendment because it takes so long to amend the Constitution and because they believe that the proposal is primarily a delaying action. President Truman told a press conference in June, 1949 that the proposed constitutional amendment was just an effort to prolong the agony.[75] During a 1956 debate on proposed changes in the method of electing the president, Senator Paul Douglas of Illinois said that he had not supported a constitutional amendment to eliminate the poll tax because he was afraid that it would not be ratified.

We are afraid that if we passed an amendment, it would be sabotaged in the State legislatures. If we can get assurance from the leaders of the South that that would not be the case, that they would actually work for its ratification, we would take a very constructive step which might enable this issue to be resolved.[76]

At hearings held on his proposal in 1949 and 1954, Senator Holland gave this assurance. He stated:

. . . in my judgment every one of the introducers of this resolution, and certainly it is true as to me, will use his best endeavors in his State to accomplish speedy ratification of the amendment.[77]

[74] Jennings and O'Mahoney introduced a poll tax amendment in several different congresses. For Jennings' proposal, see H. J. Res. 112, 77th Cong. and for O'Mahoney's, see S. J. Res. 164, 77th Cong. The measure sponsored by the 35 Republicans was S. J. Res. 132, 78th Cong.

[75] New York *Times*, June 10, 1949.

[76] 102 *Congressional Record* (daily edition) 4656.

[77] *Hearing on S. J. Res. 25*, before a subcommittee of the Committee on the Judiciary, U. S. Senate, 83rd Cong., 2d sess., p. 34. See also *Hearing on S. J. Res. 34*, before a subcommittee of the Committee on the Judiciary, U. S. Senate, 81st Cong., 1st sess.

Supporters of the federal bill also argue that since, in their opinion, Congress has the constitutional authority to repeal the tax, there is no need to attempt the tedious and uncertain method of constitutional amendment.[78]

Poll tax repeal by constitutional amendment is extremely improbable. Since only five states now have a voter poll tax, the Constitution will not be amended for this purpose. No serious consideration has been given to any of the proposed amendments, and it is evident that no significant support exists in Congress.

REPEAL BY COURTS

Another method to abolish the voter poll tax through national action is to challenge the constitutionality of state poll tax laws in federal courts. This method has been attempted in several states and has been a supplementary procedure to working for repeal by act of Congress. Some of the same groups who have supported the anti-poll tax bills instituted cases in federal district courts to challenge the constitutionality of the poll tax in their states.

Reference has been made to two cases in which the poll tax requirement was challenged, *Breedlove* v. *Suttles* and *Pirtle* v. *Brown*. The Breedlove case preceded the time when national attention first began to be seriously fixed upon the tax requirement. It originated in March, 1936, when Breedlove, a 28 year old white Georgia citizen, applied to register for voting. Suttles, a tax collector, refused to register him since he had not paid his poll tax. Breedlove brought suit in the superior court of Fulton County, Georgia, to have the Georgia poll tax provisions declared repugnant to various provisions of the national Constitution and to compel Suttles to register him for voting without poll tax payment. The court dismissed his petition and the Georgia Supreme Court affirmed.[79] The United States Supreme Court affirmed the state supreme court decision on December 6, 1937 and thereby refused to invalidate Georgia's

---

[78] See House Report No. 912, 81st Cong., 1st sess., p. 2.
[79] 183 Ga. 189 and 188 S. E. 140.

poll tax.[80]   The American Civil Liberties Union backed Breedlove in his fight against the tax.[81]

The Civil Rights Committee of the Southern Conference for Human Welfare instituted the Pirtle case.[82]   They wished to test the constitutionality of the poll tax as applied solely to an election for a member of Congress.   The Breedlove case involved an election for both state and national officers.   A special election was held in Tennessee's Third Congressional District in September, 1939 to fill a vacancy caused by death. The Southern Conference used this election to test the constitutionality of the poll tax.   Henry Pirtle, a Tennessee mountaineer and resident of Grundy County, was fully qualified to vote except that he had not paid his poll tax.   He sued the judges of election for the Fifth Civil District of Grundy County and requested a judgment that he was entitled to vote for a member of Congress.   The attorney general of Tennessee intervened and fought Pirtle's petition.   Crampton Harris, former law partner of Hugo Black and a Birmingham, Alabama, lawyer, was employed by the Southern Conference to represent Pirtle.   Federal Judges Elmer D. Davies and Leslie R. Darr denied the petition and held that the question was controlled by the Breedlove decision.   Pirtle and the Southern Conference appealed to the Sixth Circuit Court of Appeals which sustained the district court decision on March 8, 1941.[83] The Supreme Court denied *certiorari*.[84]

Moss Plunkett and the Virginia Electoral Reform League instituted a series of cases challenging the poll tax in federal courts in Virginia.   They decided to take the issue to the courts after Attorney General Abram P. Staples of Virginia testified at the 1942 hearings on the Pepper bill that whether a state had

[80] 302 U. S. 277.

[81] New York *Times*, December 7, 1937.

[82] "Origin and History of the Southern Conference for Human Welfare," SCHW File, Atlanta University.

[83] *Pirtle* v. *Brown*, 118 F (2d) 218.

[84] 314 U. S. 621 (1941). For a general account of the case, see Perry, pp. 158-63. An account of an attempt to challenge Tennessee's poll tax through the state courts is given above, footnote 54, Chapter 7.

unconstitutionally deprived its citizens of their voting rights was a question for the courts, not Congress, to decide.[85]

The Virginia League's first case, *Jones* v. *Settle,* was filed in May, 1944 in the federal district court at Roanoke. Dorothy Bentley Jones, a young Negro housewife, high school graduate, and wife of a service man who was overseas, had become 21 shortly before the case was instituted. She had not been assessed for a poll tax since she was not of age on January 1, 1944. Following her twenty-first birthday, she applied to register so she could vote in the 1944 general election. The registrar, Hazeltine M. Settle, refused to register her since she had not paid a poll tax. Mrs. Jones then challenged the constitutionality of the tax requirement in the district court and demanded damages of $3,500. Before the court ruled, Defendant Settle through Attorney General Staples amended her original answer and advised that Mrs. Jones would be allowed to register without poll tax payment since she became 21 after the time of poll tax assessment. Therefore, the constitutional question became moot and was not ruled upon in the memorandum opinion of District Judge A. D. Barksdale, handed down in September, 1944.[86]

In its second case, the Virginia League attacked the poll tax through the back door by challenging constitutionality of the Virginia Districting Act passed following the congressional reapportionment of 1941. The suit was based on Section 2 of the Fourteenth Amendment which authorizes Congress to reduce a state's representation in proportion to the number of citizens denied the right to vote. The principals were Henry L. Saunders who filed as a candidate for representative-at-large

[85] *Hearings on H. R. 29,* p. 288.

[86] *Ibid.,* pp. 288-89. See also a pamphlet containing the court record published by the Virginia Electoral Reform League and the Parents and Wives of Fighting Americans, entitled *Round One of the Virginia Anti-Poll Tax Fight in the Federal Court.* The Parents and Wives of Fighting Americans was organized early in April, 1944, and was headed by Arthur Dunn, a New York lawyer, with Moss Plunkett as vice-chairman. It was established to get a Supreme Court test of the constitutionality of the poll tax. Its name reflected the clash over the tax which occurred in connection with the 1944 debate on the soldier vote bill. See New York *Times,* April 5, 1944. Dunn and Plunkett worked together on these cases.

from Virginia and Ralph E. Wilkins, secretary of the Commonwealth of Virginia. Saunders contended that Virginia was not entitled to the nine representatives assigned by the 1941 Apportionment Act; that, therefore, her districting system was not valid; and that her representatives should be elected on an at-large basis until new districts were created. He notified the Commonwealth secretary in October, 1943 that he intended to become a candidate for representative-at-large in the November, 1944 general election. Upon the advice of the attorney general, the secretary informed Saunders that he could not certify him as a candidate since no such office as representative-at-large existed. Saunders then filed a complaint against the secretary in the federal district court for the Eastern District of Virginia. When the case came before the court, the attorney general moved that the court dismiss it on the ground that all questions relating to congressional apportionment are political in nature and reside exclusively with Congress. The district court ruled in favor of the Commonwealth secretary; the Fourth Circuit Court of Appeals affirmed; and the Supreme Court, with Justice William O. Douglas dissenting, refused to grant a writ of *certiorari*.[87]

The Virginia League's third case involved a service man's wife who had moved from West Virginia to Virginia in July, 1943. In January, 1944, Eileen S. Evans inquired at the courthouse about the procedure to qualify to vote in November, 1944. She was informed that she must register before October 7, 1944 and that she did not owe any poll taxes. She did not have to pay a poll tax for 1943 since she was not a resident of Virginia on January 1, 1943 and she did not have to pay a poll tax for 1944 since poll taxes for 1944 were not required to vote in 1944. She was advised by friends to check this matter again. This time she was told that under a 1942 amendment to Section 22 of the Virginia Tax Code it would be necessary for her to pay the 1943 tax. In September, 1944, she paid that poll tax

---

[87] Statement of Moss A. Plunkett, *Hearings on H. R. 29*, pp. 289-90; *Saunders v. Wilkins*, 152 F. (2d) 235 (1945), 328 U.S. 870 (1945), and 329 U.S. 825 (1946) (rehearing denied). Osmond K. Fraenkel and John F. Finerty filed a brief for the American Civil Liberties Union as *amicus curiae* in support of the petition.

and registered to vote. The registrar informed her that she could not vote the following November since she had failed to pay her poll tax six months before the election. After being denied a vote on election day, Mrs. Evans filed a complaint against the election judges which, among other charges, challenged the constitutionality of the Virginia poll tax requirement. The state attorney general, through local counsel, filed an answer admitting all allegations except the amount of damages and asked for a jury trial on this issue. The answer stated that the purpose was to avoid ajudication by federal courts of the legal issue raised by the complaint. The court entered judgment for the damages agreed upon. The question of whether the poll tax was a valid voting qualification within the meaning of Article I, Section 2 of the Constitution was again evaded.[88]

A fourth case of the Virginia League also concerned Dorothy Bentley Jones. Mrs. Jones was not assessed for a poll tax for either 1945 or 1946. She tried to vote in November, 1946 but was not permitted to by the election judges. She told the officials that since she qualified to vote in 1944 without poll tax payment, she considered herself qualified to vote in 1946 without paying the tax. In September, 1947, she filed a complaint in the federal district court for the Western District of Virginia against the election judges and asked damages of $3,500. She asked that the court declare her qualified to vote without being required to pay a poll tax and that the election judges be restrained from denying her the right to vote in future elections.

The attorney general, through local counsel, filed an answer in October, 1947 in which he admitted, as he had done in the Evans case, the charges of the plaintiff and requested that a jury trial be held to fix the amount of the damages. He admitted that a voter poll tax is an unconstitutional burden by taxation upon a national right. He also stated that the defendants would not deny Mrs. Jones the right to vote in future elections because of non-payment of the tax.

Mrs. Jones tested the attorney general's answer in November,

---

[88] Statement of Moss A. Plunkett, pp. 290-91.

1947 by requesting the same election judges to permit her to vote without having paid her poll taxes. They refused. She showed them a copy of the answer in this case but, after discussion among the board members, was again refused.

A supplemental complaint setting forth this occurrence was then filed with the court. Since the defendants did not answer this complaint within the time specified, Mrs. Jones moved for a summary judgment in her favor which would declare the Virginia poll tax provisions unconstitutional and enjoin the defendants and their successors from enforcing against her, or any member of the class she represented, the poll tax requirement.[89] The district court ruled against her. Her sponsors originally planned to appeal but decided against it after receiving assurances that Congress would pass an anti-poll tax bill.[90]

John Locke Green, treasurer of Arlington County and a Republican leader, instituted a case involving Virginia's poll tax in 1946. He acted as attorney for Lawrence H. Michael, then Republican candidate for Congress in the Eighth District. Candidate Michael asked that poll tax collection be enjoined in his district because its enforcement would prevent many persons from voting who would vote for him. Green argued that the primary purpose of the tax was to disfranchise Negroes in violation of the Fifteenth Amendment. He also alleged that it prevented white citizens from voting and limited the right to

---

[89] *Ibid.*, pp. 291-93.

[90] Letter to author from Moss A. Plunkett, dated April 17, 1951. In addition to attacking the poll tax through the courts, Moss Plunkett challenged the tax by attempting to unseat members of the House of Representatives from poll tax states. As president of the Southern Electoral Reform League, he contested the election of these representatives following the 1944 general election. These election contests were based on Section 2 of the Fourteenth Amendment as was *Saunders* v. *Wilkins*. They went before a House committee on elections but no action was taken. The committee sealed the documents submitted. See New York *Times*, April 4, 1945; J. Mitchell Morse, "Unseat the Poll-Taxers in Congress," *New Republic*, CXII (April 30, 1945), 574. John Locke Green instituted a similar election contest against Senator Byrd in 1947. He filed in behalf of Lester S. Parsons of Norfolk who was Senator Byrd's Republican opponent in November, 1946. Green was no more successful than Plunkett. See Richmond *Times-Dispatch*, February 19, 1947.

vote to an extent that the republican form of government was denied and the privileges and immunities of United States citizens abridged.

Federal District Judge Charles Sterling Hutcheson dismissed Michael's suit on September 30, 1946, citing the Breedlove case as precedent. It was appealed to the Fourth Circuit Court of Appeals. This court, speaking through Judge John J. Parker, dismissed the case as moot in April, 1947. When it reached the court of appeals, the election in question had already been held. Since the court could not grant relief for that election and since relief for future elections was not asked, the case was moot. With reference to poll tax collection, the court held that the case could not be entertained since the plaintiff had an adequate remedy in Virginia courts.

Although the Michael case was dismissed, Judge Parker indicated sympathy for the arguments of Attorney Green. He noted that questions of the gravest character had been raised which, if presented in a proper case, would merit careful consideration. On whether these were political or judicial questions, he stated:

We are not impressed by the argument that such grave violations of the constitutional rights of citizens as those here alleged present merely political questions with which courts are powerless to deal. In a case properly before us, it would be our duty to inquire whether upon the allegations and proofs rights of citizens guaranteed by the Constitution were being denied them and, if so, to grant appropriate relief.[91]

Perhaps because of this encouragement, Attorney Green instituted a second case, *Butler* v. *Thompson.* Jessie Butler, a Negro woman of Arlington County, brought suit against Mary A. Thompson, Central Registrar for Arlington County, and other election officials to compel them to register her and to permit her to vote without payment of poll taxes. Green used the same arguments about the connection between the poll tax and the Fifteenth Amendment as he had used in the Michael

[91] *Michael* v. *Cockerell,* 161 F. (2d) 163, 164. See also Richmond *Times-Dispatch,* October 1, 1946 and April 10, 1947. Green filed a petition for rehearing immediately after the decision but the petition was dismissed. *Ibid.,* April 17, 1947.

case. The plaintiff demanded a statutory court of three judges to rule upon the constitutional questions raised. The federal district court at Alexandria ruled that a three-judge court was not authorized because no substantial constitutional or federal question was presented. On appeal, the Fourth Circuit Court of Appeals reversed and in a per curiam opinion in October, 1950 stated that a three-judge court should be convened.[92] Circuit Judge Armistead M. Dobie and District Judges Charles Sterling Hutcheson and Albert V. Bryan composed the court. Speaking through Judge Dobie, this court dismissed the suit on February 19, 1951. The court held that the evidence was insufficient to establish any discrimination against Negroes in the administration of the poll tax requirement and that this requirement was not invalid on the basis of either the Fourteenth or Fifteenth Amendments.[93] The Supreme Court affirmed the lower court decision in a per curiam opinion on May 28, 1951 with Justice William O. Douglas again dissenting.[94]

In conclusion, a large part of recent poll tax history has involved various attempts to lift this voting requirement by action of the national government. The method which has received most attention is that of repeal by Congress. Repeal by constitutional amendment has been primarily a delaying and diverting tactic although southern supporters appear to be more sincere now than when the amendment was first proposed. Serious but unsuccessful efforts have been made to have federal courts declare state poll tax provisions invalid on the basis of the national constitution. There is little possibility that the tax will be ended by any of these methods. Repeal by Congress has had the greatest possibility of success, but it is highly improbable that a federal anti-poll tax bill will ever be approved. When support for the bill was at its peak, southern senators prevented its passage by filibustering. Demand for the measure has considerably declined, and interest has fallen as

[92] 184 F. (2d) 526.
[93] *Butler* v. *Thompson,* 97 F. Supp. 17.
[94] *Ibid.,* 341 U.S. 937.

year after year passed without adoption of the proposal. At
the same time, the state repeal movement has gone forward.
As the number of poll tax states diminishes, the possibility of
repeal by Congress decreases. Although a federal anti-poll tax
bill may never become law, although a constitutional amendment abolishing the tax may never be adopted, and although a
federal court may never rule that this voting requirement
violates constitutional rights, these efforts to remove the tax are
significant. They directed public attention to the tax and
created a public demand for its removal. In this way, they
furthered state repeal movements. Although final abolition of
the tax will undoubtedly come as the result of state action, that
action would not have come as soon without the impetus given
by the national repeal movement. The national fight for poll
tax abolition also directed much attention and thought to the
political practices of the South. V. O. Key's study of *Southern
Politics* is a significant example of this broader result of the
movement to abolish the poll tax through national action.

10. CONCLUSIONS

THE POLL TAX has had its day. It is not only obsolete as a tax but also as a suffrage requirement. Only five southern states—Alabama, Arkansas, Mississippi, Texas, and Virginia—retain a voter poll tax. North Carolina, Louisiana, Florida, Georgia, South Carolina, and Tennessee have repealed it.

Use of the poll tax in the South for suffrage restriction dates back to the disfranchising era of the 1890's and early 1900's. All former Confederate States adopted a poll tax suffrage requirement at this time, commencing with Florida in 1889 and ending with Georgia in 1908. In most instances, the tax was only one of several disfranchising measures. Indeed at the time of its adoption, the poll tax was not considered the most important method of limiting the suffrage in those states where the tax was but a component part of a general program for disfranchisement. Literacy and registration requirements aroused more popular interest and largely overshadowed the poll tax. Arkansas, Florida, Tennessee, and Texas were the only states that relied upon the tax as their major instrument of legalized disfranchisement.

A combination of factors brought about the adoption of the poll tax and other disfranchising measures. One factor was a desire to find a legal basis for Negro disfranchisement both to preserve white supremacy and ostensibly to purify elections. Another factor of major importance was the Populist party which seriously challenged Democratic supremacy. This party split the whites and led to competition for the Negro vote. The increased importance of the Negro voter produced new fears for white supremacy. The Populist movement also provoked an increased amount of violence and fraud in elections. Hence, Populism produced further demands for legalized disfranchisement of the Negro and for suffrage restrictions to purify the electoral process. The Populist challenge appears also to have fostered a wish to eliminate from the voting lists many poor and illiterate whites whose votes enabled this new party to threaten Democratic predominance. Although the poll tax was portrayed as another way to deprive the Negro of his vote, the leaders of the movement for disfranchisement appear to have regarded it primarily as a method of disfranchising that class of whites which was menacing their control of southern politics. Finally, the initiation of the disfranchising movement was encouraged by the threat of national intervention represented by the Lodge Force Bill.

Where retained as a suffrage requirement, the poll tax is not uniform. In popular discussion, the tendency is to talk about "the poll tax" as though it is identical in all states, but variety rather than uniformity characterizes the tax requirement. The annual poll tax rates range between $1.00 and $2.00 and are approximately uniform and not excessive, but some states require that the tax be paid for more than one year to qualify for voting. The cumulative feature increases the cost of the tax for the prospective voter and makes the tax more burdensome in Alabama, Mississippi, and Virginia than in Arkansas and Texas where payment only for the election year is required. In Alabama, the tax may accumulate for two years to a maximum sum of $3.00; in Mississippi, two years to a maximum sum of $4.00; and in Virginia, three years to a maximum sum of $4.50, exclusive of penalties. Mississippi has a peculiar cumulative requirement for primary elections, demanding that the tax be paid by February 1 for each of two years preceding the primary. In Texas, the amount of the annual state tax is increased by poll taxes imposed by county governments.

Lack of uniformity also characterizes poll tax coverage. All citizens of voting age are not required to pay it. The exemptions from payment greatly lessen the restrictiveness of the tax upon the suffrage. These exemptions give a special advantage to those groups which have been relieved—the aged and disabled in most states and veterans in Alabama. Where, as in

Alabama, veterans have been freed from the tax and women have not been, it has largely become a device to nullify the Nineteenth Amendment. Where large proportions of prospective voters have been excused from poll tax payment, the tax may not be as restrictive upon the suffrage as it appears to be. All states except Arkansas and Virginia exempt many persons from the tax requirement.

The time of poll tax payment also varies. Most poll tax states require payment several months before the primary and general elections and thus make it more difficult for the citizen to satisfy the tax requirement. The time of payment has an important bearing upon the restrictive nature of the tax. In many instances, more persons may be prevented from voting because of the time of payment requirement than because of the cost. Many citizens who are financially able to pay do not because the time of payment slips past without their knowing it or because their interest in an approaching election has not been aroused before the payment deadline. The length of time before an election that the tax must be paid varies for primary and general elections. Mississippi, Arkansas, and Texas have the earliest deadline for payment before primary elections, and Alabama, Mississippi, Texas and Virginia the earliest deadline before general elections. Due to the importance of the primary in the one-party South, the deadline for poll tax payment for the primary has a greater effect upon voting than the deadline for the general election.

The provisions specifying proof of poll tax payment differ, too. Poll tax opponents have laid considerable emphasis upon the presentation-of-receipt requirement and have implied that loss of the receipt is accompanied by loss of the vote. This implication is not true. There are alternative methods of proving payment. The presentation-of-receipt requirement is significant mainly because of the discriminatory manner in which it may be administered by election officials. Some persons may be asked to produce a receipt while others are not troubled. However, only in Mississippi is receipt presentation the sole means of proving tax payment. In Texas and Arkansas, the receipt may be demanded at the polls but additional ways of establishing proof of payment may be used. In Alabama and

Virginia, virtually no reliance is placed upon the use of the receipt as a method of establishing poll tax payment.

Poll tax revenue is used for a similar purpose in all poll tax states. The revenue is reserved for the schools except in Texas and Virginia, where part of the proceeds are used for other purposes. Allotment of poll tax revenue to the schools has served as a justification for its continuance as a voting requirement but the amount is so small that the tax is of little importance as a source of school funds. This use confuses the tax as a suffrage restriction with the tax as a revenue measure. Where the poll tax is tied to the suffrage, its purpose is to limit the electorate and not to raise revenue.

Based upon poll tax rates, coverage, time of payment, and proof of payment, the most burdensome poll taxes are found in Virginia, Mississippi, and Alabama, in that order. Those of Arkansas and Texas are more moderate yet not without their significance as suffrage restrictions.

Southern experience with the poll tax differs widely not only in terms of rates, coverage, proof and time of payment but also in terms of administration. Where the tax is a suffrage requirement, it is not a tax in the usual sense of the word. Its payment is voluntary. Some states have laws to compel poll tax payment but these laws are infrequently and inadequately enforced. Few officials try to encourage poll tax payment but indications are that more and more steps are being taken to make payment somewhat easier. This fact reflects the decreasing significance of the tax as a suffrage restriction. Many groups, such as women's, veteran's, labor, and Negro organizations engage in campaigns to urge their fellow citizens and their members to satisfy the tax requirement. Contrary to general belief, Negroes are not ordinarily prevented from paying their poll taxes when they offer to pay them.

The manner of administering tax collection may disfranchise as many individuals as the cost of the tax. Collection procedures tend to encourage real property owners to pay more than non-property holders since property taxes and poll taxes are usually collected simultaneously. In this way, as well as because of the cost of the tax, the requirement helps to keep political power in the hands of conservative, propertied interests.

A number of corrupt practices are associated with the poll tax voting requirement. The most common and most serious abuse is paying the tax of others to buy votes. Laws prohibiting this practice are not effective. Vote buying through poll tax payment occurs in varying degrees, with the extent fluctuating according to the intensity of election contests. There are indications that the practice is not as serious now as poll tax opponents claim, and also that it is less common and less serious than in earlier years. Candidates and their supporters engage in the practice most frequently but management and labor resort to it also. With the rise of unions, management lost much of its control over labor's vote and so largely ceased paying employees' poll taxes. In some instances, union leadership assumed this function from management. The extent to which the tax is paid for corner loafers and machine supporters makes a mockery of one of the classic arguments used in its support, i.e., that the tax keeps government in the hands of upstanding, able, and intelligent citizens and excludes corrupt, illiterate, disinterested, and ignorant persons from the polls.

Additional corrupt practices are associated with the poll tax requirement. They include acceptance of payment for voting purposes after the deadline and back-dating tax receipts; excusing part of the cumulative amount due (mainly in Alabama before reduction of the cumulative period in 1953); allowing persons to vote without payment; and interpreting exemption provisions liberally.

The tax lends itself to several distinctive dishonest practices which may be used by particular political groups to their advantage. It is not, however, the actual cause of political corruption. The cause is more deep-seated and exists within the society which permits such conduct. Poll tax repeal eliminates particular dishonest practices associated with the tax but it does not result in any overnight purification of electoral processes just as its adoption did not purify elections. If the society condones corrupt methods, poll tax removal simply means that other dishonest election procedures will be used.

The poll tax is not the sole, nor even the chief, cause for low voter participation in southern poll tax states. Opponents of the tax have considerably over-stated the amount of disfranchisement caused by the tax. No single factor affects the turnout of voters; the poll tax is only one of several. Although repeal advocates have over-stated the case against the tax, it should not be concluded that the tax is of no importance as a voting restriction. Especially where the tax is cumulative, it discourages and prevents many citizens from participating in the political process. The number varies from state to state in accordance with particular conditions and with the severity of the tax. Participation rates tended to decline before poll tax adoption and to increase prior to repeal. In both instances, action taken with respect to the tax seemed to help along a movement already in progress; the tax was not responsible for initiating the trend. No great upsurge in voting followed elimination of the tax requirement. In addition, only part of the increase that occurred can be attributed to abolition of the tax. However, repeal was responsible for a proportion of the increase and, given the low level of electoral participation in the South, any increase is a significant one. Therefore, the poll tax helps to maintain a restricted suffrage and its repeal gives encouragement to many to qualify as voters.

The Louisiana and Alabama analyses disclosed that poll tax repeal or a reduction in the cumulative period did not result in an immediate, sizeable increase in Negro voters although these changes did produce a significant increase in the number of white women registered as voters. Repeal in other states has not meant Negro office holders and a significant increase in political activity on the part of Negroes. The poll tax has been a deterrent to voting by Negroes but it has not been the major one. It affects white citizens more directly than Negroes.

The extent of poll tax payment is affected by urbanism, density of population, the number of Negroes or some other unassimilated group in the population, and the economic conditions of the area. The urban voter, the Negro voter, and the economically depressed voter may be affected more adversely by a poll tax requirement than other groups in the society. But southern urbanites, Negroes, and those at the bottom of the economic scale are poor voters in non-poll tax states, and it may be that they fail to pay the tax simply because they are not interested in elections. The tax undoubtedly helps to discourage them from voting, and may bear upon them more harshly than upon country people, non-Negroes, and economically prosperous groups. But the tax is not alone responsible for their failure to vote.

No final or complete answers to the questions of who pays and who does not pay the poll tax resulted from the methods used in this study. The answers obtained would be more meaningful and trustworthy if the county-by-county analysis could have been applied in more states. Since usable information on the number paying the tax on a county-by-county basis is available only for Arkansas and Texas, the analysis had to be restricted to these states. The attempt to discover the relation between economic status and poll tax payment disclosed the inadequacy of comparative data which adequately measures economic well-being.

Nothing of significance about the effects of the tax upon voting was learned from comparing voting behavior in poll tax and non-poll tax states. Conclusions about the suffrage effects of the tax based on interstate comparisons are of little or no value.

The movement to abolish the poll tax through act of Congress directed national attention to the tax and brought about charges which led to this study. The repeal movements on both state and national levels are interrelated. Although North Carolina repealed her tax requirement in 1920, the movement to repeal the tax by either state or national action did not begin in earnest until the 1930's. Two states, Louisiana and Florida, lifted the tax in 1934 and 1937 before the attention of Congress was turned to it in 1939. Agitation of this issue before Congress helped to foster repeal movements in the remaining poll tax states. Since Congress turned attention to the tax requirement, Georgia eliminated it in 1945, South Carolina in 1951, and Tennessee in 1953, while Alabama significantly modified her cumulative provision in 1953 by reducing the cumulative period from 24 to two years. Active, but thus far unsuccessful, movements to abolish the tax have been carried on in the remaining poll tax states.

The threat of national action has pushed along state repeal movements. Mississippi is the only state where little has been done to obtain poll tax abolition. The Magnolia State is also the only one where the threat of national action has appeared to harm, rather than benefit, the state repeal movement. However, in claiming that a federal anti-poll tax bill has delayed repeal of their tax requirement, Mississippians are simply seeking an excuse to justify their failure to act. Mississippi probably would not have considered removing her tax requirement if a federal anti-poll tax bill had not been introduced. One of the most important results of the national poll tax battle is the encouragement it has given repeal movements within the poll tax states. When this voting requirement has finally been wiped off the books, the end will come through state, rather than national, action. Possibility of enactment of a federal anti-poll tax bill becomes more remote as the tax is eliminated or greatly modified in additional states.

The state and national movements to abolish the poll tax are also interrelated because similar groups have been sponsoring both movements. In the poll tax states, opponents of the tax requirement are members of the liberal, progressive wing of the Democratic party. In large measure, they are the ones who have not had the predominant voice in southern affairs. They support poll tax repeal because they believe that removal of the tax will result in broadening the suffrage which in turn will enable them to capture control of the party and carry out their social welfare programs. Because some southern leaders despaired of state action while others hoped that the possibility of national action would lead to state repeal, they initiated a federal anti-poll tax bill. When the issue was introduced on the national stage, liberals seized upon it as a way to rid the nation of conservative and demagogic southern representatives. When the poll tax question was before Congress, support for its removal by national action had to be given by the liberal wing of the Democratic party because of the importance of the northern Negro vote. Since the poll tax has long been regarded as a means to disfranchise southern Negroes, Democratic left-wingers, especially those from the North, have had to stand up and be counted against the tax and technically for passage of an anti-poll tax bill.

Before the poll tax was abolished in any state, the support of practical politicians had to be won. In several instances, this support was given most reluctantly. Reform groups have played important roles in applying pressure and in creating an opinion favorable to repeal. However, in large measure, repeal has been accomplished because hard-headed politicians decided that such action would be beneficial to them or because they were pushed into this position by the threat of national action. In those states retaining the tax—Alabama, Arkansas, Mississippi, Texas, and Virginia—repeal will not be achieved until professional politicians acquiesce. They may be needled into approving abolition by making it appear that passage of a federal bill is imminent. The work of labor, Negro, veterans', women's, and other organizations for repeal has been and will be important in keeping the issue before the public and in creating a favorable opinion. The tax will probably be eliminated first in Arkansas and Texas. Racial tension resulting from the school segregation controversy will have to be abated before it will be removed in Virginia and Alabama. Repeal will come last in Mississippi.

In addition to the effort to abolish the poll tax by act of Congress, attempts have been made to outlaw it by constitutional amendment and by court action. Opponents of a federal bill used the suggestion for a constitutional amendment primarily as a diverting tactic to delay action on the bill. In recent years, sincere support for the proposed amendment has come from the South, but there is little possibility of its adoption. Some poll tax opponents, especially in Virginia, have made serious efforts to challenge the constitutionality of the tax requirement through federal courts.

No attempt to remove the tax either through Congress or the courts has been successful, but these attacks made the nation so aware of the tax that its removal in all states cannot long be delayed. The assaults upon the tax through agencies of the national government also aroused an interest in the political

processes of the South. This interest led to important studies
of southern political behavior which in turn raised questions
about political behavior in other regions of the nation.

In this study, the writer has attempted to present an objective and factual picture of the southern poll tax voting
requirement. To this end, the origins, form, administration
of collection, relation to political corruption, suffrage effects,
and movements for repeal of the tax were examined. The study
was concerned with what the tax requirement is and how it
operates. The question of whether a tax requirement is
"good" or "bad" in relation to the suffrage has not been
directly raised or considered. But the writer began the study
with the belief that a tax requirement for the suffrage has no
place in a nation which calls itself a democracy. Nothing that
was learned about the tax during the study caused any change
in this fundamental point of view. A tax requirement for the
suffrage is contrary to the democratic ideals which underlie
the American governmental system. It is based upon an
assumption that the suffrage should be limited to an élite group
and that those who pay the tax will be the ones who are
capable of participating in the affairs of their government. The
tax does not operate in this fashion. There is considerable
truth in the remark that the poll tax is used to "enfranchise the
dishonest poor and to disfranchise the honest poor." Although
the tax may not prevent as many persons from voting as its
opponents claim, it does prevent and discourage many citizens
from participating. Since the democratic process is symbolized
by the act of voting, a democratic regime should exercise
extreme care in placing restrictions upon voting. In such a
regime, a poll tax on the suffrage has no place.

INDEX

en, 43-44, 232; not a valid qualification for voting, 258-59; results in election of officials unresponsive to popular needs, 201-02, 242-43, 267-68, 288; subverts republican form of government, 264-65; unimportant as source of school revenue, 55-57, 284; violates equal protection of the laws, 265

arguments for poll tax: general, 268-69; a means of purifying elections, 7-10, 281-82; disfranchises Negroes, 4-7, 28, 30-31, 51-52, 189-90, 229, 231, 235, 239-40, 281-82, 286-87; important source of school revenue, 55, 184-85, 220, 224-26, 228, 239-40, 284; keeps government in hands of elite, 22-24, 28-31, 104, 231, 240, 282, 285, 290; person unwilling to pay small tax should not vote, 220, 240; substitute for voter registration system, 218, 225, 228-29

Arkansas: Good Government League of Crittenden County, 87

Arkansas poll tax: adopted, 2-4, 3n, 16-17, 281; adoption and Force Bill, 30; adoption and Populist party, 16-17; areas supporting repeal of, 226, 229; arguments against repeal of, 224-25; assessment of, 46-47, 61-62; collection of, 61-63; collections of compared with amount spent for education, 56; counties having highest rates of payment compared with counties having lowest rates of payment, 146-47, 153; coverage, 38-39, 41, 44, 283; delinquent collection of, 47n; disfranchising effects of, 113-14, 122, 137; disposition of proceeds from, 55; distribution of counties by percentage of all adults 21 and over paying in 1949, 145; increase in rate of payment, 153-54; intercounty comparisons of payments, 144-54; non-payment of, 107; payment and cash receipts from farming, 170-71; payment and density of population,

146-49, 153; payment and economic well-being, 146n; payment and Negroes, 146-47, 149-51, 153-54; payment and per capita income, 169-70; payment and political party competition, 151-54; payment and price of cotton, 171-73; payment and urbanism, 146-48, 153; payment by agent, 62, 83-87; payment campaigns, 63; proof of payment, 53, 283; purification of elections by, 9; rates, 32-33, 37-38, 282; repeal and education groups, 224-26, 228, 230; repeal and federal anti-poll tax bill, 227; repeal and labor unions, 224, 228, 230, 238-39; repeal and League of Women Voters, 228, 230, 238-39; repeal and Negroes, 226, 229-30, 239; repeal and segregation controversy, 229-30, 239; repeal and urbanism, 229-30; repeal movement, 201, 224-30, 238-39, 289; time of payment, 45-48, 283; vote buying through payment of, 83-89

Arkansas Democrat, 229
Arkansas Gazette, 86, 229
Arnall, Ellis, 185-88, 199
Arnold, Remmie L., 210n
Aycock, Charles A., 15

Bankhead, William B., 37
Barkley, Alben, 247, 256n
Barksdale, A. D., 274
Battle, John S., 210n, 211, 214
Battle, Laurie C., 135, 255n
Beacham, John R., 183
Belden, Joe, 221n
Bellinger, Charlie, 91
Bender, George H., 248, 250, 267n
Benson, Mary Lou, vi
Berry, William D., 103n
Bethune, Mary McLeod, 250
Biggs, Broughton, 195n
Biggs, Burch, 194-97
Biggs v. *Beeler*, 194-98
Bilbo, Theodore G., 237, 242, 247
Birmingham *News*, 9, 235

Dombrowski, James, 250n
Douglas, Paul, 271
Douglas, William O., 275, 279
Downs, L. McCarthy, 93-94
Duncan, Alderman, 191n
Dunn, Arthur, 274n
Durr, Virginia F., 244n, 250

Eaton, Amasa M., 7n
Edelman, John W., 36n
education groups: poll tax repeal and,
 184-85, 215n, 224-26, 228, 230, 239-40
Edwards, Horace H., 210n
Egger, Rowland, 186n
Ellender, Allen, 125, 270n
Ellison, William M., Jr., 175n
employers: payment of employees' poll
 taxes by, 100-04, 285
Ethridge, Mark, 186
Evans, Eileen S., 275-76
Evans, Silliman, 193-94, 197, 199-200
Ex parte Yarbrough, 262-63

Farm Security Administration, 103n
Farmer, Hallie, 233
Farris, Charles D., 115n
Faubus, Orval E., 228
Faulkner, James H., 234
federal anti-poll tax bills: analysis of
 votes in House of Representatives
 on passage of, 252-55; analysis of
 votes in Senate on cloture applicable to, 256-57; arguments for and
 against, 257-69; Bender bill, 248,
 253-54, 256n; Geyer bill, 244-47,
 253-56; Marcantonio bill, 247-48,
 253-56; New Deal and, 242-43; Norton bill, 248, 253-56, 257n, 270; Pepper bill, 245-47, 273-74; segregation
 controversy and, 249; Senate filibus-
 ters and, 247-48; state repeal movement and, 185-86, 188-91, 197, 212-
 13, 215-16, 219, 227, 237, 238-39, 243,
 280, 287-89; supporters and opponents of, 249-57, 288-89
Fenwick, Charles R., 213
Finerty, John F., 275n

Fletcher, Allan A., 80
Fletcher, John L., 85n, 227n
Florida: Farmers' Alliance in, 11n,
 116; multiple ballot box law, 115
Florida poll tax: adopted, 2, 4, 115,
 281; adoption and Populist party,
 11; coverage, 38n; disfranchising effects of, 114-18, 122, 126-29, 137-38;
 rates, 34n, 115; repeal and labor
 unions, 184; repeal and Negroes,
 184; repeal and schools, 184-85; repeal movement, 2, 182-85, 199, 287;
 time of payment, 45n, 115
Folsom, James E., 134, 230, 234, 237
Force Bill: 17, 29-31, 282
Foreman, Clark, 143n, 186n, 245n, 250
Foreman, Kenneth J., 190n
Fraenkel, Osmond K., 275n

Gailor, Frank H., 195
Gard, Wayne, 217n
Garner, John N., 37
Gasque, J. Ralph, 191n
Gaston, William A., 128
Gavagan, Joseph A., 246
Gelders, Joseph, 244n, 245n, 246n
George, David G., 93-94, 202, 205n,
 210n-11n, 250
George, Walter F., 131n, 270n
Georgia Electoral Reform League,
 202n
Georgia poll tax: adopted, 2-4, 281;
 adoption and Populist party, 12, 19-
 20; constitutionality of, 260-64, 272-
 73, 278; coverage, 38n, 41n; disfran-
 chising effects of, 129-31, 138; non-
 payment and partial payment of,
 106-07; rates, 34-36, 38; repeal and
 Negroes, 130; repeal and the press,
 186; repeal movement, 2, 185-88,
 199, 287; time of payment, 45n; vote
 buying through payment of, 95-96
Georgia Voters' Registration Act of
 1949, 131
Geyer, Lee E., 244-46
Gilmer, Henry G., 49, 93
Glass, Carter, 8, 245n

of persons per motor vehicle, 155-
57, 165-68; payment and per capita
income, 169-70; payment and political party competition, 167-68; payment and price of cotton, 171-73;
payment and Progressive Voters
League, 71; payment and urbanism,
155-61, 168; payment by agent, 89;
payment campaigns, 70-71; penalty
for delinquent payment, 68; proof
of payment, 53, 283; rates, 32-33, 35,
37-38, 282; repeal and bar associations, 219-20; repeal and Chamber
of Commerce, 217, 219; repeal and
churches, 218-19; repeal and federal
anti-poll tax bill, 216, 219, 238; repeal and labor unions, 218-19, 222;
repeal and League of Women Voters, 217; repeal and Mexican-Americans, 217, 218n, 221-22; repeal and
Negroes, 223-24, 238; repeal and the
press, 219; repeal and urbanism,
223; repeal and veterans, 217-19; repeal movement, 201, 215-24, 238-39,
289; revenue receipts, 36; time of
payment, 45-46, 48-50, 283; vote buying through payment of, 89-92
Thomas, Calhoun, 189-90
Thomas, Rex, 234n
Thompson, Gus, 234
Thompson, Mary A., 278-79
Thompson, Melvin E., 130-31
Thrasher, Max B., 24n
Thurmond, J. Strom, 189, 191, 270n
Tillman, Benjamin R., 5-6, 13, 25
Tinsley, J. M., 67, 209
Truman, Harry S., 241-42, 248, 271
Tuck, William M., 211-12

United States v. *Classic*, 261-63
University of Alabama Research Committee, vi
urbanism: poll tax repeal and, 199,
223, 229-30, 231, 235-36, 255

Vaden, Robert C., 204n, 207, 211
Vardaman, Claude O., 233

veterans: poll tax payment and, 284;
poll tax repeal and, 191, 209, 217-19,
239, 250-51, 289
Virginia: Association Against the Suffrage Amendments, 210-11; Byrd
machine, 141, 201-15, 238; College of
William and Mary Voters League,
211; constitutional convention of
1901-02, 6-8, 18, 21-22, 26-27, 49-51,
64-65; Readjuster party, 3n, 18;
Richmond Citizens' Association, 211;
voting in compared with voting in
North Carolina, 143-44
Virginia Advisory Legislative Council,
92, 202-04, 207n
Virginia Civil Rights Organization,
209
Virginia Commonwealth League, 211
Virginia Electoral Reform League, 68,
202-05, 212, 273-77
Virginia poll tax: adopted, 2-4; adoption and Negro disfranchisement,
5-7; adoption and Populist party,
12, 18; adoption and purification of
elections, 8-9; adoption and white
disfranchisement, 21-22, 26-27; assessment of, 65-66; collection of, 64-
68; collections compared with
amount spent for education, 56-57;
coverage, 38-41, 44, 283; disposition
of proceeds from, 55, 284; non-payment of, 107; payment and labor
unions, 101; payment campaigns,
67-68; penalty for delinquent payment, 65; proof of payment, 54,
283-84; rates, 32-38, 57, 282; repeal
and Campbell commission, 204-14;
repeal and churches, 209; repeal and
federal anti-poll tax bill, 212-13,
215, 238; repeal and Gooch report,
203-04; repeal and labor unions,
209; repeal and Negroes, 209, 215,
238; repeal and Republican party,
210-11; repeal and school segregation controversy, 215, 238, 289; repeal and the press, 208; repeal and
veterans, 209; repeal and Wise

County scandals, 212-13; repeal movement, 201-15, 238-39, 289; time of payment, 45-46, 48-51, 283; vote buying through payment of, 3n, 49-50, 92-95

Virginia Right to Vote League, 210

Virginia Voters League, 67, 209

vote buying through poll tax payment, 3n, 49-50, 77-104, 183, 222, 245, 285

voter registration fee, 188, 201, 207, 218-20, 224

voting in southern poll tax and non-poll tax states compared, 139-44, 287

Wallace, David D., 13n

Wallace, Henry, 188

Wallace, O. T., 191n

Wallace, W. Lewis, 191

Walthall, Edward C., 25

Waring, J. Waties, 190

Watson, J. Tom, 117

Watson, Tom, 9, 19-20

Weeks, Stephen B., 3n

Wharton, Vernon L., 30n

White, Melvin J., 13n, 27n

Whitehead, Robert, 207, 210

Whittington, William M., 237n, 268n

Wilcox, Mark, 128

Wilkins, Ralph E., 275

Williams, Henry N., 193n, 198

Willbern, York, vi

Wilson, Homer, 98-99

women's organizations: poll tax payment and, 61, 64, 70-71, 284; poll tax repeal and, 43-44, 194, 215n, 217-18, 224, 228, 230, 232-33, 238-39, 251, 289

Woods, Robert H., 208n

Woods, James P., 202-04

Woodward, C. Vann, 9n, 20n

Wright, Fielding L., 64

Wysor, J. C., 6-7

Wysor, J. Frank, 204n

Zweifel, Henry, 219